Following the Crowd: Psychological Drivers of Herding and Market Overreaction

Kok Loang Ooi • Norazlin Binti Ab Aziz
Wee Yeap Lau

Following the Crowd: Psychological Drivers of Herding and Market Overreaction

Springer

Kok Loang Ooi
Department of Finance, Faculty of Business and Economics
Universiti Malaysia
Kuala Lumpur, Malaysia

Norazlin Binti Ab Aziz
Department of Finance, Faculty of Business and Economics
Universiti Malaysia
Kuala Lumpur, Malaysia

Wee Yeap Lau
Department of Decision Science, Faculty of Business and Economics
Universiti Malaysia
Kuala Lumpur, Malaysia

ISBN 978-981-95-0791-7 ISBN 978-981-95-0792-4 (eBook)
https://doi.org/10.1007/978-981-95-0792-4

This Springer imprint is published by the registered company Springer Nature Singapore Pte Ltd.
The registered company address is: 152 Beach Road, #21-01/04 Gateway East, Singapore 189721, Singapore

To those who seek truth amidst market noise,
To the silent observers who dare to question the crowd,
To the scholars, mentors, and pioneers of behavioural finance,
Whose insights continue to illuminate the irrational corners of our decisions
This work is for you.
And to our family and loved ones,
whose unwavering support and encouragement
have been the quiet strength behind each chapter
Thank you for believing in us when the journey seemed uncertain.

Acknowledgement

This book would not have been possible without the invaluable support and encouragement of many individuals and institutions. First and foremost, we would like to extend our sincere gratitude to the Faculty of Business and Economics at the University of Malaya for their generous provision of a book grant, which made this work a reality. Their commitment to supporting scholarly research and knowledge dissemination has been instrumental in the completion of this book. We are deeply grateful to our academic colleagues, research collaborators, and mentors who have shared their insights, critiques, and encouragement throughout this journey. To our family and loved ones, thank you for your patience, understanding, and unconditional support. Lastly, we dedicate this work to all readers and future scholars who seek to explore the fascinating interplay between psychology and financial markets. May this book serve as a foundation for deeper inquiry and thoughtful reflection.

About this Book

This book provides a comprehensive and critical examination of behavioural finance, highlighting the psychological and cognitive mechanisms that shape investor behaviour and impact market outcomes. Departing from the assumptions of rationality embedded in traditional financial theories, the study highlights how biases such as overconfidence, overreaction, and affective responses frequently drive deviations from expected utility models. Central to the discussion is the phenomenon of herding behaviour, conceptualised through rational, informational, reputational, and compensational frameworks. Rather than acting independently, investors often respond to the actions of others, especially during periods of heightened uncertainty, market volatility, or informational ambiguity. Such collective behaviour contributes to mispricing, excess volatility, and the formation of financial bubbles or crashes. The analysis further investigates how modern information channels, particularly digital media and social platforms, intensify these behavioural patterns, accelerating the spread of sentiment and reinforcing feedback loops. Through a synthesis of theoretical insights, empirical evidence, and practical implications, this book contributes to a deeper understanding of market inefficiencies rooted in human psychology. Its findings offer value to scholars seeking to expand behavioural finance theory, practitioners aiming to interpret market dynamics more effectively, and policymakers interested in enhancing the stability and resilience of financial systems in an increasingly complex global environment.

Funding This publication was supported by a book grant awarded by the Faculty of Business and Economics, Universiti Malaya. The author gratefully acknowledges the financial assistance provided, which enabled the completion and dissemination of this academic work. The views expressed in this book are solely those of the author and do not necessarily reflect the official policy or position of the faculty or the university.

Contents

About the Authors

Kok Loang Ooi is a distinguished scholar in finance with expertise in behavioural finance, market psychology, and investor behaviour. He is currently affiliated with the Faculty of Business and Economics at Universiti Malaya, where he is actively involved in empirical research, postgraduate supervision, and academic leadership. He holds a PhD in Behavioural Finance, an LLM from the International Islamic University Malaysia (IIUM), and a Master of Finance from Universiti Sains Malaysia (USM). His research addresses key areas, including herding behaviour, investor sentiment, overreaction, and cognitive biases in financial markets. He previously served at KPMG, where he handled audit and advisory work for both domestic and international clients. He serves as a Trustee of the Malaysia Game Changer Foundation under the Legal Affairs Division (BHEUU) of the Prime Minister's Department. He is a professional member of the Institute of Internal Auditors Malaysia and frequently invited to speak at international academic, experienced, and policy-related forums.

Norazlin Ab Aziz is a Senior Lecturer at the Department of Finance, Faculty of Business and Economics, Universiti Malaya. Prior to her academic career, Dr. Norazlin served in various capacities within the unit trust industry, leveraging knowledge gained from her Bachelor of Economics (Hons) degree from the International Islamic University Malaysia. She transitioned into academia while pursuing her Master of Economics at the University of Malaya and later earned a PhD in Accounting and Finance from the University of Glasgow. At the University of Malaya, she teaches Islamic finance, economics, fixed income, and corporate ethics. Her current research reflects a strong commitment to advancing knowledge at the nexus of sustainable finance, economics, Islamic finance, and the evolving carbon market in Malaysia. She also investigates the role of language in business communication and its impact on financial decision-making. Beyond academia, Dr. Norazlin actively supports inclusive economic development through micro-entrepreneurship training initiatives. She also contributes to the scholarly community as an Associate Editor of the *Journal of Islamic Accounting and Business Research*.

Wee Yeap Lau is a Professor at the Faculty of Business and Economics and an Academic Board Member of the Asia-Europe Institute, Universiti Malaya. He was an MEXT Scholar at Osaka University, an AUA Scholar at UAE University, and a Visiting Scholar at the NUS RMI. He received his PhD and Master's degree in Economics from Osaka University, as well as a Master of Science in Financial Engineering from the National University of Singapore. He also attended an Executive Education program at the Bendheim Centre for Finance, Princeton University. He has authored two books published by Palgrave Macmillan, a professional text for the Malaysian Insurance Institute, and edited two books for University Press, in addition to 70 journal articles indexed in the Web of Science collection. He is a member of CPA Australia and an Elected Member of the International Statistical Institute.

List of Figures

List of Tables

Chapter 1
The Psychology of Herding

1.1 Introduction

Herding behaviour is one of the most intriguing and contradictory phenomena in financial markets. This psychological inclination is profoundly embedded, originating from ancestral survival impulses, but is now evident in stock market exuberances, real estate bubbles, and cryptocurrency surges. Herding fundamentally occurs when investors relinquish their autonomous judgements to emulate the behaviour of the majority. This behaviour, influenced by fear, greed, or uncertainty, may incite an exuberant market rise and devastating falls. The importance of herding is paramount as it influences investment choices at both the individual and institutional levels, affecting asset prices and regulatory measures. Comprehending this phenomenon is crucial for investors navigating market cycles, regulators striving to avert financial instability, and behavioural economists analysing the psychology of economic decision-making.

In financial markets, herding often serves as the unseen force driving some of history's most infamous booms and calamities. Throughout history, from the Tulip Mania of the seventeenth century to the dot-com crisis of the early 2000s, collective investor behaviour has consistently contradicted rationality, driving prices to illogical extremes before succumbing to the pressures of reality. The subprime mortgage crisis is a significant instance: driven by the widespread conviction that house prices would continue to rise, individuals and institutional investors invested heavily in mortgage-backed securities without fully understanding the associated risks. As the market eventually reversed, the crowd surged in the opposite direction, precipitating one of the most severe financial catastrophes in contemporary history. The cycles of extreme optimism, followed by widespread fear, illustrate the significant impact of herd behaviour on financial stability and economic progress.

At the psychological level, herding is influenced primarily by two interrelated factors: social proof and compliance (Loang 2024). Social proof, a concept introduced by social psychologist Robert Cialdini, refers to the human tendency to seek

K. L. Ooi et al., *Following the Crowd: Psychological Drivers of Herding and Market Overreaction*, https://doi.org/10.1007/978-981-95-0792-4_1

help from others when making decisions, especially in ambiguous situations. In financial markets, investors often rely on the insights of peers, analysts, or media sensationalism rather than conducting their basic research. Conformity, as notably demonstrated in Solomon Asch's research, explains why people are inclined to disregard their judgement in order to conform to the majority. Asch's research showed that, even when individuals recognised the group's consensus as erroneous, many chose to comply rather than asserting their independence. This behavioural tendency is particularly perilous in financial markets, where fear of missing out may lead to widespread irrational decision-making.

Three prominent individuals have significantly influenced our understanding of herding behaviour in financial markets. Solomon Asch's studies on social influence laid the groundwork for understanding how people yield to collective pressure, a phenomenon that is distinctly evident in speculative investing tendencies. Nobel laureate Robert Shiller elaborates on this concept by introducing the notion of 'irrational exuberance', which describes how investor confidence can escalate uncontrollably, leading to unsustainable asset bubbles. His research in behavioural finance has been essential in elucidating the reasons why markets often diverge from rational economic models (Ooi 2024). Amos Tversky, in collaboration with Daniel Kahneman, developed the heuristics and biases framework, which explains why investors usually rely on cognitive shortcuts and emotional instincts rather than logical analysis. His study has yielded profound insights into the persistence of herding behaviour in advanced financial markets despite the availability of enormous data and expert views.

1.2 The Evolutionary Basis for Herd Behaviour

1.2.1 Herding as a Survival Mechanism

Herding behaviour is not only a peculiarity of contemporary financial markets; it is a profoundly ingrained survival strategy that has influenced human decision-making for millennia. Prior to the advent of stock markets and economic crises, our ancestors relied on communal decision-making to navigate an uncertain and sometimes perilous environment (Liu et al. 2022). The capacity to align with the collective and adhere to the majority during times of uncertainty was not only beneficial but also vital for existence. In a realm where a single erroneous choice may result in a fatality, remaining with the group enhances the likelihood of evading predators, locating sustenance, and securing safety via collective strength. Individuals who deviated excessively from the group were often the first casualties of nature's severe conditions. Over time, this urge for uniformity has become ingrained in the human brain, affecting both physical survival and social and economic behaviour.

In early human cultures, herding behaviour significantly influenced decision-making. When faced with uncertainty, whether it is the optimal hunting position, the edibility of specific plants, or the route to water, individuals observe the behaviours of others. When the bulk of the group proceeded on a particular path, it was often more prudent to follow than to risk a solitary investigation (Loang et al. 2024). The repercussions of an erroneous decision may be disastrous. This entrenched dependence on communal knowledge establishes the basis for societal unity and stability. Groups displaying pronounced herding behaviours tended to be more robust since synchronised movement and collective knowledge conferred an evolutionary benefit. Despite conflicting personal inclinations, the capacity to rely on the group's judgement was a characteristic that enhanced the probability of survival and, eventually, reproduction.

In modern times, this primordial survival instinct persists, as evidenced in boardrooms, trading floors, and digital investment platforms. The contemporary financial market is, in several respects, a perilous environment characterised by prevailing uncertainty. Just as ancient people relied on the communal knowledge of their tribe to evade danger, contemporary investors observe the actions of others when formulating financial decisions (Choijil et al. 2022). During periods of heightened uncertainty, such as market crashes, economic recessions, or speculative bubbles, investors tend to conform to prevailing trends, often neglecting a comprehensive risk assessment. The apprehension of standing alone and the potential for erroneous decision-making in solitude can be formidable. It seems more secure to align with the majority, purchasing when others are acquiring and divesting when others are selling, despite logical counterarguments. This explains why financial markets display pronounced cycles of booms and busts; investors often react to herd behaviour rather than fundamental economic indicators.

Risk aversion, a fundamental survival driver, exacerbates herding behaviour in financial markets. In antiquity, avoiding unnecessary risks was crucial; selecting an inappropriate hunting area or consuming a toxic plant could result in lethal consequences. Currently, the same aversion to risk is manifested in financial decision-making. Investors prioritise the dread of losses over the appreciation of gains, a psychological phenomenon termed loss aversion. Upon seeing others leave the market, their instinct compels them to follow suit to avert certain disasters. This elucidates why market declines often escalate swiftly; panic disseminates quickly, prompting the masses to flee. Conversely, in bull markets, the fear of missing out prevails, prompting investors to flock to assets only because of others' actions, thus generating unsustainable bubbles.

The potency of this dynamic is amplified by the social reinforcement inherent in herding. When an individual conforms to the majority, and the choice proves to be accurate, the behaviour is reinforced, enhancing the propensity for future conformity (Loang, 2023). This reinforcing cycle makes herding a particularly challenging habit, especially in contexts that encourage autonomous thinking. In financial markets, this suggests that even experienced investors and analysts—individuals who, in principle, should rely on facts and logical analysis—can exhibit a herd mentality (Komalasari et al. 2022). They saw others as profiting and fearful of exclusion. They see others in a state of panic, and dread becomes the last one, retaining a failing investment. The irony lies in the fact that, whereas herding historically enhanced survival prospects in ancient settings, it often resulted in financial devastation in contemporary markets. Conforming to the majority may have aided early humans in evading predators; however, in modern, intricate financial systems, it may direct investors towards market collapses and speculative bubbles. The issue for contemporary investors lies in discerning when the survival instinct of herding is detrimental rather than beneficial. Mastering the ability to resist the need to conform and engage in independent thought amidst uncertainty is essential for evading the severe financial repercussions associated with unrestrained herd behaviour.

As Table 1.1 shows, herding behaviour is not a novel creation of financial markets; it is a timeless survival mechanism that traces back to humanity's earliest days. Long before there were stocks to buy or sell, our ancestors faced life-or-death decisions in the wilderness. In those times, uncertainty was not theoretical; it was immediate and deadly. A wrong turn in the search for food or water could lead to starvation or the jaws of a predator. In such a perilous world, following the crowd was not a weakness but wisdom. The collective movement increased safety, and communal knowledge saved lives. When a tribe moved toward a water source or avoided a dangerous path, it did so with the force of the lived experience. Over generations, the instinct to conform became neurologically hardwired; those who followed the group tended to survive and pass on their genes. This evolutionary inheritance is still with us today, quietly guiding our behaviours, even in contexts where the original threats no longer exist.

Today, ancient instincts play out in the high-stakes theatre of financial markets, often with disastrous consequences (Kennedy 2025). When uncertainty arises, whether in the form of inflation spikes, economic downturns, or geopolitical shocks, investors often do not act as purely rational agents. Instead, they scan their environment for cues from others, much like their ancestors, once they watch the herd for survival signals. This is where the psychology of loss aversion and fear of missing out kicks in. Investors see others selling and fear being left behind; as they observe others profiting and rushing to join the trend, they also enter the trend themselves. The emotional mind screams louder than the rational mind. However, sophisticated tools, algorithms, and real-time data do not sufficiently dampen the impact of instincts. Despite decades of financial education and access to information, market participants often act in lockstep, mimicking behaviours, not out of analysis, but out of deeply rooted fear and desire to belong. In modern boardrooms and online trading platforms, the survival instinct still whispers follow the herd, and you will be safe.

Ironically, what once ensured our survival may accelerate our downfall. As Table 1.1 underscores, herding once helped humans avoid danger and make sound group-based decisions. However, in financial markets, the exact mechanism can lead to the formation of asset bubbles, sudden panic, and massive sell-offs. The consequences are not just personal; they ripple across all economies. What begins with the cautious imitation of snowballs into systemic risk? And the cruel twist? Investors who follow the herd may feel secure at the moment, but by doing so, they often overlook fundamentals, overprice assets, and contribute to market inefficiency. The key challenge for modern investors is to recognise when the urge to conform is

Table 1.1 Herding as survival mechanism vs. financial behaviour

Aspect	Herding as a survival mechanism (primitive human context)	Herding in financial behaviour (modern financial markets)
Purpose and function	The core function of herding in early human societies was survival. Individuals followed the group to avoid threats such as predators, natural disasters, or dangerous terrain. Herding increased the chances of finding food, water, and safety through collective action	In financial markets, herding often serves the psychological function of security through consensus. Investors follow the crowd to minimise regret, avoid isolation, and reduce perceived decision-making risk during uncertainty, especially in volatile or unfamiliar market conditions
Environmental uncertainty	Ancient humans faced high environmental volatility unpredictable weather, scarce resources, and dangerous wildlife. In such environments, collective movement was often safer than individual exploration	Financial markets are similarly characterised by uncertainty and complexity. Rapid shifts in economic indicators, global news, and investor sentiment create conditions in which people mimic others' trading decisions rather than relying solely on independent analysis
Risk aversion and loss aversion	The evolutionary instinct to avoid danger made risk aversion a dominant trait. Taking unnecessary risks, such as venturing alone, could lead to death. Hence, staying with the group was a low-risk strategy that enhanced survival	In modern finance, this translates into loss aversion the tendency to fear losses more than valuing equivalent gains. Investors often follow the herd to avoid losses, especially when others are selling during a downturn, even if fundamental analysis suggests otherwise
Learning and information processing	Early humans relied heavily on observational learning watching others to learn which plants were safe, which paths led to water, or where to hunt. The group acted as a knowledge repository	Today, investors rely on social signals, media coverage, analysts' opinions, and market momentum as informational shortcuts (heuristics). Instead of processing all information independently, many investors assume the crowd must know something, thus follow the trend
Social reinforcement and feedback loops	Herding was often rewarded socially and evolutionarily. Those who followed the group and survived passed on their genes. Conformity became a socially valued behaviour that enhanced group cohesion	Investors who follow the herd and initially profit (e.g. during a market rally) are positively reinforced, making it harder to break the cycle in future. The fear of being wrong alone outweighs the fear of being wrong with the majority

(continued)

Table 1.1 (continued)

Aspect	Herding as a survival mechanism (primitive human context)	Herding in financial behaviour (modern financial markets)
Psychological biases at play	Behaviour was shaped by instincts, fear, and the need for social acceptance. Deviation from group norms could result in being ostracised or endangered	Modern herding is influenced by cognitive biases such as confirmation bias, availability bias, FOMO (fear of missing out), and social proof. These biases override rational analysis and push individuals to mimic others' financial actions
Outcome and consequences	In early societies, herding usually led to greater group survival, better decision-making under uncertainty, and cohesive societal structures	In finance, however, herding can lead to market inefficiencies, asset bubbles, and crashes. While short-term gains may occur, long-term consequences include systemic risks and wealth loss when collective behaviour detaches from fundamentals

Source: Authors' work

helping and when it is hurting. In today's world, survival is no longer about escaping predators but about escaping the psychological traps that come with them. To thrive in modern markets, we must learn not only to think independently but also to override the instincts that once kept our ancestors alive.

1.2.2 Neurological and Psychological Foundations

The human brain is an extraordinary organ engineered to analyse extensive information, identify patterns, and frequently make swift decisions without conscious awareness (Tversky and Kahneman 1992). However, underneath its brilliance lies a fundamental flaw: it is predisposed to shortcuts (Bennett and Hacker 2022). In an unpredictable environment, the brain seeks efficiency. Instead of meticulously evaluating every potential consequence with flawless reasoning, it relies on cognitive biases and mental shortcuts that streamline intricate decision-making. While beneficial in several facets of life, these biases significantly contribute to herd behaviour in financial markets, often resulting in illogical decisions, speculative bubbles, and severe downturns.

A significant bias that drives herding is the availability heuristic, a cognitive shortcut wherein individuals assess the likelihood of an occurrence based on the ease with which instances are recalled. When a particular stock has experienced significant gains in recent weeks, it is more likely to continue its ascent, as previous achievements are vividly recalled by investors (Humphrey et al. 2021). They recall headlines of unprecedented stock prices, social media messages touting the next significant opportunity, and acquaintances boasting about their investment profits. These dramatic, readily remembered instances eclipse more objective elements such as earnings reports, industry trends, or economic realities. What is the outcome? Investors enter the market not because of meticulous study but because their instincts suggest this is the next significant opportunity to observe the number of individuals profiting!

The same bias operates inversely during a market decline. As markets decline, panic ensues as adverse news predominates headlines (Shiller 2000). Investors often overlook long-term trends and firm fundamentals, instead focusing on the rapid decline in their portfolios. The availability heuristic leads individuals to overestimate the probability of ongoing losses owing to the prominence of instances such as crashes, bankruptcies, and financial crises in their thoughts. Herd impulse prevails, prompting them to sell without considering the justification for their response.

Another cognitive bias that reinforces herding behaviour is anchoring, which is the tendency to rely excessively on an initial piece of information when making a judgement. In financial markets, anchoring emerges in several forms, often ensnaring investors in irrational behaviours. Envision is a stock valued at $100 per share but has since declined to $60. An investor tied to the $100 price will persist in seeing $60 as 'cheap', regardless of contrary indications from the company's fundamentals. Rather than objectively evaluating a stock's intrinsic worth, they concentrate on its historical price, assuming it will revert to that level, which leads them to purchase alongside others with similar views. The stock may have been initially overpriced, and its current price may only indicate a long-awaited correction. However, anchoring skews judgements, causing investors to conform to the majority rather than re-evaluating their own beliefs.

This dependence on cognitive heuristics is not only detrimental; it is a fundamental aspect of human cognition embedded in survival mechanisms (Banerjee 1992). Neuroscience studies have shown that when people engage in collective behaviour, the brain secretes dopamine, a neurotransmitter associated with pleasure and reward. Participating in the collective and adhering to the majority elicits a sense of satisfaction. This explains why individuals experience a surge of exhilaration when investing in a thriving market alongside numerous others. Financial trends evolve into self-fulfilling prophecies as mass involvement bolsters confidence and drives up prices.

Nonetheless, the brain's reaction to herding encompasses both pleasure and terror. The amygdala, the brain's centre for fear, significantly influences financial decision-making, particularly in unstable markets (Picone et al. 2021). When an investor observes others in a state of panic liquidating their assets, the amygdala activates, signalling a threat and cautioning that inactivity may result in significant losses. This elicits a fight-or-flight reaction when the impulse to conform to and avoid imminent danger supersedes logical cognition. This explains why market collapses often rise rapidly: fear disseminates like an emotional contagion, intensified by the brain's innate sensitivity to perceived dangers.

In ambiguous situations, the brain grapples with uncertainty, prompting a natural inclination to seek directions from others. In conditions of greater uncertainty, individuals are more likely to imitate the behaviours of their peers. Research using fMRI scans has shown that conformity to group choices activates the brain's reward centres, thus reinforcing behaviour. Simultaneously, when people deviate from the majority, the anterior cingulate cortex, linked to social grief and discomfort, becomes activated, rendering nonconformity psychologically taxing. This neural unease explains why few investors possess the fortitude to act independently, while the majority proceed on a different path.

In financial markets, this neurological configuration creates a perfect storm: cognitive biases propel investors toward groupthink, the brain's reward system reinforces conformity, and the fear of losses exacerbates the challenge of independent thought (Clark et al. 2022). The outcome is a loop in which individuals invest not because of trust in their analysis, but because their cognition suggests that conforming to the majority is the most secure option. However, history has consistently shown that most cases are often mistaken. Those who uncritically adhere to it are overwhelmed when the rush changes.

1.3 Early Examples of Collective Behaviour in Pre-Industrial Markets

1.3.1 Medieval and Renaissance Markets

In the extensive narrative of financial history, few events compared to the remarkable silliness and exhilaration of speculative bubbles emerged in the medieval and Renaissance markets (Kaye 2024). These were the first documented occurrences of widespread financial hysteria, characterised by the abandonment of logic in favour of uncritical optimism, as the compelling force of herd behaviour engulfed investors. They endure cautionary tales, illustrating that markets, regardless of their sophistication, are subject to human psychology, avarice, and the compelling forces of social influence.

The Tulip Mania in 1637 is often considered the first documented speculative bubble. In seventeenth-century Holland, tulips symbolised wealth, elegance, and social status. The Dutch, famous for their commercial expertise, transformed these exotic blooms into a speculative investment, with rare tulip bulbs fetching prices that defined reason (Graham 2014). As news of the potential riches was disseminated, the number of individuals, including farmers, merchants, artists, and even ordinary labourers, invested their funds in tulip bulbs, confident that prices would continue to rise. The market surged as fear of missing out intensified, and at the peak of the frenzy, a single bulb of the rarest type might fetch the price of an entire home in Amsterdam.

However, like all the bubbles, the illusion could not last. In early 1637, the demand for tulips abruptly diminished. The cause of this collapse remains unclear; nonetheless, once prices began to plummet, panic ensued swiftly. Investors who purchased inflated prices urgently sought to divest, although no purchasers were willing to perpetuate the facade. In a matter of weeks, the tulip market collapsed, resulting in the overnight loss of fortunes and leaving many tulip bulbs valueless. The absurdity of the situation became a mere fable or speculative excess, emerging as a symbol of financial folly. Nonetheless, while Tulip Mania is often referenced as an instance of economic imprudence, it includes more than just avarice, illustrating the influence of social proof and the psychological inclination to emulate others in decision-making. The Dutch did not invest in tulips because of a fundamental belief in their long-term value; instead, they participated due to widespread societal interest in the flowers.

Almost a century later, history recurred on a larger scale with the South Sea Bubble of 1720, a financial catastrophe characterised by governmental intervention, rampant speculation, and fraudulent assurances of immense wealth (Leonard 2022). The South Sea Company was founded in England and has promising trading prospects in South America. Investors were confident that the firm would generate substantial profits, leading to a significant increase in its stock price. British nobles, parliament members, and King George I himself were entangled in the speculative fervour, giving an aura of legitimacy to the idea. Company shares surged from £100 to over £1000, prompting many to incur debt to invest, believing they would attain unprecedented wealth.

However, beneath the façade, the South Sea Company had little genuine earnings and limited operational viability (Bikhchandani et al. 1992). The entire bubble was constructed on hype, political manipulation, and confirmation bias, the inclination to pursue information that corroborates a pre-existing opinion while disregarding opposing facts. Investors often disregard cautionary indicators due to their desire to believe in the allure of effortless prosperity. However, for all bubbles, it ultimately collapsed. By the conclusion of 1720, the South Sea stock had plummeted to its initial value, obliterating wealth and precipitating financial devastation across England. The incident revealed extensive corruption inside the government and economic organisations, resulting in public indignation and the subsequent enactment of more stringent restrictions.

Tulip Mania and the South Sea Bubble exemplify a fundamental aspect of human nature: the collective irrationality that arises when greed, optimism, and social influence converge. They demonstrate that financial markets are not only logical systems governed by logic and fundamentals; instead, they are profoundly emotional environments where fear and euphoria significantly influence their dynamics. Although these historical occurrences may seem distant, their lessons remain pertinent in contemporary times. The psychological mechanisms that influenced tulip and South Sea investors persist to shape financial markets, as seen in phenomena such as the dot-com boom, cryptocurrency surges, and real estate bubbles. The names may change, and the assets may transform, but human nature endures, perpetually attracted to the allure of effortless wealth and perpetually susceptible to the influence of the collective.

1.3.2 Eighteenth and Nineteenth Century Financial Crises

By the eighteenth and nineteenth centuries, financial speculation had developed into a formidable force capable of transforming whole economies and dismantling them with equal rapidity (Sufi and Taylor 2022). The development of global commerce, colonial ventures, and industrial advancements has provided investors with opportunities to increase their wealth. Repeatedly, these prospects deteriorated into widespread speculation fuelled by unrestrained optimism, avarice, and the conviction that prices would continue to rise. The Mississippi Bubble of 1720 and the Railway Mania of the 1840s, two notorious financial catastrophes, provide similar insights into the perils of speculative excess and collective behaviour.

The Mississippi Bubble was a significant financial deception engineered by the great economic visionary John Law (Cialdini 2001). Law, a Scottish economist and gambler, persuaded the French authorities that his unconventional theories might alleviate the nation's severe financial crisis. He offered a bold plan to establish a national bank that would issue paper currency and associate this currency with a trading firm that would capitalise on the vast, unexplored wealth of French Louisiana, the Mississippi firm. The narrative was irresistibly compelled to do so. The law promised immense prosperity from commerce in the Americas, prompting individuals from many backgrounds to hasten their investments in the company's shares. Indeed, they were securing a stake in France's future economic supremacy.

As demand surged, the prices of Mississippi Company shares escalated dramatically, resulting in one of the first documented stock market panics. At the zenith of the frenzy, the shares increased by more than 20 times their initial value. Investors sold their properties, incurred debt, and invested all their resources in the venture, confident that Louisiana's wealth would make them billionaires. Paris was engulfed in a frenzy of speculation, with accounts of ordinary individuals suddenly amassing vast fortunes. John Law was seen as a financial prodigy, a figure who seemed to have redefined the principles of wealth generation.

However, underneath the ostentatious exterior, Mississippi was founded on hollow assurances and speculative exaggeration. Louisiana lacks extensive gold mines and abundant wealth to be exploited. The company's actual trading activities were negligible, and when investors began to recognise the absence of anticipated earnings, their confidence diminished (Fligstein 2021). A sense of terror ensued. Individuals who were previously eager to purchase shares are now equally eager to divest. Share prices plummeted almost instantaneously, erasing wealth and thrusting France into an economic catastrophe. Riots erupted in the streets, and John Law, formerly esteemed as a financial saviour, departed France in ignominy. The Mississippi Bubble is a remarkable instance of financial exhilaration culminating in catastrophe, illustrating how uncritical belief in an overly optimistic investment may result in devastation.

Just over a century later, the world witnessed another episode of financial insanity, this time during the Industrial Revolution, when the allure of new infrastructure initiatives sparked a speculative frenzy known as Railway Mania. The introduction of steam engines and the rapid construction of railway networks in the early nineteenth century transformed transportation. For the first time in history, individuals and commodities can traverse vast distances with unparalleled rapidity. The potential for economic expansion was substantial, and investors saw railroads as the next most significant opportunity.

By the 1840s, railroads had emerged as the most lucrative investment trend in Britain. Everyone seeks a share of opportunities. Newspapers amplified excitement, disseminating ambitious projections of a future in which trains would link every city, village, and rural area, ushering in unprecedented riches. Politicians advocated railway development, and Queen Victoria herself was an ardent proponent. Numerous new railway companies have been established, so far with little than aspirational plans and unfulfilled commitments. Investors invested their assets in railway stocks, regardless of their financial status, believing that it was a sure path to prosperity.

At its zenith, several railway lines were planned, and speculative capital inundated the industry. While several projects were genuine, numerous others were merely financial illusions, representing businesses without any viable potential for actualising railway construction. Financial institutions enthusiastically extend credit to railway speculators, exacerbating a cycle of indebtedness and excessive investment. The bubble expanded swiftly, with railway stocks attaining excessively inflated prices.

However, many manias are unsustainable. By 1846, fissures had begun to emerge. Overconstruction and rampant speculation have led to financial instability, prompting investors to question the viability of several railway enterprises. As uncertainty proliferated, stock prices began to decline. The market, formerly characterised by excitement, transitioned to panic. Railway stocks collapsed, erasing wealth and leaving several investors insolvent. The British economy entered a recession, resulting in the abandonment of several railway projects, with incomplete rails serving as haunting memories of imprudent investments.

Railway Mania was not only a financial catastrophe, but also a pivotal moment that transformed investment practices and economic policy. The crisis led to more stringent restrictions, compelling enterprises to demonstrate financial sustainability before acquiring capital. It also functioned as a clear admonition that even the most transformative technology might become an instrument of speculative excess when hope surpasses reality.

The Mississippi Bubble and Railway Mania, separated by more than a century, convey a similar cautionary narrative: when avarice and collective behaviour dominate, financial markets become disassociated from reality, resulting in an eventual collapse that causes widespread devastation (Notteboom et al. 2021). These historical crises are not just remnants of the past; their tendencies are repeatedly observed in contemporary markets. The dynamics that propelled dot-com stocks in the 1990s, property markets in the 2000s, and cryptocurrencies remained vigorously active. The lesson is unequivocal: when conjecture supplants reason, history tends to recur.

1.4 Financial Implications of Herding Tendencies

1.4.1 Impact on Asset Pricing and Market Efficiency

An asset's price should theoretically represent its genuine intrinsic worth, which is a careful equilibrium of financial performance, future earnings potential, and macroeconomic circumstances (Lewellen and Shanken 2002). However, financial markets theoretically do not function. They operate in an environment where psychology, conjecture, and irrational enthusiasm skew prices to an unrecognisable extent. When herding behaviour prevails, rational valuation is disregarded, and emotion rather than facts drives asset values. This mispricing may present significant opportunities for those who identify it, while for the rest, it becomes a perilous entrapment, leading to market instability and financial turmoil.

Central to asset mispricing is a perilous fallacy: the belief that prices accurately represent reality. Ideally, a stock's price accurately represents its profitability, growth potential, and industry dynamics. However, markets are influenced by perception, which is often susceptible to manipulation. When investors become convinced that a particular asset, such as a stock, cryptocurrency, or real estate, will appreciate alone, they cease to evaluate its intrinsic worth. This is the point at which irrational exuberance, a phrase used by economist Robert Shiller, prevailed. Investors are convinced that the market has entered a new era, rendering previous regulations obsolete and that concerns about overvaluation are outdated.

This kind of uncritical optimism inflates bubbles, causing assets to be valued much beyond their intrinsic worth. In the late 1990s, dot-com bubbles and technology firms with little or no income saw their stock values double or triple overnight due to their association with the Internet revolution. Investors were hesitant to purchase due to concerns about profitability; instead, they acquired based on the conviction that others were also making similar purchases. A similar process occurred during the 2008 housing bubble when the sentence that 'home prices will perpetually increase' incited a reckless surge of speculation. In recent years, we have seen such occurrences with cryptocurrency surges, where digital assets have appreciated significantly not because of their inherent value, but due to a collective influx of investors.

This mispricing provides misleading market signals. When an asset is overpriced, investors mistakenly perceive it as a secure investment, which attracts more buyers and exacerbates bubble inflation. However, when unavoidable corrections occur, the repercussions are rapid and severe. Investors who purchased at the zenith, believing they were entering an opportune period, now find themselves with assets that are swiftly losing value. This is the point at which herding behaviour transitions from avarice to panic, just as swiftly as individuals enter the market, they exit, resulting in market collapses that obliterate billions in value overnight.

The influx and exodus of investors in markets not only impact individual assets but also undermine the overall underpinning of financial stability. Stock market stability relies on logical and predictable behaviour, with prices fluctuating in accordance with supply and demand driven by genuine economic data. However, when herding behaviour prevails, markets undergo extreme volatility characterised by significant fluctuations that may erode trust and generate systemic problems. During the 2008 financial crisis, panic selling triggered a cascade effect, causing financially sound firms to experience a significant decline in stock prices due to widespread market anxiety. Likewise, during the COVID-19 market crisis of 2020, the first sell-off was not grounded in fundamentals; it was a response to pervasive uncertainty and mass investor exodus, resulting in unprecedented declines in global stock indices.

The danger of this instability is its self-perpetuating nature. During periods of significant market instability, institutional investors such as hedge funds, pension funds, and prominent asset managers tend to withdraw, thereby diminishing liquidity and exacerbating the challenges faced by individual investors in liquidating their holdings. This intensifies the downward pressure, causing prices to fall below their underlying values. In severe instances, this may result in liquidity crises, causing the collapse of all financial institutions due to forced liquidations, as exemplified by Lehman Brothers in 2008.

Notwithstanding the disorder generated by herding behaviour, several investors repeatedly succumb to the same psychological pitfalls. What is the reason? During market upswings, it seems more secure to conform to the majority rather than be solitary. Investors assure themselves that as long as others are profiting, they will also achieve financial gain. History demonstrates that genuine market stability arises from autonomous rather than collective movements. Individuals who pursue asset bubbles ultimately become casualties of their optimism, but those who identify mispricing before the herd's awareness are the ones who truly reap the rewards.

The true struggle was to reject the allure of the masses. Herding may provide short-term gains; however, it compromises long-term market efficiency, making it more challenging to accurately price assets. For markets to operate effectively, they must represent actual worth rather than widespread speculation. Until investors adopt a more detached perspective and assess assets with clarity, the cycle of bubbles and crashes will continue as it has historically.

1.4.2 Institutional and Retail Investors' Role in Herding

Herding behaviour is sometimes seen as a psychological pitfall for retail investors: average folks caught in market frenzies, purchasing at the zenith and divesting at the nadir (Chen et al. 2015). However, some of the most influential factors propelling herding behaviour are not individual traders but institutional investors, such as hedge funds, mutual funds, pension funds, and colossal asset management firms. These financial behemoths, equipped with billions of dollars and advanced algorithms, were not immune to the influence of groupthink. They often exacerbate market tendencies, thereby inciting booms and collapses.

At the institutional level, herding is influenced by a combination of professional incentives, risk aversion, and competitive pressures. Fund managers are evaluated based on their performance in comparison with their peers, creating a significant incentive to adhere to market trends rather than diverge from them. A fund manager adopting a contrarian approach, eschewing a flourishing stock or sector on which others are capitalising, faces the risk of underperformance and potential loss of investors. This explains why even adept investors who identify inflated assets may choose to capitalise on the trend instead of risking obsolescence. In extreme instances, this creates a self-perpetuating loop when institutional investors converge on identical bets to avoid the appearance of error in the short term, despite being aware that the long-term fundamentals do not warrant such actions.

Nevertheless, hedge funds, known for their assertive and autonomous trading techniques, are highly vulnerable to herding behaviour. Numerous hedge funds rely on similar mathematical models, technical indicators, and risk-management procedures, leading to similar findings. When a hedge fund executes a significant transaction, such as shorting a company, investing in a high-growth area, or reallocating from an asset class, its funds promptly follow suit. This occurred during the 2008 financial crisis when hedge funds invested significantly in mortgage-backed securities. They were convinced that as long as other funds were profiting in that sector, they could not afford to forgo participation. The collapse of the housing market initiated a chain reaction through the unwinding of these investments, exacerbating the crisis.

A notable catalyst of institutional herding is the proliferation of passive investing, where substantial funds replicate stock indices instead of engaging in active investment strategies. As exchange-traded funds (ETFs) and index funds proliferated, more capital was directed towards a particular group of equities solely because of their inclusion in the index. This suggests that when investors allocate capital to an S&P 500 index fund, all 500 firms experience inflows, regardless of their unique fundamentals. This may result in artificial inflation of stock prices since demand is influenced not by corporate performance but by automated capital movements.

Although institutional investors significantly influence market movements, the advent of social media has altered herding behaviour among retail investors, resulting in novel speculation in the digital age. Platforms such as Reddit, Twitter, TikTok, and YouTube have provided retail traders with an unparalleled capacity to coordinate, disseminate market insights, and stimulate widespread engagement in specific stocks, cryptocurrencies, and speculative transactions.

The most notable example of this phenomenon is the 2021 GameStop episode, in which a collective of retail investors on Reddit's r/WallStreetBets significantly inflated the price of GameStop's shares, resulting in substantial losses for hedge funds engaged in short selling. What started as a specialised transaction among a limited number of retail investors rapidly evolved into a significant financial movement as social media magnified the message and hundreds of new traders inundated the market. What is the outcome? A company that traded at $4 per share in 2020 surged to over $500 in early 2021, driven only by digital herding. However, for all earlier speculative frenzies, momentum was indefinitely not sustainable. After the frenzy subsided, stock prices plummeted, resulting in substantial losses for many late investors.

Social media herding is distinctive due to its rapid dissemination, driven by viral content, memes, and influencer-generated enthusiasm. A solitary tweet from Elon Musk, a trending hashtag, or a popular TikTok video may prompt hundreds of investors to engage in a transaction without consideration for fundamental analysis. This behaviour has significantly influenced the Bitcoin market. Meme currencies such as Dogecoin and Shiba Inu have surged dramatically, not due to technical advancements or intrinsic economic worth, but rather because of communal fervour and online momentum.

In contrast to conventional market herding, which is influenced by institutional authority and professional motivations, digital herding is propelled by emotions such as excitement, greed, and the exhilaration of participating in a significant movement. Retail traders today view investment not just as a financial choice, but as a social and cultural phenomenon, where participating in the right transaction at the right moment can integrate them into an online revolution.

What is the issue? Herding, influenced by social media, often results in significant instability. The prices of highly sought-after items may surge dramatically within days, only to plummet swiftly afterwards. In contrast to institutional investors, who employ risk management measures, retail traders sometimes invest all of their capital without safeguards, resulting in severe financial repercussions when enthusiasm wanes.

1.5 Case Studies

1.5.1 The Tulip Mania (1637)

The Tulip Mania of 1637 is a renowned incident in financial history, characterised by the exorbitant prices of a little flower, to the extent that the whole economy seemed to be dependent on it. Despite the ongoing discussion on the specifics of the crisis, it is indisputable that herd behaviour, social proof, and overconfidence contributed to an unsustainable bubble that ultimately burst, resulting in one of the most notorious cautionary tales in market speculation.

During that period, the Netherlands was among the most affluent countries globally, serving as a centre for commerce, finance, and innovation. The Dutch pioneered capitalism, controlling global trade through the Dutch East India Company and amassing substantial wealth from their naval empire. In this thriving economy, tulips, previously an exotic luxury imported from the Ottoman Empire, transformed into a symbol of prestige for the affluent. The more vivid and uncommon the tulip, the higher its perceived value. Dutch aristocracy and wealthy merchants started vying for the acquisition of the most coveted bulbs, transforming tulip possession into a symbol of distinction.

What started as a specialised luxury commodity for the affluent rapidly evolved into a comprehensive speculative market. As the price of tulip bulbs escalated, an increasing number of individuals, including artisans, farmers, and tradespeople, began purchasing tulips not for ornamental purposes but as financial investments. The rationale was straightforward: since prices had consistently increased over the years, they would continue in their upward trajectory. This encapsulates herding behaviour: investors ceased to rely on fundamentals and instead conformed to the majority, thinking that collective purchasing indicated correctness.

Social proof has significantly contributed to the escalation of the frenzy. In ambiguous circumstances, individuals often observe others' behaviour to inform their choices. The continuous increase in tulip prices reinforced the perception that tulips were a guaranteed investment. Even the initially sceptical individuals came to feel pressure to engage. They saw their neighbours acquiring wealth rapidly and worried about being excluded fear of missing out that continues to have a significant influence on contemporary financial markets.

Overconfidence, the conviction that the market will continue to ascend, exacerbates the situation. Investors deluded themselves into believing that the worth of tulip bulbs would rise perpetually, despite the disconnect from reality. This excessive excitement has led to a surge in speculative trading, with individuals borrowing funds, mortgaging properties, and liquidating assets to purchase more tulip bulbs. Contracts for tulips were transacted several times before the bulbs bloomed, establishing a primitive form of a futures market based only on speculation rather than intrinsic worth.

During the frenzy, the prices of the rarest tulips reached heights that contradicted all economic rationales. Sure, bulbs were allegedly sold at a cost exceeding that of the entire home in Amsterdam. Common labourers resigned from their positions to engage in tulip trading, believing that they had discovered a means to attain enduring prosperity. Chaos seemed inexorable until it stopped.

In early 1637, faith in the tulip market diminished abruptly. A customary tulip auction does not attract buyers willing to pay exorbitant sums. Doubt begins as a whisper and escalates to a shout. What sustained the market if price increases were not assured? A sense of panic ensued. Individuals who had invested substantial sums in tulip bulbs hastened to sell before the price declined; however, unexpectedly, there were no purchasers. The once-thriving market collapsed within weeks, resulting in financial ruin. Wealth was obliterated, contracts lost value, and several speculators were left with valueless flower bulbs.

The fascination of Tulip Mania lies not only in the ridiculousness of the bubble but also in its unsettling resemblance to contemporary events. The psychological mechanisms that propelled Dutch merchants into a speculative frenzy herding, social validation, and overconfidence recurred throughout history, from the dot-com bubble of the 1990s to the cryptocurrency surges of the 2010s and the 2020s. What is the lesson? The dynamics of collective psychology influence financial markets. Regardless of whether it pertains to tulip bulbs, technology equities, or digital currencies, when individuals cease to pose basic enquiries and begin to conform to the majority, they jeopardise their financial stability.

1.5.2 *The South Sea Bubble (1720)*

The South Sea Bubble of 1720 was a remarkable financial catastrophe characterised by unrestrained speculation, political machination, and the perilous influence of information asymmetry. In contrast to Tulip Mania, which was fuelled by a frenzy about a physical asset, the South Sea Bubble centred on something far more elusive: assurances of future riches. The crisis fundamentally arose from the conviction that a corporation devoid of tangible assets or profits could inexplicably produce unlimited wealth. When the illusion dissipated, it obliterated fortune, undermined investor confidence, and reverberated across the British economy.

The South Sea Company, a British commercial entity, played a central role in the frenzy and was awarded a monopoly on commerce with South America. The proposition was enticing: the business would exploit vast, uncharted markets, returning gold, silver, and rare commodities from the New World. Investors were informed that they were acquiring stakes in a venture that would make them affluent. There was a singular issue: Britain lacked substantial authority over South American commerce. The Spanish, who dominated the majority of the territory, had little intention of allowing profitable British commerce to thrive under their oversight. However, in public perception, such subtleties were of little significance.

Speculative frenzy was not entirely spontaneous; it was orchestrated. The British government contributed significantly to the bubble inflation. The South Sea Corporation was authorised to oversee national debt, enabling investors to convert government bonds into shares of the corporation. This created a semblance of financial credibility. Even King George I, members of Parliament, and other prominent personalities from Britain participated, thereby enhancing public confidence. If elites are investing, the enterprise must be a secure investment. This governmental backing served as social validation, attracting an increasing number of individuals to the conjecture.

However, the primary catalyst of the South Sea Bubble was information asymmetry, which refers to the disproportionate allocation of knowledge between insiders and the broader public. While average investors were misled into thinking the firm was poised for extraordinary success, those in authority, including government officials and corporate insiders, were aware of this reality. The South Sea Company engaged in a few legitimate economic activities; however, its management fervently marketed its stock, making extravagant claims and employing misleading financial strategies to enhance its valuation. Market manipulation was pervasive; insiders disseminated false rumours of imminent trade agreements, while corporate leaders clandestinely liquidated their shares as prices escalated.

Due to restricted access to credible information, ordinary investors relied on social proof, observing others accumulate wealth and assuming they could profit similarly. This established a self-reinforcing loop whereby escalating prices attracted additional buyers, further inflating share values. Stock prices surged from £100 to £1000 within a few months. Ordinary people, eager to engage, depleted their savings and secured loans and wagered all their assets, believing that this was their pathway to affluence.

Figure 1.1 shows that the company's stock price began a meteoric rise, fuelled by extravagant rumours of potential profits and aggressive marketing strategies in early 1720. Starting at approximately £128 in January, shares soared to £175 in February, £330 in March, and reached a peak of £1000 in August. This unprecedented surge was not supported by the company's fundamentals but was driven by speculative mania and the allure of quick riches. However, by September, the bubble burst, and the stock price plummeted back to £100, wiping out the fortunes of countless investors and leading to widespread financial ruin.

However, as with other speculative bubbles, the illusion was disintegrated. As uncertainties over the company's true profitability proliferated, confidence began to diminish. Insiders, who had already amassed their wealth, began liquidating their shares, sparking fear among investors. The market swiftly reversed, and what ascended rapidly plummeted. Stocks that were formerly highly valued became almost suddenly valueless. The crash ravaged many people, from nobles to labourers, and plunged Britain into financial disarray.

The South Sea Bubble was not only a financial debacle but also served as a significant lesson in market psychology. This revealed how governmental intervention may exacerbate speculative bubbles, conferring illusory legitimacy to precarious enterprises. It also highlights the risks of information asymmetry, where the privileged have access to authentic financial information while regular investors are left to pursue illusions. The legacy of the South Sea Bubble serves as a cautionary story that resonates in contemporary financial markets. The recurrence of deceit, widespread speculation, and insider benefit has been seen from Enron's accounting problems to the 2008 housing crisis. What is the lesson? Exercise caution when evaluating exaggerated claims, particularly when proponents are the primary beneficiaries.

1.5.3 The 2008 Financial Crisis

The 2008 financial crisis was a catastrophic economic collapse, erasing billions of dollars in global wealth, leading to the bankruptcy of significant financial institutions and leaving millions unemployed and homeless. This was not only a narrative of substandard loans and insolvent banks; it exemplified herding behaviour, whereby investors, financial institutions, and even average homebuyers were ensnared in the conviction that the housing market was infallible. The disaster arose from a communal miscalculation of risk, fuelled by unwarranted confidence, social validation, and the perilous assumption that widespread participation equated to safety.

The U.S. housing market, which had an unparalleled boom in the early 2000s, was at the core of the catastrophe. Home prices have been consistently increasing for years, and the prevailing notion is that real estate is a secure investment. This asset is expected to appreciate over time. This established a self-perpetuating loop whereby an increasing number of individuals sought to purchase properties, thereby

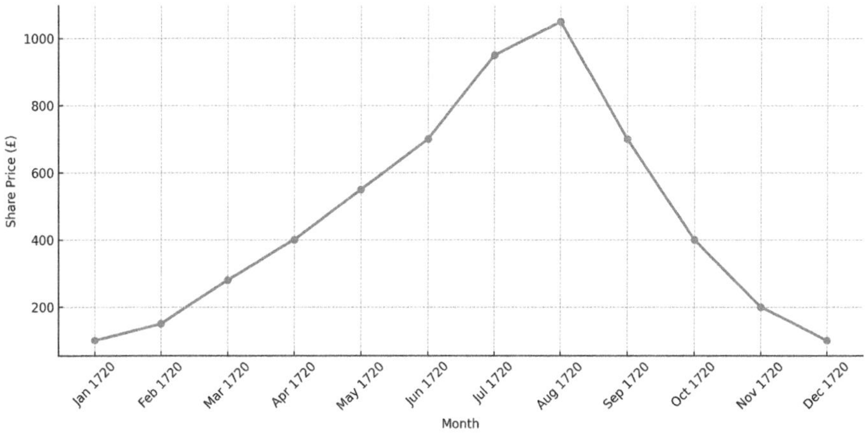

Fig. 1.1 South Sea Company share price. Source: Authors' work

driving up prices and enticing further buyers. Lenders eager to capitalise on the surge began providing mortgages to nearly everyone, including individuals with limited credit histories and restricted repayment capacity. These high-risk loans, known as subprime mortgages, became the foundation of the financial time bomb.

This swarming behaviour extended beyond that of home buyers. Banks, hedge funds, and institutional investors all adhere to the same perilous rationale, seeing real estate as a secure investment. They consolidated these high-risk mortgages into intricate financial instruments known as mortgage-backed securities (MBS) and marketed them to global investors. The securities were then restructured into more hazardous instruments, known as collateralised debt obligations (CDOs), which credit rating agencies classified as high-quality assets despite their composition of toxic debt. All parties benefited; hence, no one paused to consider the essential study: What happens if house prices cease to escalate?

The psychological factors behind the crisis were influenced by social proof and overconfidence. Investors saw banks generate billions of mortgage securities and thought they were secure. Homebuyers saw their neighbours purchasing houses with little or no down payments and inferred that they should emulate this practice. Banks saw their rivals extend precarious loans and experienced pressure to conform and remain competitive. The fear of missing out perpetuated the cycle: if others were profiting in real estate, why did they not participate? The notion that millions, including Wall Street experts, could simultaneously be erroneous was implausible.

However, fissures began to emerge in 2007. Housing prices remained static before declining. Homeowners who secured unaffordable mortgages suddenly discovered that they owed more than the value of their properties. Defaults increased, and ostensibly 'safe' mortgage-backed securities transformed into hazardous assets instantaneously. Banks that had overextended themselves started incurring substantial losses. However, due to the widespread distribution of these toxic assets across the global financial system, panic has rapidly intensified into a comprehensive financial crisis.

In 2008, Lehman Brothers, a prominent investment bank, collapsed due to its detrimental mortgage investments, triggering a chain reaction that led to a decline in global markets. Stock markets collapsed, significant banks required government assistance, and the global economy experienced its most severe recession since the Great Depression. Organisations that promoted herding, such as credit rating agencies, investment banks, and regulators, miscalculated the aggregate risk entirely.

The psychological ramifications of this catastrophe undermined trust in financial markets. Investors, who were formerly elated, are now gripped by fear of withdrawing their capital from equities, real estate, and many other assets. Governments were compelled to intervene in substantial bailouts, while central banks reduced interest rates to stabilise the economy. Millions of individuals lost their employment, residences, and life savings due to collective adherence to misguided convictions that property values were impervious to decline.

The 2008 crisis served as a stark reminder of the perilous nature of herding behaviour when it permeated an entire institution. The exact psychological mechanisms that compelled investors to engage in the South Sea Bubble and Tulip Mania were once again in effect. However, this time, the repercussions were of a global magnitude. The main lesson? When a consensus emerges that something is a 'certainty', it is often anything but. Markets are not infallible, and when the collective masses take risks, the repercussions may be disastrous.

1.6 Conclusion

The examination of herding behaviour in financial markets reveals a persistent pattern of human psychology, which has led to both remarkable profits and disastrous failures throughout history. From the speculative frenzy of Tulip Mania in 1637 to the systemic collapse of the 2008 financial crisis, herding has been one of the most significant and perilous forces in economic decision-making. This book analyses the methods, causes, and effects of herding, providing profound insights into why both institutional and ordinary investors often conform to the majority instead of using rational judgement.

This investigation highlights that herding is fundamentally influenced by psychological biases, including social proof, conformity, overconfidence, and the fear of missing out. Investors often do not rely on independent analysis; instead, they observe the actions of others and presume that these actions are the appropriate course of action. This inclination is exacerbated by the influence of the media, technological advancements, and digital communication platforms, which accelerate the dissemination of both rational and irrational financial trends. The emergence of social media-induced speculation, exemplified by the 2021 GameStop incident, has led to a rapid escalation of herding behaviour in the digital era.

However, herding is not intrinsically detrimental to the environment. Occasionally, this may result in market efficiency when investors jointly recognise attractive sectors or technical advancements. Nonetheless, when unregulated, herding can exacerbate asset bubbles, promote excessive speculation, and trigger panic-induced sell-offs. The collapse of financial bubbles, exemplified by the burst of the dot-com bubble in 2000 and the real estate downturn in 2008, has consistently demonstrated the catastrophic effects of widespread miscalculation. When investors collectively engage without scrutinising the viability of their investments, market distortions emerge, resulting in economic instability that may require years, if not decades, for recovery.

References

Banerjee AV (1992) A simple model of herd behaviour. Q J Econ 107(3):797–817

Bennett MR, Hacker PMS (2022) Philosophical foundations of neuroscience. Wiley, Hoboken

Bikhchandani S, Hirshleifer D, Welch I (1992) A theory of fads, fashion, custom, and cultural change as informational cascades. J Polit Econ 100(5):992–1026

Chen HL, Chow EH, Shiu CY (2015) The informational role of individual investors in stock pricing: evidence from large individual and small retail investors. Pac Basin Financ J 31:36–56

Choijil E, Méndez CE, Wong WK, Vieito JP, Batmunkh MU (2022) Thirty years of herd behaviour in financial markets: a bibliometric analysis. Res Int Bus Financ 59:101506

Cialdini RB (2001) Influence: science and practice, 4th edn. Allyn & Bacon, Boston

Clark CN, Edwards MJ, Ong BE, Goodliffe L, Ahmad H, Dilley MD, Jenkins PO (2022) Reframing postconcussional syndrome as an interface disorder of neurology, psychiatry and psychology. Brain 145(6):1906–1915

Fligstein N (2021) The banks did it: an anatomy of the financial crisis. Harvard University Press, Cambridge

Graham B (2014) The Mediterranean in the medieval and renaissance world. In: The Mediterranean. Routledge, London, pp 75–93

Humphrey RH, Massis AD, Picone PM, Tang Y, Piccolo RF (2021) The psychological foundations of management in family firms: emotions, memories, and experiences. Fam Bus Rev 34(2):122–131

Kaye J (2024) Introduction to the medieval and renaissance period. In: The Palgrave handbook of philosophy and money: volume 1: ancient and medieval thought. Springer, Cham, pp 523–531

Kennedy CA (2025) Biggest bankruptcy ever! Viewing a drama written in verse about investment banking through the lens of behavioural economics (Master's thesis, Harvard University)

Komalasari PT, Asri M, Purwanto BM, Setiyono B (2022) Herding behaviour in the capital market: what do we know and what is next? Manage Rev Q 72(3):745–787

Leonard A (2022) London marine insurance 1438–1824: risk, trade, and the early modern state. Boydell & Brewer, Martlesham

Lewellen J, Shanken J (2002) Learning, asset-pricing tests, and market efficiency. J Financ 57(3):1113–1145

Liu S, Zhao Y, Zhu Q (2022) Herd behaviours in epidemics: a dynamics-coupled evolutionary games approach. Dyn Games Appl 12(1):183–213

Loang OK (2023) Sustainable development goals, herding, and risk-averse behavior in Muslim countries. J Islam Monet Econ Financ 9(2):313–336

Loang OK (2024) Risk avoidance, macroeconomic indicators and bank performances in developing economies. Ann Fin Econ 19(4):2450018

Loang OK, Candra S, Naveenan RV (2024) Stability in chaos: impact of monetary, fiscal, and firm characteristics on investor sentiment in Asian emerging markets. Int J Business Soc 25(3):1145–1164

Notteboom T, Pallis T, Rodrigue JP (2021) Disruptions and resilience in global container shipping and ports: the COVID-19 pandemic versus the 2008–2009 financial crisis. Maritime Econ Logist 23(2):179

Ooi KL (2024) Analyst forecasting and market liquidity dynamics: a comparative analysis of US and Chinese markets pre and post COVID-19. J Gen Manag. https://doi.org/10.1177/03063070231225603

Picone PM, De Massis A, Tang Y, Piccolo RF (2021) The psychological foundations of management in family firms: values, biases, and heuristics. Fam Bus Rev 34(1):12–32

Shiller RJ (2000) Irrational exuberance. Princeton University Press, Princeton

Sufi A, Taylor AM (2022) Financial crises: a survey. Handb Int Econ 6:291–340

Tversky A, Kahneman D (1992) Advances in prospect theory: cumulative representation of uncertainty. J Risk Uncertain 5(4):297–323

Chapter 2
Market Overreaction Explained

2.1 Introduction

Market overreaction is a compelling and extensively discussed phenomenon in behavioural finance. This describes a scenario in which investors react disproportionately to new information, leading to significant deviations in asset prices from their underlying values. In contrast to efficient market theory, which posits that stock prices consistently reflect all available information rationally, market overreaction suggests that emotions, cognitive biases, and herd behaviour may drive financial markets into severe and often illogical fluctuations. This inclination may lead to transient price distortions, resulting in mispricing, speculation, and economic instability in extreme cases (Loang 2024a). Comprehending market overreaction is crucial for investors navigating volatile markets, as well as for politicians and regulators seeking to mitigate systemic risks.

In contrast to sensible price changes that align asset values with fresh information, overreactions disrupt this mechanism. In a perfectly efficient market, investors evaluate new information impartially and adjust their values accordingly, thereby minimising undue volatility. In reality, financial markets are influenced by human psychology, where emotions and biases often supersede logical analysis. Investors often overemphasise recent occurrences, misread indicators, and respond excessively to news regardless of their nature. This emotional intensification may drive prices to unsustainable heights, fuel asset bubbles, or trigger significant sell-offs. The primary difference is in the scale and persistence of price fluctuations; sensible adjustments tend to stabilise over time, but overreactions may lead to extended volatility and financial instability.

Central to market overreactions are the many psychological biases that influence investor behaviour. Availability heuristics lead people to rely on easily retrievable information, resulting in an exaggerated emphasis on current or sensational events rather than evaluating past patterns or essential facts (Loang 2025). Anchoring bias causes investors to remain focused on a reference point, such as historical stock

K. L. Ooi et al., *Following the Crowd: Psychological Drivers of Herding and Market Overreaction*, https://doi.org/10.1007/978-981-95-0792-4_2

prices or analyst predictions, rendering them hesitant to modify their expectations despite fresh evidence indicating a different outcome. Loss aversion, a significant principle in behavioural finance, leads investors to dread losses more than they value similar profits. This tendency often leads to panic selling during market declines and excessive risk-taking in favourable environments. Collectively, these cognitive distortions create an environment in which asset values tend to fluctuate between irrational and extreme pessimism.

The repercussions of market overreaction are extensive, often resulting in financial crises, speculative bubbles, and heightened investor emotion. Historical events, such as the 1929 Stock Market Crash, the late 1990s dot-com bubble, and the 2008 financial crisis, illustrate how collective overreaction may propel markets to unsustainable peaks before collapsing with catastrophic repercussions. These incidents highlight a cyclical tendency toward overreaction, where speculative excess is followed by swift corrections, resulting in extensive economic turmoil. In addition to large-scale crises, overreaction influences individual investors, often leading them to purchase at market peaks and sell at troughs, rather than adhering to prudent investment strategies.

In the high-octane world of financial markets, investors pride themselves on rationality, portraying themselves as cold and calculating strategists driven by logic and data. However, beneath spreadsheets and algorithms, human psychology quietly governs the market's heartbeat. Table 2.1 reveals three of the most potent and persistent cognitive biases: the availability heuristic, anchoring bias, and loss aversion, each subtly distorting investor judgement, often without the investor's awareness. The availability heuristic is the mental trick our brains play when visibility is confused with validity. If a story is loud, recent, or emotionally intense, we assume that it is essential. A crisis splashed across every headline, or a sudden market rally filling our social media feeds, can hijack our decision-making. Instead of weighing fundamentals, we react impulsively to noise. The mind clings to what it can recall most vividly, not what is most relevant. This explains why a minor event, excessively covered in the media, can trigger disproportionate investor panic or euphoria, launching markets into irrational overdrive.

However, deception does not stop. Anchoring bias traps investors in psychological time warps. We anchor our expectations to an initial number stock's purchase price, a previous market high and unconsciously allow it to dictate our present decisions. When a share dips from $100 to $70, many investors stubbornly hold on, not because the fundamentals justify it, but because they believe it will eventually return to 'what it used to be'. Conversely, when a stock rallies beyond what we are accustomed to seeing, we hesitate, suspicious that it has gone 'too far', even if today's reality supports a higher valuation. Then, there is the king of all biases, loss aversion, the reason market corrections often descend into full-blown crashes. Investors hate losing more than they love winning. The moment red numbers appear on their screens, the fear reflex kicks in. Rational analysis is abandoned in favour of emotional escape. Sell now, think later. This primal fear response turns regular market cycles into self-fulfilling ones. These psychological traps do not just affect

Table 2.1 Cognitive biases that shape investor behaviour

Bias	What it means	How it affects investors	Illustrative example
Availability heuristic	Investors tend to judge the likelihood of an event based on how easily an example comes to mind usually recent, dramatic, or emotionally charged news	Heightens emotional reactions and clouds rational judgement. Investors focus on eye-catching headlines instead of long-term trends or fundamental data	A sudden geopolitical conflict dominates the news cycle. Even though the affected region has minimal economic ties to the investor's portfolio, the constant media attention causes panic selling across global markets. The fear is not rooted in analysis but in mental accessibility
Anchoring bias	The human mind latches onto an initial piece of information (often the purchase price or a past market high) and uses it as a reference point, even when it no longer makes sense	Investors become mentally 'stuck'. They delay selling poor-performing assets or resist buying valuable stocks just because prices deviate from past norms	An investor buys a stock at \$120. Months later, the stock falls to \$85 due to sector-wide changes. Despite new data suggesting the company is now overvalued, the investor refuses to sell clinging to the belief it will return to \$120, even though that figure is now irrelevant
Loss aversion	The emotional pain of losing money is far stronger than the joy of gaining the same amount. This causes people to avoid losses at all costs even at the expense of future gains	Triggers fear-based decisions, such as panic selling during downturns or hesitating to invest in promising assets. This leads to missed opportunities and irrational exits	During the 2008 financial crisis, many investors saw their portfolios drop and exited the market in panic. Had they stayed invested, they could have recovered handsomely during the subsequent bull market. Instead, their fear of further losses caused them to lock in losses permanently

Source: Authors' work

amateurs; even seasoned traders fall prey to them. Recognising their pull is the first step toward making wiser, more composed decisions in a world that rewards not just intelligence but also emotional discipline.

2.2 Behavioural Triggers Leading to Overreaction

2.2.1 Availability Heuristics and Market Sentiment

Investors want to see their decision-making as grounded in logic, analysis, and rational thinking. However, markets repeatedly convey another narrative (Barberis et al. 1998). Emotions dominate, logic diminishes, and the price of a company or the entire market fluctuates in a manner that contradicts its essential worth

(Haritha 2024). The availability heuristic is a potent, although often unnoticed, influence on behaviour. It serves as a cognitive shortcut that leads individuals to excessively depend on the most recent or striking information they receive. In the realm of investment, when a prominent firm fails, a financial scandal arises, or a significant geopolitical crisis occurs, investors tend to focus excessively on a single event, often disregarding broader historical patterns or underlying facts. Their risk perception becomes distorted, leading them to make judgements driven by fear or exhilaration instead of rationality.

Envision an investor who experienced the 2008 financial crisis. This event, characterised by dramatic market downturns and the imminent collapse of the global financial system, is indelibly etched in their minds (Loang 2024b). Years later, despite the significantly altered economic circumstances, a slight market decline or adverse news may elicit an exaggerated response. The recollection of previous crises skews their assessment of current dangers, resulting in excessive reactions, such as hastily liquidating equities, withdrawing from the market altogether, or eschewing prudent investments that meet all rational criteria. Conversely, the same concept applies: when a stock has been rising for weeks, headlines are favourable, and social media is replete with narratives of substantial profits, investors begin to assume that the rise is perpetual. The latest and most salient information influences decision-making, causing people to pursue trends at opportune moments.

Media significantly enhanced these psychological inclinations. Financial news networks, social media, and online investing forums function on a fundamental principle: attention generates engagement, which yields profits (Kliger and Kudryavtsev 2010). Consequently, spectacular headlines, hyperbolic predictions, and emotionally charged tales prevail in financial reporting. A solitary earnings shortfall from a prominent corporation may spark media uproar, with experts warning about potential declines and traders responding to the alarm. Conversely, as markets ascend, news sources amplify enthusiasm, often portraying speculative rallies as inexorable phenomena and prompting ordinary investors to engage in inflated valuations. This creates a perilous feedback loop: media magnifies investor mood, investor sentiment drives market fluctuations, and market fluctuations elicit more media attention, accelerating the cycle.

Social media have elevated this phenomenon to an unprecedented degree. Professional journalists and experts have historically disseminated financial news (Shefrin and Statman 1994). Currently, anyone with Internet access can influence market sentiment. Platforms such as Twitter, Reddit, and YouTube have created retail investor groups in which speculation, rumours, and hype disseminate with unparalleled rapidity. A single viral article may propel a stock upward or downward within hours and is often disconnected from any fundamental rationale. The GameStop phenomenon in 2021 exemplifies this. A modest gathering of retail traders discussing short squeezes in Reddit's WallStreetBets community has evolved into a global financial phenomenon. Availability heuristics were prominently at play. Investors were drawn to news stories such as 'the underdogs triumphing over Wall Street', narratives of substantial overnight profits, and forecasts of perpetual growth. The overwhelming magnitude and fervour of the story made it an irresistible phenomenon, prompting many individuals to engage without comprehending the associated hazards.

The Genuine Danger of Availability Heuristics in Financial Markets: When investors excessively depend on the latest or sensationalised information, they become captives of the present (Chen et al. 2017). They pursue euphoria, evade despair, and eventually make choices that jeopardise enduring prosperity. Identifying this prejudice is the first step to surmounting it. Accomplished investors cultivate the ability to detach, examine historical data, assess fundamentals, and withstand the emotional influences of transient news cycles. The capacity to disengage from distractions and preserve perspective distinguishes individuals who succeed in the market from those who succumb to psychological pitfalls.

2.2.2 Anchoring Bias and Price Fixation

Investors prefer to believe that they are adaptable thinkers who can modify their expectations in response to new information (Odean 1998). However, actuality often diverges significantly (Wang 2023). The human mind has a persistent inclination to cling to specific reference points, such as numerical values, historical pricing, and prior trends, while finding it challenging to transcend these benchmarks even in the face of significant changes. This cognitive prejudice is referred to as anchoring bias, and in the realm of investment, it may constitute one of the most perilous and expensive errors.

Envision an investor who acquires shares of a corporation at a price of $100 per share. Subsequently, the stock undergoes market declines, sector disturbances, or disappointing results, resulting in a price reduction of $70. Investors must reassess new knowledge. Does a company's forecast support its present valuation? Is this a prudent investment? Instead, they remained tethered to an initial purchase price of $100. They convince themselves that I will divest when the price returns to $100, despite the threshold being entirely dissociated from the company's true worth. This obsession may lead to illogical decisions, such as clinging to underperforming equities excessively, disregarding superior investment prospects, or even exacerbating a poor wager in the hope of recouping losses.

This bias affects investors during periods of stock appreciation. Assume that a company's stock, which has traditionally traded at about $50 per share, unexpectedly escalates to $90 on favourable news (Ali 2023). Numerous investors may exhibit reluctance, believing that $50 represents the 'true' price and that the present value is an overreaction despite the company's fundamentals now warranting the elevated valuation. This indecision may lead individuals to forfeit lucrative investment opportunities due to their fixation on outdated pricing. In both instances, whether choosing to sell a depreciating stock or refraining from purchasing an appreciating one, anchoring bias compels investors to base their judgements on historical figures rather than current circumstances.

Anchoring bias influences not only individual investors but also significantly affects the entire market dynamics, particularly during periods of rapid transformation. In stock market falls, many investors are preoccupied with the prior peaks (De Bondt and Thaler 1995). During the 2008 financial crisis, stock values declined significantly universally; however, investors who based their expectations on pre-crisis levels often overlooked the fundamental changes that had occurred. Consequently, they either retained depreciating stocks excessively or were reluctant to re-enter the market during low-price periods, thus forgoing the subsequent rebound.

Conversely, in speculative bubbles, anchoring bias can lead to perilous levels of overconfidence. Examine the cryptocurrency surge of 2017, during which Bitcoin escalated from approximately $1000 to over $20,000 within a single year. Investors who had seen Bitcoin at $5000 several months prior attached their expectations to that price, persuading themselves that $20,000 was merely a starting point. When the price ultimately plummeted to $3000 in 2018, many were astonished and were unable to comprehend that their benchmarks had been illusory highs rather than enduring prices.

The potency of anchoring bias resides in its capacity to supersede rationality and confine investors to antiquated beliefs. However, recognising this prejudice may serve as a potent instrument. Experienced investors cultivate the ability to counteract anchoring by persistently re-evaluating their beliefs. They circumvent the cognitive bias of obsessing over historical price levels and concentrate instead on fundamentals, such as corporate profits, economic conditions, and overarching market trends. Adaptability is key. Markets are dynamic, evolving in reaction to new information, and successful investors are those who can modify their strategy without adhering to predetermined price points. Releasing obsolete anchors is not the only talent; it is essential for sustained success in the financial realm.

2.2.3 Loss Aversion and Panic Selling

Fear has a far more significant influence than greed on financial markets. Investors may like profits, although they detest losses. Psychological studies indicate that the anguish of financial loss almost doubles the satisfaction derived from an identical gain (Kuramoto et al. 2024). This entrenched prejudice, known as loss aversion, significantly influences investor behaviour, particularly during times of market decline. It elucidates the reasons for the uncontrollable nature of sell-offs, the capacity of tiny losses to incite widespread panic, and the tendency of even experienced investors to engage in irrational behaviour when confronted with potential financial losses.

Loss aversion predisposes investors to overreact to negative information. Participants may exhibit confidence and optimism in steady or ascending markets. However, once a downturn commences, whether instigated by a disappointing earnings report, geopolitical strife, or economic instability, anxiety prevails. Investors often focus on potential losses and sometimes exaggerate the dangers. Rather than assessing their portfolios judiciously, they hastily sell before the conditions deteriorate, sometimes liquidating solid stocks in the process. This fear-induced reaction seldom relies on a basic understanding. This is an emotional response to the immediate distress of seeing negative figures in their accounts.

The danger of this behaviour is exacerbated by herd mentality, the inclination of investors to emulate the crowd's behaviours instead of exercising independent judgement. Panic is infectious. When investors initiate sales, others see a downturn and conclude that a significant issue must be present. Instead of delaying an analysis of the problem, they participated in the evacuation, anticipating the mitigation of losses before the harm escalated (Kahneman and Tversky 1996). This chain reaction may transform the mild fall into a comprehensive market meltdown. The greater the panic among individuals, the more severe the sell-off, perpetuating a detrimental cycle of fear and declining prices.

Historical instances abound in which loss aversion and herd-induced panic selling disrupt financial markets. The 1929 Stock Market Crash is a classic case study. In the months preceding the crisis, the market experienced a boom characterised by speculative fervour that propelled stock values to unprecedented levels. However, once the market started its downturn in October, dread ensued. Investors who had leveraged funds to acquire equities were forced to divest, triggering further panic. The psychological anguish of financial loss, coupled with the urgent need to withdraw from the market prior to additional price declines, precipitated one of the most severe economic crises in history.

The 2008 financial crisis illustrates how loss aversion may precipitate a market collapse. With the collapse of the housing bubble and the onset of bank failures, global stock markets experienced a significant decline. Investors apprehensive about the possibility of a subsequent Great Depression divested their assets at an extraordinary rate. Even those with robust, well-diversified portfolios experienced terror upon seeing others liquidate their holdings. Rather than retaining significant assets, they succumbed to fear, thereby realising losses that might have been recuperated with patience.

Even in moderate instances, loss aversion and herd behaviour influence daily market fluctuations. A single adverse news piece might diminish a company's value by billions of dollars. A market downturn may trigger automatic stop-loss orders, exacerbating drops in the absence of any fundamental cause for alarm. In an era of algorithmic trading and continuous financial news, panic selling may spread rapidly and often exacerbate short-term losses beyond what market fundamentals warrant.

2.3 The Financial Toll of Exaggerated Market Responses

2.3.1 The Impact on Market Volatility

Market volatility is the heartbeat of the financial realm, occasionally stable and foreseeable, at others, unpredictable and tumultuous. Although several variables contribute to price fluctuations, one of the most significant, but often undervalued, influences is market overreaction (Dhingra et al. 2024). When investors allow emotions and cognitive biases to influence their judgements, prices may surge or fall irrationally far above or below fair value within days or even hours. These drastic variations generate uncertainty, undermine investor confidence, and more critically propagate a self-sustaining cycle of volatility that may destabilise all markets.

Overreaction skews stock values by inducing disproportionate fluctuations in reactions to fresh information. Rather than assimilating news judiciously, investors often overreact, either by hastily acquiring assets at inflated prices or precipitously divesting in a state of panic. A solitary earnings report that slightly underperforms expectations may trigger a substantial sell-off, despite the company's robust long-term outlook. A rumour or optimistic projection may elevate stock values dramatically, only for reality to precipitate a decline. These overreactions are not logical responses to essential evidence; instead, they are driven by investor psychology, characterised by fear, greed, and a herd mentality.

The influence of overreactions on volatility is most evident in historical market movements. The Black Monday catastrophe of 1987 exemplified one of the most significant and spectacular events in financial history. On October 19, the Dow Jones Industrial Average plummeted by 22.6% in a single day, marking the most important one-day percentage decline in history. Although apprehensions over trade deficits and inflation had been brewing, the speed and magnitude of the downturn were much beyond what economic principles could rationalise. The fall was primarily fuelled by panic selling, computerised trading systems exacerbated anxiety, and investors responded to market indicators. What was intended as a temporary adjustment evolved into a monumental downfall as terror supplanted it.

The dot-com boom in the late 1990s served as a compelling example. Driven by exuberant speculation, investors allocate capital to online startups, inflating value to irrational heights despite several firms lacking profitability or sustainable business plans (Liu et al. 2023a). Each successful IPO (initial public offering) confirmed the notion that the Internet was an inexhaustible source of wealth. However, when reality emerged and corporations failed to fulfil expectations, the market responded excessively. Between 2000 and 2002, the NASDAQ Composite experienced a decline of approximately 78% in value, erasing billions of dollars in wealth. The collapse was not only a correction of inflated stock prices but also an overreaction to a prior overreaction, illustrating the bidirectional nature of volatility.

Overreaction contributed significantly to the 2008 financial crisis. As the housing market started to deteriorate, investors experienced panic, liquidating mortgage-backed assets and equities at any cost. The fear of systemic failure has resulted in some of the most severe market fluctuations in history. The Dow Jones experienced daily movements of 5–10%, a level of volatility seldom seen, except during wars or economic crises. Numerous price fluctuations are driven by pure uncertainty and loss aversion, rather than by changes in the asset's underlying value.

The phenomena of overreaction and volatility are not confined to market collapse; they also account for abrupt rallies. Examine the GameStop phenomenon in 2021. A modest assembly of ordinary traders, opposed to Wall Street short sellers, has evolved into a global financial phenomenon. The stock price surged over 1700%

within weeks, propelled not by changes in the firm's fundamentals but by excitement, social media discourse, and a shared conviction that prices could only continue to rise. However, as the mood changed, the bubble collapsed, and the stock declined sharply. This kind of drastic price fluctuation, disconnected from the underlying value, epitomises the market overreaction that exacerbates volatility.

The danger of volatility caused by overreaction lies in its ability to generate a feedback cycle. As market volatility increases, investors tend to overreact to fewer events (Zhang et al. 2023). A slight decline can escalate into a panic sell-off, whereas a slight rise can transform into an unsustainable bubble. Every new fluctuation underscores the notion that markets are erratic and tumultuous, leading to more emotional decision-making. Understanding this trend is essential for investors, analysts, and policymakers. Individuals who understand how overreaction exacerbates volatility may avoid being overwhelmed by unreasonable market fluctuations. The most successful investors do not pursue trends or succumb to panic at the first indication of adversity; they remain anchored in fundamentals, understanding that volatility, while unavoidable, is often amplified by human behaviour. The essential strategy for enduring and prospering in financial markets is not to avoid volatility, but to manage it from a clear and sensible perspective.

2.3.2 Impact on Institutional and Retail Investors

The impact of market overreaction is not uniform across investors. Retail investors often succumb to emotional decision-making, whereas experienced traders, hedge funds, and institutional investors tend to excel in turbulent environments (Liu et al. 2023b). The considerable disparity in the reactions of these two groups to severe market fluctuations explains why retail investors often incur losses while astute market participants capitalise on their errors. Overreactions provide possibilities for those who maintain rationality and discipline, but those who allow fear and greed to dictate their choices often incur significant losses.

Professional traders and hedge funds possess a unique advantage over individual investors: they understand that markets are influenced by psychology and have the tools to exploit irrational behaviour (Badía et al. 2021). When excessive reactions lead to stock values soaring to unreasonable levels or falling below the intrinsic value, institutional investors intervene to capitalise on these discrepancies. A quintessential illustration is contrarian trading, in which hedge funds acquire inexpensive equities during panic sell-offs and short, overvalued assets during speculative booms. This method is effective because overreaction is often transient; markets generally self-correct after emotions diminish. Substantial investors with significant capital and advanced models can withstand volatility, wagering on the ultimate reversion to an intrinsic value.

Institutional investors also capitalise on overreactions via high-frequency trading (HFT). These companies use computers to identify and capitalise on small, illogical price fluctuations within milliseconds. During instances of panic selling, high-frequency trading algorithms identify undervalued assets and acquire them before a typical investor has a chance to respond. Likewise, when ordinary investors pursue a stock driven by enthusiasm, these algorithms capitalise on the momentum by selling, thus securing gains before the inevitable price decline. This high-frequency trading approach exploits the emotional volatility of inexperienced market participants, yielding billions of dollars in profits for hedge funds, while individual investors incur substantial losses.

Conversely, retail investors often fail in turbulent markets because they tend to let emotions dictate their trading decisions. Fear, greed, and herd mentality result in purchasing at elevated prices and divesting at diminished values, the very antithesis of prudent investment. A prevalent error is panic selling, whereby an investor liquidates equities at a loss just by seeing negative figures on their display. Motivated by loss aversion, this response overlooks the reality that many market falls are transient and that long-term investors often recuperate their losses by maintaining their investments. However, fear obscures judgement, prompting several individuals to withdraw from the market at the most opportune moment.

Conversely, FOMO (fear of missing out) may be as detrimental. When a stock experiences a sudden surge, ordinary investors often rush to participate, believing they are missing a rare opportunity. They base their forecasts on recent price fluctuations, assuming that the pattern will continue forever. This cognitive bias was prominent during the 2021 GameStop short squeeze, when several retail investors rushed to the stock as it surged, only to see its decline as momentum dissipated. The hedge funds that initially shortened the company's position incurred early losses; however, after the bubble burst, institutional investors profited from the downturn, while several retail traders were left with worthless shares.

The financial sector is structured to exacerbate the emotional characteristics of regular investors. Financial news networks, social media influencers, and trading applications promote impulsive behaviour (Jones et al. 2021). Inflated headlines, hyperbolic predictions, and sensational stock recommendations foster short-term thinking, complicating individual investors' ability to maintain rationality. The emergence of commission-free trading platforms, which gamify investing via push alerts and confetti animations, promotes fast, emotion-driven transactions over deliberate, long-term decision-making.

However, ordinary investors are not destined to fail. To avoid the pitfalls of overreaction, it is essential to adopt a disciplined, data-driven investment strategy. Long-term investors who disregard daily price fluctuations, eschew speculative fervours, and adhere to basic research often surpass those who pursue trends or respond emotionally. Renowned investors such as Warren Buffett have amassed their fortunes by capitalising on market overreactions rather than succumbing to them. Buffett's adage, 'be fearful when others are greedy and greedy when others are fearful', underscores the need for patience and reason in an erratic market.

2.3.3 *Impact on Regulatory and Economic*

Market overreaction is not only an issue for individual or institutional investors; it also has extensive ramifications for the entire financial system (Aghion et al. 2023). Excessive volatility driven by overreaction may undermine investor confidence, destabilise the economy, and, in severe instances, compel governments and regulatory authorities to intervene to re-establish order. Financial markets form the foundation of the global economy, and when they exhibit excessive instability, the repercussions extend far beyond Wall Street, affecting companies, consumers, and governments.

Regulatory intervention is often required when excessive reactions jeopardise financial stability or generate inequitable market circumstances. During market crashes caused by panic selling or uncontrollable surges driven by speculative mania, authorities encounter increasing demand to take action. A common reaction is the deployment of circuit breakers, devices intended to halt trade when prices fall precipitously temporarily. Following the Black Monday crisis of 1987, during which the Dow Jones Industrial Average plummeted by 22.6% in a single day, U.S. authorities implemented circuit breakers to prevent future market collapses. These protections were activated several times during the COVID-19 market turmoil in March 2020, underscoring their function in mitigating excessive overreactions and allowing investors to re-evaluate their selections judiciously.

A significant regulatory measure to counteract overreactions is the imposition of short-selling limits. In times of increased volatility, authorities may implement temporary prohibitions on short selling to avert the significant downward pressure on stock prices. This was apparent during the 2008 financial crisis, when some governments, notably the United States and the United Kingdom, temporarily prohibited short selling in bank equities to mitigate panic-induced falls. Although these restrictions help avert abrupt, panic-induced sell-offs, they often incite controversy, as they are contended to undermine market efficiency and may result in unexpected repercussions, such as artificially sustaining expensive equities.

In addition to direct market interventions, regulatory authorities enhance financial monitoring when overreactions reveal systemic weakness. The excessive risk-taking that precipitated the 2008 crisis triggered comprehensive changes, notably the Dodd-Frank Act in the U.S.A., designed to deter financial institutions from engaging in imprudent speculation. Likewise, after the collapse of the dot-com bubble in the early 2000s, more stringent corporate governance measures were implemented to mitigate the deceptive financial reporting that had driven speculative excess. These initiatives demonstrate how excessive responses can alter the regulatory framework, leading to stricter regulations and increased monitoring that may persist for an extended period.

The economic ramifications of overreaction transcend stock prices, which may jeopardise long-term financial stability. Market crashes induced by investor fear lead to elevated borrowing rates for firms, a decline in consumer confidence, and a reduction in investment. An exemplary case is the Great Depression, which was triggered by the 1929 stock market collapse, instigating a cascade of economic deterioration that resulted in widespread unemployment, bank insolvencies, and a protracted economic recession. The 2008 financial crisis, driven by excessive exuberance in the housing market and subsequent overreactions in financial markets, resulted in one of the most severe recessions in contemporary history worldwide. These examples demonstrate that market overreaction is not only an economic issue; it can also permeate the economy, affecting employment, salaries, and sustainable development.

Even when overreaction does not culminate in complete financial crises, it engenders inefficiencies that destabilise the market equilibrium. When asset values fluctuate erratically due to speculative trading rather than intrinsic value, capital allocation is affected. Companies may struggle to secure capital at fair values, and volatile market conditions may deter long-term investors. Additionally, economic expansion may decelerate as financial uncertainty undermines companies and erodes consumer confidence. In severe instances, excessive reactions may erode faith in financial markets entirely, leading to reduced engagement from ordinary investors and a shift toward alternative assets, such as real estate or cryptocurrency, which also entail their associated risks.

To mitigate these consequences, governments and regulators have continually adjusted their policies to manage market volatility. Central banks often intervene during financial crises by changing interest rates, providing liquidity, or implementing quantitative easing to stabilise markets. The Federal Reserve's assertive measures during the COVID-19 crisis, reducing interest rates to nearly zero and acquiring billions of dollars in assets, averted a financial catastrophe, illustrating policymakers' response to economically disruptive overreactions.

2.4 Lessons from History's Biggest Market Collapses

2.4.1 The 1929 Stock Market Crash

The 1929 Stock Market Crash was not only a financial failure; it was a psychological catastrophe (Gordon 2023). A historical moment occurred when fear supplanted reason, speculation was divided into anarchy, and millions of investors watched helplessly as their wealth dissipated overnight. Although several economic causes led to the crisis, behavioural triggers significantly exacerbated one of history's most catastrophic financial collapses, thereby precipitating the Great Depression.

During the 1920s, the U.S. stock market experienced an unprecedented surge in activity. The economy thrived, industrial output increased, and consumer confidence reached its peak. However, underneath this wealth was a foundation constructed by excessive speculation. Numerous Americans, from Wall Street magnates to local merchants, were investing in stocks, confident that prices would continue to rise. The notion that stock market investment was a 'guaranteed success' has become firmly ingrained in widespread awareness. Newspapers sensationalised the success narratives of average individuals acquiring wealth rapidly, while financial consultants urged investors to leverage borrowed funds to purchase stocks on margin to optimise their profits. By 1929, over 40% of all stock market transactions had been conducted using borrowed funds, a degree of leverage that rendered the market a precarious situation.

This unreasoned confidence exemplified irrational exuberance, as investors disregarded cautionary indicators and invested in equities driven solely by greed. Availability heuristics significantly influenced investors who anchored their expectations of recent profits, assuming that the bull market would last indefinitely. As stock prices increased, public confidence increased, thereby perpetuating the myth of market infallibility. Few studies investigate whether fundamentals support these escalating prices.

However, when fissures emerged, market sentiment transitioned from elation to acute terror. By mid-1929, the economic signs indicated impending difficulties. Industrial productivity decelerated, business earnings diminished, and consumer debt increased (Fleming 2021). Nevertheless, most investors disregarded these cautions, believing that the market's momentum would continue. The tipping point occurred in September 1929 when stock values fluctuated, leading to a succession of modest drops that undermined investor confidence. The market's vulnerability was starkly demonstrated on October 24, known as Black Thursday, when panic selling began. A surge in margin calls compelled overleveraged investors to liquidate their holdings, instigating a self-perpetuating cycle of trepidation.

On October 29, known as Black Tuesday, the market experienced a precipitous decline, with the Dow Jones Industrial Average plummeting over 12% in a single day. The rapidity and magnitude of the collapse were exacerbated by herd behaviour; when investors saw plummeting prices, they hastily sought to liquidate their holdings at any cost, eager to escape before the conditions deteriorated further. The concept of 'riding out the storm' dissipated as the fear of complete financial devastation seized the market. Banks, having extended credit imprudently to stock speculators, then panicked and demanded loan repayments and liquidated assets to mitigate losses. The cycle of compelled liquidation intensified this collapse, resulting in an overall market depreciation of approximately 90% during the subsequent 3 years.

The psychological repercussions of the crisis were as catastrophic as the financial losses. Investors who envisioned boundless prosperity now view the stock market as a perilous and erratic entity. The abrupt and severe decline in wealth undermined public confidence in Wall Street, prompting several individuals to cease investing entirely. This psychological pain had a cascade impact on the broader economy: businesses collapsed, unemployment surged, and consumer expenditure declined sharply. As apprehension extended beyond financial markets, a temporary economic downturn evolved into the Great Depression, a prolonged economic catastrophe that lasted for nearly a decade.

2.4.2 The Dot-Com Bubble (1999–2000)

The late 1990s represent an era of unparalleled technical optimism. The Internet was revolutionising the world, novel tech businesses were rising rapidly, and investors were sure they were witnessing the inception of a new economic era. Capital was readily invested in any enterprise, including those with '.com' in their title, but conventional valuation criteria, such as profitability, cash flow, or a sustainable business model, were largely disregarded. Stocks ascended not because of their underlying robustness, but because investors had faith in the boundless possibilities of technology. It was a classic instance of market overreaction, where excessive exuberance elevated asset values to untenable levels, subsequently leading to a precipitous decline upon the return to reality.

The dot-com boom was driven by a confluence of the fear of missing out, speculative exuberance, and the pervasive conviction that traditional economic principles were obsolete. Investors saw technology firms doubling or tripling in value within months, and rather than scrutinising the durability of these increases, they hastily purchased shares, worried that they might miss the next significant chance. The financial media significantly contributed to the escalation of this hysteria, with experts and pundits perpetuating the idea that 'this time is different'. Silicon Valley was lauded as the epitome of wealth generation, with any enterprise linked to Internet technology seen as an immediate success story.

The core of the bubble was an exaggerated response to the Internet's promises. Although digital transformation really altered sectors, investors underestimated the pace and profitability of this upheaval. Numerous Internet businesses launched initial public offerings (IPOs) without achieving profitability, although their stock prices surged solely due to speculation, excitement, and momentum. Valuations reached ludicrous heights, as seen in the case of Amazon, which exhibited a price-to-earnings (P/E) ratio above 1000, while several enterprises with no sales were appraised in billions. People thought growth was more important than making a profit, so they put money into companies that couldn't actually earn money..

Nonetheless, no bubble can last indefinitely, and by early 2000, fissures started to manifest. Investors began to scrutinise the justification of these exorbitant values, and as scepticism permeated the market, a rush to leave ensued. The succession of unsatisfactory earnings announcements from prominent technology firms triggered a flurry of sell-offs. Suddenly, the same investors who had inflated prices to exorbitant levels recognised their excessive response to the Internet boom and subsequently overreacted once more, this time in the opposite direction.

The subsequent event was one of the most remarkable market crashes in history. The Nasdaq Composite, which escalated from 1000 points in 1995 to over 5000 points in early 2000, plummeted over 78% by 2002. Firms formerly favoured by Wall Street vanished instantaneously. Pets.com, a prominently marketed firm that spent millions of dollars advertising without a sustainable route to profitability, declared bankruptcy 9 months after its first public offering. Other technology behemoths, such as Cisco, Intel, and Amazon, experienced stock price declines exceeding 80%, although they ultimately recovered. The most catastrophic aspect of the catastrophe was the erosion of investor wealth: trillions of dollars were wiped out when the bubble collapsed, resulting in substantial financial losses for both institutions and private investors.

The rise of the Dot-Com Bubble in the late 1990s was not just a financial phenomenon; it was a cultural moment. It marked the first time that Silicon Valley overtook Wall Street as the global centre of economic imagination. As shown in Fig. 2.1, the NASDAQ Composite Index began its ascent in 1994 at a modest 752 and then gained incredible momentum over the next 6 years. By 1999, the index had surpassed 4000, and by March 2000, it had reached its all-time peak of 5048.62, driven by insatiable investor appetite for anything remotely connected to the Internet. Traditional valuation metrics, such as earnings, profit margins, and even revenue, were discarded in favour of sheer potential. Companies with no business model, no income, and often no products were valued in billions. The rally was not about performance but about perception. Investors were convinced that the rules of finance had changed forever and that missing out in this new era was more dangerous than participating unthinkingly. Financial media fuelled the frenzy, and Silicon Valley startups became overnight rock stars; venture capital flowed like champagne.

However, as Fig. 2.1 illustrates, the higher the climb, the harder it is to fall. By the second quarter of 2000, the narrative had begun to unravel. Reality crept through weak earnings reports, missed expectations, and the dawning realisation that many of these startups were not building sustainable businesses; they were burning cash faster than they could raise it. The following is a brutal correction: The NASDAQ plummeted from over 5000 to just 1139.90 by October 2002, erasing nearly 77% of its value. This was not just a market crash; it was an economic reckoning. Firms that had once symbolised the future, such as Pets.com, eToys, and Webvan, vanished almost overnight. Tech giants, such as Amazon and Cisco, saw their stock prices collapse by over 80%, although some would eventually recover. Trillions of dollars in investor wealth evaporated. The emotional arc of the bubble is embedded in the curve in Fig. 2.1: a euphoric climb fuelled by collective optimism, followed by a devastating plunge triggered by overvaluation, herd behaviour, and the unforgiving return of financial gravity. It remains one of the most cautionary episodes in modern investment history, a stark reminder that dreams may drive markets, but they are anchored in reality.

The dot-com crisis underscored the perils of market overreaction and speculative excess. Investors base their expectations on historical gains, assuming that the excellent performance of tech companies in prior years would continue forever. They disregarded essential warning signals and believed that conventional financial concepts were obsolete in the digital era. Upon realising the truth, they succumbed to panic, liquidated their equities at any valuation, and instigated a comprehensive market collapse.

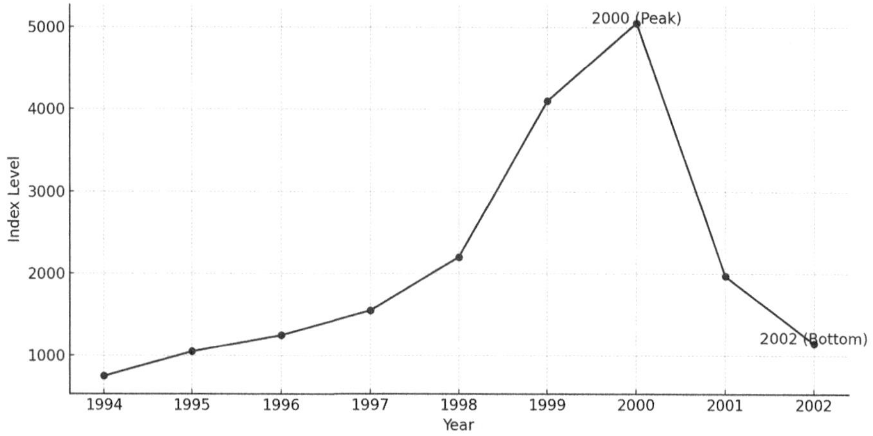

Fig. 2.1 NASDAQ Composite Index during the dot-com bubble. Source: Authors' work

2.5 Empirical Experiment

It began not in a trading pit on Wall Street, nor a Bloomberg terminal glowing in some New York hedge fund, but in a quiet lab room inside a business faculty in Malaysia (Authors' experiment). Yet what happened in that room told a story as old as markets themselves: that humans, regardless of age or background, are deeply susceptible to perception, emotion, and the influence of the crowd.

The goal of the experiment was deceptively simple: to investigate whether everyday people, young students with modest exposure to finance, would display classic patterns of market overreaction and herding behaviour when placed in simulated investing conditions. More specifically, would they react too strongly to irrelevant but emotionally charged news? Would they abandon their judgement when told the majority was thinking otherwise? And perhaps most importantly: how far could their minds be swayed in a matter of minutes?

To answer these questions, the research team designed a live experiment using fundamental market elements. A sample of 90 undergraduate students majoring in finance, economics, and business volunteered to participate. None were professional traders. Some dabbled in stock apps or followed financial influencers on Instagram or TikTok, but none claimed advanced market knowledge. They were, in every way, perfect analogues for the new class of digital-era retail investors: eager, informed, but often driven more by instinct than discipline.

To construct a believable simulation, the researchers selected five publicly listed companies from Bursa Malaysia, the country's primary stock exchange. These weren't high-flying global titans like Apple or Amazon, but real mid-cap Malaysian firms with active trading volume and stable visibility. The companies were:

- Top Glove Corporation Berhad—a global rubber glove manufacturer.
- Genting Malaysia Berhad—a hospitality and resort conglomerate.

- Sime Darby Plantation—a major player in palm oil production.
- Berjaya Food Berhad—a consumer-facing F&B operator, owning Starbucks Malaysia.
- Press Metal Aluminium Holdings—an industrial metals producer.

These firms were chosen for three reasons: first, they reflected a mix of industries familiar to students; second, they were not obscure, so participants had some surface familiarity; and third, their real-time stock volatility was neutral to moderate, which helped ensure that any reactions were more likely driven by the experiment's stimuli not pre-existing bias or hype.

The experiment unfolded in three distinct phases, across three carefully structured groups. Each group consisted of 30 randomly assigned students and was seated in identical lab environments to minimise distractions and external influences.

In Phase One, all participants were presented with the same investment briefing packet, which included summaries of the financial metrics for the five companies. The data was simplified into dashboard-style presentations, including earnings per share, price-to-earnings ratios, five-day and one-year stock trends, and a brief company background. Significantly, the financial health of all five companies was normalised and deliberately balanced to ensure no clear outperformer emerged. The goal was to create an 'even field' so that no particular company appeared objectively superior. Students were instructed to rate each stock on a scale from 1 to 10 based on attractiveness and indicate whether they would 'Buy', 'Hold', or 'Sell' if given a mock RM10,000 to invest.

This initial round served as the behavioural baseline. Phase Two introduced the stimuli.

The first group (Control Group A) received no new information. They were asked to repeat the same exercise, using only their memory or notes from the First Round. This allowed researchers to measure how much judgement drift might occur naturally without external influence. The second group (Treatment Group B) was exposed to a set of fabricated news headlines. These headlines were modelled closely on real Malaysian financial journalism, short, emotive, and plausible. They included headlines such as:

- 'Genting Malaysia gains bullish momentum after tourism minister's upbeat forecast'.
- 'Top Glove under fire over ESG concerns in new viral social media campaign'.
- 'Berjaya Food sees analyst downgrade amid soft consumer spending'.

Crucially, none of the news pieces reflected fundamental shifts in company performance. They were pure framing stimuli designed to test how perception, rather than reality, alters investment choices. The third group (Treatment + Social Group C) received the same news as Group B. Still, with a twist: they were also shown fabricated social sentiment data, designed to simulate the effect of market consensus. On-screen prompts informed them of what 'the majority of investors' were doing:

- '74% of investors are currently selling Top Glove'.
- '68% of traders have increased positions in Sime Darby Plantation'.
- 'Most retail investors are neutral on Press Metal holding steady'.

The consensus data was not genuine but engineered to reflect believable herd movements, positive, negative, or neutral, aligned with the tone of the headline. What followed was fascinating.

In Group A, the Control group, participants showed minimal drift. Their scores fluctuated by an average of 3–5%. Their decisions remained largely consistent, suggesting that without external influence, these students primarily relied on financial indicators and rationality. In Group B, however, the impact of emotionally framed news was profound. Ratings for stocks associated with positive headlines increased by an average of 17%, while those for negatively framed stocks declined by 22%. What was remarkable was that the financial data had remained unchanged. Students were reacting entirely to the narrative, rather than the fundamentals of the material. This was textbook market overreaction triggered not by performance metrics but by storylines that 'felt' absolute, even if they weren't.

But the most striking results came from Group C.

When both news and social consensus were combined, the shifts in decision-making accelerated and clustered. Students who initially rated a company as a 'Buy' in Round One reversed their decision to 'Sell' after seeing that 74% of others were selling, even if the headline was only mildly negative. Others admitted that after the experiment, they felt uncertain and followed the group because 'everyone else can't be wrong'. Some even confessed to not reading the company data at all in the second round, choosing instead to copy what 'the market' was doing.

The data confirmed what behavioural finance theorists have warned for years: the combination of media framing and herd influence creates a psychological storm where rationality is quickly overwhelmed. The average deviation in Group C reached 30% nearly double that of the news-only group. More than half of the students changed their initial decision in response to social cues, not because of new information, but because they feared being out of step with their peers.

This wasn't just data. It was a mirror. These were smart, capable students trained in corporate finance and market valuation, yet, even in a low-stakes simulation, they fell prey to the same traps that have shaped financial history: the dot-com bubble, the 2008 collapse, and meme stocks. They didn't need billions at stake to react emotionally. All it took was a few words on a screen and the whisper of what 'everyone else' was doing.

Ultimately, this experiment not only proved that market overreaction is a universal phenomenon but also demonstrated its significance. It proved that it is natural. That humans, even the educated ones, don't evaluate value in a vacuum. We anchor on headlines. We scan for consensus. We doubt ourselves and defer to others. We herd, not because we're foolish, but because we are wired to survive uncertainty through imitation. Markets may move on numbers, but people move on narratives. And when enough people move together, even fiction becomes fact, at least for a while.

2.6 Conclusion

Market overreaction is a pivotal element that significantly influences financial markets, often leading to pronounced price volatility, speculative bubbles, and panic-induced disasters. This phenomenon is influenced by cognitive biases, such as availability heuristics, anchoring, and loss aversion, which skew investor decision-making. Emotional reactions from investors, as opposed to reasoned responses, lead to pronounced price fluctuations that may destabilise markets and the entire economy. Overreaction affects not only individual investors but also institutional trading methods, regulatory measures, and financial stability.

The ramifications of investors' market overreactions are significant. Retail investors often succumb to the hype by purchasing at inflated prices and then panic-selling during market downturns, resulting in subpar returns. Institutional investors usually capitalise on these behavioural inclinations through contrarian tactics, short selling, and algorithmic trading. Comprehending overreaction may help investors formulate more disciplined strategies, circumvent herd behaviour, and identify when markets diverge from their intrinsic values.

From a regulatory perspective, overreaction poses a barrier to financial stability. Market collapses often compel authorities to implement interventions, such as circuit breakers, short-selling prohibitions, and liquidity infusions. Nonetheless, interventions may have unintended consequences, such as distorting price discovery or encouraging excessive risk-taking. Policymakers must strike a balance between fostering efficient markets and mitigating severe volatility, which can precipitate economic catastrophes.

References

Aghion P, Bergeaud A, Van Reenen J (2023) The impact of regulation on innovation. Am Econ Rev 113(11):2894–2936

Ali MA (2023) Anchoring bias and financial security: a study of KSE markets. J Financ Secur 1(1):20–42

Badía G, Ferruz L, Cortez MC (2021) The performance of social responsible investing from retail investors' perspective: international evidence. Int J Financ Econ 26(4):6074–6088

Barberis N, Shleifer A, Vishny R (1998) A model of investor sentiment. J Financ Econ 49(3):307–343

Chen CS, Cheng JC, Lin FC, Peng C (2017) The role of house money effect and availability heuristic in investor behaviour. Manag Decis 55(8):1598–1612

De Bondt WFM, Thaler RH (1995) Financial decision making in markets and firms: a behavioural perspective. Handb Oper Res Manag Sci 9:385–410

Dhingra B, Batra S, Aggarwal V, Yadav M, Kumar P (2024) Stock market volatility: a systematic review. J Model Manag 19(3):925–952

Fleming M (2021). Productivity growth and capital deepening in the fourth industrial Revolution (No. 010)

Gordon C (2023) In many possible worlds: an interdisciplinary history of the world economy since 1800. Springer, Singapore, pp 495–529

Haritha PH (2024) The effect of heuristics on Indian stock market investors: investor sentiment as a mediator. Manag Labour Stud 49(1):43–61
Jones CM, Shi D, Zhang X, Zhang X (2021) Understanding retail investors: evidence from China
Kahneman D, Tversky A (1996) On the reality of cognitive illusions. Psychol Rev 103(3):582–591
Kliger D, Kudryavtsev A (2010) The availability heuristic and investors' reaction to company-specific events. J Behav Financ 11(1):50–65
Kuramoto Y, Khan MSR, Kadoya Y (2024) Behavioural biases in panic selling: exploring the role of framing during the COVID-19 market crisis. Risks 12(10):162
Liu H, Peng L, Tang Y (2023a) Retail attention, institutional attention. J Financ Quant Anal 58(3):1005–1038
Liu F, Umair M, Gao J (2023b) Assessing oil price volatility co-movement with stock market volatility through quantile regression approach. Resour Policy 81:103375
Loang OK (2024a) Risk avoidance, macroeconomic indicators and bank performances in developing economies. Ann Financ Econ 19(4):2450018
Loang OK (2024b) Stability of shariah-compliant stocks in Indonesia, Malaysia, AND GCC: the roles of monetary and fiscal policies and contagion. J Islam Monet Econ Financ 10(1):155–176
Loang OK (2025) Can machine learning surpass human investors? Evidence from adaptive herding behaviour in US, China and India. J Appl Econ 28(1):2435796
Odean T (1998) Are investors reluctant to realize their losses? J Financ 53(5):1775–1798
Shefrin H, Statman M (1994) Behavioural capital asset pricing theory. J Financ Quant Anal 29(3):323–349
Wang B (2023) The impact of anchoring bias on financial decision-making: exploring cognitive biases in decision-making processes. Stud Psychol Sci 1(2):41–50
Zhang Y, He J, He M, Li S (2023) Geopolitical risk and stock market volatility: a global perspective. Financ Res Lett 53:103620

Chapter 3
The Cost of Following the Crowd

3.1 Introduction

Financial markets are often seen as being driven by rational decision-making, whereby investors evaluate data, assess risk, and allocate resources effectively. However, history has consistently shown that markets are not entirely logical. Instead, they are profoundly affected by collective human behaviour, whereby people, organisations, and even governments succumb to the psychological phenomenon of conformity. This phenomenon of herding results in market inefficiencies, causing asset prices to diverge markedly from their underlying values, misallocating capital, and undermining economic stability.

Herding is particularly dangerous because it fosters a false sense of assurance. When several investors enter a burgeoning market, their combined confidence reinforces the conviction that prices will continue to rise (Loang 2025a). This self-sustaining cycle results in overvaluation, creating speculative bubbles that ultimately implode their mass. Conversely, when panic ensues, the same investors hastily divest, causing markets to decline beyond what fundamentals warrant. The outcome is a cycle of prosperity and decline, marked by overwhelming optimism followed by profound fear, ultimately resulting in extensive financial devastation.

Herding behaviour fundamentally arises from ingrained psychological tendencies. Humans are inherently sociable organisms that are predisposed to seeking security in groups. This inclination was advantageous in early human history, as collective adherence often ensured survival. However, in financial markets, the inclination to comply may be catastrophic. Investors are usually influenced more by others' choices than by their autonomous evaluations. This is especially apparent in speculative manias when logical scepticism is overshadowed by the prevailing belief that an asset will continue to appreciate. The fear of missing out supersedes the fear of financial loss, prompting people to engage in actions that they would often eschew.

K. L. Ooi et al., *Following the Crowd: Psychological Drivers of Herding and Market Overreaction*, https://doi.org/10.1007/978-981-95-0792-4_3

Nevertheless, when circumstances change, and the audience transitions from elation to hysteria, the repercussions may be catastrophic (Loang 2025b). Market collapses often stem not from deteriorating fundamentals but from the collective psychology of fear and dread. Investors, seeing the fear of others, conclude that they must also withdraw from the market to avoid becoming the last holders of devaluing assets. The resultant response may obliterate billions in market value overnight, destabilising not just individual portfolios but all economies.

3.2 Examples of Wealth Destruction Due to Crowd Behaviour

3.2.1 The Role of Herding in Financial Bubbles

However, financial bubbles do not develop instantaneously (Cividino et al. 2023). They begin as small ripples, often driven by genuine economic innovation or optimism, before intensifying into formidable waves of speculation that inflate asset values to unsustainable levels. Central to every bubble is a fundamental yet perilous phenomenon known as herding. When investors cease to evaluate the intrinsic value of an asset and instead rely on the actions of the majority, the market enters a perilous period where reason is overshadowed by emotion.

Herding psychology is fundamentally embedded in human nature. Individuals perceive greater security in collective movements than in isolation (Riaz and Iqbal 2015). When asset values rise rapidly, whether in equities, real estate, or cryptocurrency, investors initially reap significant profits (Danial 2023). Their success narratives proliferate rapidly, media sources amplify their achievements, financial experts label the trend as the new standard, and everyone seeks to be a part of it. What is the outcome? An increasing number of investors are entering the market, allocating capital to assets not because of an understanding of their intrinsic worth, but rather due to observing others' profits and a fear of missing opportunities. This self-perpetuating loop continually raises prices, thereby dissociating them from economic reality.

History is replete with remarkable instances of a speculative boom driven by excessive exuberance. The Dutch Tulip Mania of the 1630s was one of the most notable and infamous events (Öztürk 2022). What originated as a specialised market for exquisite and uncommon tulips transformed into widespread mania, as individual tulip bulbs were exchanged for sums sufficient to purchase a whole house. The delusion of infinite worth propelled prices upward until reality intervened. Upon the decision of some traders to liquidate their assets, panic ensued, resulting in a market crash within weeks, leaving several individuals financially devastated.

By the late 1990s, the same psychological dynamics were evident during the dot-com bubble (Delossantos 2023). The emergence of the Internet was an undeniably transformative event in history, although the excitement soon gave way to imprudent conjecture. Investors allocate billions of dollars to technology firms without established business plans, profitability, or even a definitive product. The conviction that 'this time is different' prevailed, persuading everybody that conventional valuation measurements were no longer relevant. The stocks of firms with only a dot-com in their name saw extraordinary increases. This exemplified herd behaviour, as investors purchased shares not because of the firms' understanding but rather in response to rising stock prices. When the bubble collapsed in early 2000, billions of dollars in market capitalisation were almost instantaneously obliterated.

The Bitcoin surge in 2017 exhibited a similar trend. Bitcoin and other digital assets saw a dramatic rise in value, with values increasing several-fold within months (Harju 2024). New investors entered the market, motivated by the fear of missing out (FOMO), rather than a comprehensive understanding of blockchain technology or the fundamentals of Bitcoin. Social media and online forums have evolved into fertile environments for speculative enthusiasm, as influencers and self-styled authorities have said that Bitcoin will reach values of $100,000 or even $1 million (Limongi Concetto and Ravazzolo 2019). However, for all bubbles, the revelry could not endure indefinitely. By early 2018, the market had experienced a crash, resulting in Bitcoin's value depreciating by over 80% and erasing billions of dollars in speculative investments.

The cycle recurs repeatedly: an initial wave of optimism, followed by increasing media attention, an influx of new investors, and a subsequent tipping point when mood changes, precipitating a swift and catastrophic decline. The rationale for the recurrence of these bubbles is straightforward: humans are inherently predisposed to rely on collective judgement. We presume that if the majority engage in an action, it is intrinsically correct. However, in financial markets, conforming to the majority often results in a calamity. Understanding the impact of herding on speculative bubbles is crucial for investors seeking to avoid the next financial crisis. Individuals capable of identifying warning indicators, such as unsustainable price escalations, sensationalist media attention, and neglect of intrinsic valuation, can use the chance to withdraw prior to the collapse of the bubble. The stark truth is that when markets diverge from reality, correction is always severe. It is rapid, ruthless, and arbitrary, penalising those enticed by the mirage of effortless wealth.

3.2.2 *Overreaction and Market Crashes*

A market collapse does not occur during isolation. They do not stem from a single adverse earnings announcement, abrupt policy change, or discrete economic deceleration (Loang and Ahmad 2022). Instead, they are the manifestation of mass psychology at its most extreme surge of anxiety that escalates into complete panic, whereby logical thought is forsaken and primal survival instincts dominate. The same herding behaviour that drives speculative booms during ascents also intensifies the decline during descent. Upon perceiving danger, the crowd's dash for the exits transforms into a stampede, resulting in devastation.

Overreaction is a fundamental component of every significant market decline (Zahera and Bansal 2018). A single dismal economic report, prominent bankruptcy, or a political upheaval can undermine market confidence. Initially, the decrease was controllable; nevertheless, as losses accumulated, anxiety proliferated rapidly. Investors who observe a decline in stock prices often presume that a catastrophic event has occurred, despite the underlying fundamentals remaining unchanged. The impulse to prioritise sales over enquiries prevails. No one wants to be the last holder of a declining asset.

This panic-induced sale creates a detrimental loop. As an increasing number of individuals divest their assets, prices decline further, instigating margin calls and compelling leveraged investors to sell their positions at reduced prices (Loang 2025a). Financial institutions, hedge funds, and individual investors all rush to withdraw from the market before incurring intolerable losses. The higher the sales, the more rapid the fall. A self-perpetuating feedback cycle emerges, whereby anxiety generates further fear, culminating in market devastation beyond all expectations.

Historically, numerous examples of excessive reactions have led to financial disasters. The collapse of 1929 was one of the most notorious instances (Gordon 2023). The preceding decade was characterised by economic growth and a stock market boom, marked by wild speculation and widespread borrowing for investment purposes. However, when fissures emerged in the economy, apprehension ensued. On October 24, 1929, known as Black Thursday, investors hastily divested, inundating the market with sell orders. Alarm disseminated. By Black Tuesday, just a few days later, the stock market had declined by over 25% of its value, initiating a downward trajectory that eventually led to the Great Depression (Kinari 2016). A correction rapidly escalated into an economic disaster, as fear immobilised investors and consumers, depleting liquidity and hindering development over the last decade.

However, overreaction is not confined to protracted economic crises. This can occur within a few hours. On October 19, 1987, known as Black Monday, the Dow Jones Industrial Average experienced a 22.6% decline in value within a single day, marking the most significant one-day percentage decrease in history. The crisis was precipitated by automated trading algorithms and a surge in panic selling, as investors believed that the decline indicated a more profound economic collapse. However, in contrast to the Great Depression, the economic fundamentals were not as severe. Within months, markets recovered, demonstrating that the intensity of the crisis was more indicative of psychological reactivity than of economic fundamentals.

The most notable instance of fear-driven markets spiralling uncontrollably occurred in March 2020, coinciding with the COVID-19 epidemic (Ooi 2024a). As the virus spread worldwide, financial markets responded with significant turbulence. Investors concluded that economic shutdowns would incapacitate enterprises, resulting in a decline of almost 30% in the S&P 500 within weeks (Ooi 2024b). The pace of collapse was unparalleled, driven by uncertainty, sensationalised media reporting, and algorithmic trading that expedited sell orders. Companies with robust financial statements, consistent income streams, and no pandemic risk were excluded, along with underperforming enterprises. It was a state of blind fear and an emotional reactivity that neglected any underlying analysis. However, when the world adapted to the epidemic, markets recovered rapidly, underscoring the irrationality of the first downturn.

The message is unequivocal: market collapses seldom stem from rationality; emotions primarily drive them. Once established, fear proliferates more rapidly than anticipated by any financial model. Investors, consumed by anxiety, forsake long-term strategies and concentrate only on current survival. They divest not because they believe their holdings are worthless but rather because they cannot endure the prospect of more losses. The herd operates cohesively, exacerbating volatility and driving prices to extremes that contradict economic reality.

Opportunities exist for individuals to discern these patterns. Most astute investors understand that the peak of fear coincides with the peak of opportunity (Kumar and Prince 2022). In times of peak panic, when headlines proclaim catastrophe and markets seem to plummet uncontrollably, the foundations of recovery are established. Individuals who can resist the allure of the masses and respond to situations with independent, rather than emotional, reactions are those who ultimately prevail.

3.3 Case Study: The Housing Bubble and Its Cascading Effects

3.3.1 The Rise of the Housing Bubble

The early 2000s represented an era of optimism and limited potential for the American home market. Homeownership ceased to be an aspiration; it was seen as a definitive route to affluence. The conviction that 'real estate invariably appreciates' became a widely accepted doctrine echoed by lenders, investors, and ordinary purchasers. Financial institutions promoted this. Financial institutions support this. The media idealised individuals who refrained from purchasing a house or many properties, deeming them imprudent for overlooking easy financial gains. However, underneath this gilded facade, a perilous bubble developed and burst with catastrophic repercussions.

The origin of the housing bubble was established during the period of inexpensive credit. Following the dot-com bust and the September 11 attacks, the Federal Reserve lowered interest rates to unprecedented lows in an effort to stimulate economic growth. Instantly, borrowing became very easy, resulting in a surge of capital in the housing market. Banks motivated to capitalise on the credit surge started providing mortgages to almost all applicants, irrespective of their income, credit history, or repayment capacity. Previous lending regulations, which required evidence of financial soundness, were discarded in favour of high-risk loans, including introductory rates and negligible down payments.

However, accessible credit alone has been insufficient to sustain one of the most significant financial booms in history. The primary catalysts of the crisis were speculative investment and collective behaviour. As residential property values began to rise, individuals saw their neighbours, colleagues, and acquaintances profiting from property ownership. The rationale was compelling: purchase a property now, and in a few years, its value will increase substantially. Investors, keen to capitalise on the trend, began acquiring many residences, not for habitation but to 'flip' for rapid profit. The surge in speculative purchasing has caused housing values to soar.

The media have contributed to exacerbating the situation. Television programmes romanticised property flipping, depicting average individuals transforming small investments into million-dollar gains instantaneously. News sites have published articles on the thriving housing market, reinforcing the belief that prices will continue to increase. Banks and mortgage brokers promote unconventional lending packages, assuring customers that they can purchase houses far beyond their financial capabilities. Adjustable-rate mortgages (ARMs), interest-only loans, and 'NINJA' loans (No Income, No Job, No Assets) became prevalent. While housing prices continued to rise, the viability of these lending methods remained unchallenged.

Communal elation established a feedback cycle. Escalating prices led to increased borrowing, which in turn facilitated further purchasing and, consequently, further price inflation. Economists cautioned that the market was overheating, although their apprehensions were overshadowed by the collective assertions of real estate brokers, mortgage bankers, and Wall Street executives who claimed that the boom would last indefinitely. Even those who saw danger struggled to withstand the allure of the throng. If others are profiting, why does it remain inactive?

The most dangerous aspect of herding behaviour is that it engenders a false feeling of security until it ceases to do so. By 2006, fissures had begun to manifest in the foundation. Residential property prices escalated far beyond the financial reach of the majority, and the first indications of distress started to emerge. Nevertheless, several individuals persisted in their purchases, believing that the market would correct itself and continue to rise. Some individuals frequently refinanced their homes, using their properties as personal ATMs to drain equity for vacations, luxury cars, and other investments. Lenders continued to provide high-risk mortgages, while Wall Street persistently aggregated them into mortgage-backed securities, marketing these investments to global investors as secure, high-yield assets.

Many failed to see that the entire housing market was founded on precarious fiction. Prices were increasing not due to genuine demand or robust economic fundamentals, but rather as a result of speculation and readily available capital. The phenomenon of herding behaviour has engendered a significant imbalance, poised to collapse imminently. Like its predecessors, the bubble was fated to implode. When it occurs, the repercussions would be even more severe than anticipated.

3.3.2 The Collapse of the Subprime Mortgage Market

The housing market collapse did not occur abruptly. It was not a sudden eruption but a gradual, insidious awareness that something was profoundly off. In the first stage, murmurs of caution arose from a select group of contrarian experts who saw fissures emerging behind the polished veneer of ever-rising property prices. However, the audience was not prepared to heed the warning. Real estate has long served as a primary means of achieving affluence. They stated that home prices never experienced a nationwide drop. Consequently, despite the emergence of troubling indications, the herd continued to advance until the earth under it collapsed.

By mid-2007, the first significant warning indicator was undeniable. Home values ceased to increase, and several homeowners with adjustable-rate mortgages (ARMs) faced escalating monthly payments that were unaffordable. Mortgage defaults increased, especially in the subprime sector, the most precarious segment of the housing market, where loans were extended to borrowers with inadequate credit, little income, and no evidence of financial stability. Suddenly, lenders who had invested years in granting mortgages with little monitoring began to worry. The premise that property prices will perpetually increase underpins the entire system. However, the foundation deteriorated, and anxiety escalated.

Financial firms that had fervently fuelled the housing craze were overwhelmed by toxic debt. For years, banks have been aggregating mortgages, both favourable and unfavourable, into mortgage-backed securities (MBS) and collateralised debt obligations (CDOs), marketing them to global investors as secure, high-yield investments. These assets were assigned an AAA rating by credit agencies, creating a facade of stability. However, when mortgage defaults escalated, reality emerged; these investments were far more perilous than previously acknowledged. As almost all significant financial institutions had these assets, the banking system became vulnerable to an imminent crisis.

As the market began to decline, apprehensions ensued. Institutional investors, hedge funds, and pension funds that invested billions in mortgage-backed securities abruptly recognised their ignorance of the actual value of these assets. Their reactions were prompt and harsh, liquidating all the assets. Panic-induced sell-offs ravaged Wall Street, erasing billions in value within weeks. Banks hastily sought to divest their mortgage assets; however, they encountered a shortage of purchasers. The same herd mentality that fuelled the bubble's expansion also contributed to its downfall. When one institution was divested, others followed suit, not because of a comprehensive understanding of the hazards, but because they could not afford to be the last remaining entity.

The rapid erosion of trust made this catastrophe even more devastating. Financial institutions that had been invulnerable just a few months earlier were suddenly teetering on the edge of insolvency. Bear Stearns, once a powerhouse on Wall Street, was one of the first casualties; the deleterious mortgage security compromised its financial statements. In March 2008, the Federal Reserve conducted an emergency sale to JPMorgan Chase, although this served as a temporary solution. The actual shock occurred in September when Lehman Brothers, one of the most prominent and most respected investment banks globally, filed for bankruptcy.

Lehman's failure marked the transition from panic to comprehensive financial turmoil. If a 158-year-old organisation with billions of assets could collapse overnight, then no bank would be secure. The economic system was on the brink of collapse as banks ceased lending to one another, fearing that their counterparties may be the next to fall. Stock markets collapsed, erasing billions of investors' wealth. Global markets mirrored this trend, as the interdependence of the financial system caused the first housing crisis in the U.S.A. to extend to Europe, Asia, and beyond.

Upon reflection, the indicators were evident from the first. These warning signals had been illuminated for years; however, the herd remained engrossed in the delusion of boundless profits to heed them. When the collapse occurred, it was not a slow adjustment; instead, there was a frenzied rush for the exits, a frantic endeavour to flee before it was too late. However, for several individuals, this has already been the case. Homeowners forfeited their homes, banks incurred billions in losses, and the globe descended into the most severe economic crisis since the Great Depression, entirely due to the perilous fallacy that the collective could never err.

3.4 Lessons for Future Market Participants

3.4.1 Recognising and Avoiding Herding Traps

The financial realm has an unwavering propensity to recur. Markets experience fluctuations, economic booms transition into downturns, and cyclical patterns of elation and distress recur again. The 2008 financial crisis was not the first instance of herd behaviour resulting in economic calamity, nor will it be the last one. Individuals who comprehend the potency of collective opinion and, crucially, how to counteract its sway, possess a significantly enhanced likelihood of not only surviving the subsequent financial upheaval but also flourishing within it.

The first step in evading herding traps is to identify them. Herding is alluring. It insinuates assurances of effortless profit, comforting investors that if the majority engage in it, it must be a prudent course of action. Bubbles develop when individuals cease to scrutinise the rationale behind investment and instead conform to the collective behaviour of the herd. An astute investor recognises that if an opportunity seems too advantageous, it is likely to be deceptive.

A prominent indicator of the herding trap is the disconnection of asset prices from fundamental values. When equities, real estate, or cryptocurrencies ascend at an unsustainable rate, driven more by speculation than by intrinsic economic worth, caution should be exercised. Investors must consider whether individuals purchase an investment due to its rationale or if they are acquiring it simply because of prevailing trends. If the response favours the latter, the prudent course of action is to withdraw before the bubble collapses.

Another method of evading the majority is to adopt contrarian thinking. In each financial cycle, the population tends to err at extremes, exhibiting irrational exuberance at the peak and unreasoning terror at the nadir. Renowned investor Warren Buffett succinctly articulated this notion by stating, 'Be fearful when others are greedy, and greedy when others are fearful'. This entails refraining from the impulse to engage while others are hastily pursuing investment and instead seeking opportunities where others are retreating.

Contrarian investors recognise that financial markets are influenced by their emotions. They understand that exhilaration can lead to overvaluation, and fear can lead to undervaluation. During market crashes and episodes of panic selling, the contrarian perceives the opportunity to avoid catastrophe. He seeks robust firms whose stock valuations are adversely affected by the overall market decline. He purchases, whereas others are too apprehensive. Upon completing the cycle, he reaps the benefits.

However, discipline is required to avoid conformity. This signifies the fortitude to remain passive while others capitalise on a surging bull market. It also means tolerating criticism associated with opposing the dominant narrative. During the dot-com boom, those who declined to invest in inflated Internet stocks were derided as antiquated and disconnected. However, as the bubble collapsed, they remained intact, whereas others forfeited everything.

Autonomous research is a crucial tool for countering herd behaviour. Investors who rely solely on news headlines, social media trends, or anecdotal endorsements are significantly more susceptible to engaging in speculative frenzies. Successful investors conduct their due diligence by analysing financial accounts, examining market cycles, and understanding the actual value of an asset before making decisions.

An additional crucial method is to preserve the long-term perspective. Herd behaviour is driven by short-term thinking, with individuals pursuing immediate gains and shifting rapidly between trends. However, the most proficient investors use a long-term strategy. They understand that market cycles fluctuate and adjust their positioning appropriately. Rather than attempting to time the market precisely, they focus on building a robust portfolio, diversifying their assets, and adhering to a plan, even when short-term trends suggest otherwise.

The most challenging aspect of evading herding traps is the psychological obstacle. Humans are predisposed to affirmation by others. The need for affiliation and conformity is profoundly embedded in our impulses. Resisting the collective is problematic because it often requires solitude under significant pressure. History demonstrates that the most successful investors, those who consistently outperform the market over time, are capable of distinguishing between emotion and rationality, maintaining composure amidst widespread fear, and withdrawing while others eagerly invest.

Herding behaviour always exists in financial markets. A further bubble emerges, followed by the ensuing collapse. Individuals who discern warning indications, engage in independent thought, and possess the discipline to withstand societal pressures will not only escape financial disasters but also capitalise on the errors of others. Most people do not earn money. It was constructed by discerning when to withdraw.

3.4.2 Risk Management Strategies

Each financial crisis yields two types of investors: those who succumb to their losses and those who emerge resilient, having grasped the essential lesson that markets are inherently unpredictable, but the risk can be effectively managed. The distinction between these two groups is not a matter of chance; it is a deliberate strategy. Effective risk management is essential for navigating unpredictable markets, preventing catastrophic losses, and ensuring long-term success. Nevertheless, investors repeatedly disregard it, deceived by the fallacy that bull markets are perpetual, that effortless profit is but a transaction away, and that the majority must be correct. Through difficult experiences, they discover that markets are more ruthless than they initially thought.

Diversification is one of the most successful risk mitigation strategies. Although it may seem too simplistic, historical evidence demonstrates that diversifying assets across several asset classes, sectors, and regions is one of the most effective safeguards against market volatility. Investors who allocated their entire portfolios to technology companies before the dot-com disaster, real estate before the 2008 financial crisis, or cryptocurrency ahead of the 2022 crypto winter experienced significant losses. Conversely, those who diversified their portfolios by including a combination of equities, bonds, commodities, and real estate were able to withstand setbacks and recover more swiftly.

The rationale for diversification is clear: various assets do not fluctuate in the same way concurrently. When equities decline, fixed-income securities are often appreciated. When an industry falters, another may thrive (Tuckman and Serrat 2022). Diversifying assets substantially mitigates the risks associated with a single-market collapse. However, notwithstanding the clarity of this idea, avarice often obstructs it. When a particular industry yields substantial profits, the allure of investing entirely is challenging to resist. Why do mediocre returns when you may treble your investment? That is, until the bubble collapses, when individuals who neglected diversification come to realise too late that they should diversify their investments.

Diversification alone is not sufficient. Investors should adopt a long-term perspective, viewing market downturns not as causes for alarm but as opportunities for acquisition (Sutton 2025). Short-term traders, who are influenced by emotions, sometimes respond impulsively to market volatility. They pursue high-performance equities at their zenith and abandon reliable investments at the first indication of difficulty. They overlook the inevitability of market cycles and the transience of collapses. Those who remain steadfast often emerge victorious.

However, financial education is the most often neglected risk-management instrument. Significant market losses typically arise not from poor investments but from erroneous decisions and choices made based on ignorance, disinformation, and uncritical reliance on unreliable sources. Investors lacking financial literacy are particularly susceptible to herding behaviour, succumbing to hype, and experiencing panic at the most inopportune times. They assume excessive leverage, neglect asset value, and disregard previous trends that may help circumvent significant losses.

A greater comprehension of financial markets reduces an investor's susceptibility to prevalent pitfalls. An astute investor remains composed during market declines, understanding that such downturns often provide opportunities. They eschew speculative bubbles and examine their fundamentals. They do not conform uncritically to the majority; they engage in independent thinking. This discipline originates from education, studying investment literature, analysing market history, understanding economic cycles, and acquiring knowledge from those who have adeptly navigated financial adversities in the past.

3.4.3 The Role of Policy and Regulation

Markets, when unregulated, exhibit unpredictable behaviour. They ascend to unreasonable peaks, propelled by exhilaration and conjecture, and only plummet catastrophically when reality intervenes. The financial sector has often witnessed this phenomenon, from the Dutch Tulip Mania of the 1600s to the 2008 financial crisis. Although investors' emotions and herd behaviour significantly influence these cycles, regulation is one of the paramount drivers of economic stability. In the absence of controls, speculation escalates uncontrollably, resulting in bubbles that burst, with disastrous repercussions. However, appropriate regulations may mitigate market excesses before they become irreversible.

Regulation is often seen as an undesirable intrusion, an impediment to free markets and innovation. Historically, uncontrolled greed has had devastating consequences. Imprudent lending practices, excessive leverage, and a total breakdown of regulatory control precipitated the 2008 crisis. Banks granted subprime loans with little regard to borrowers' repayment capacity, while financial entities restructured these hazardous debts into intricate securities marketed as secure investments. Regulators, either oblivious to the magnitude of danger or reluctant to take action, failed to react promptly. What is the outcome? A worldwide economic collapse eradicated billions of dollars in wealth, obliterated millions of jobs, and inflicted enduring damage to the banking system.

Subsequently, governments worldwide attempted to enact regulatory measures to prevent the recurrence of this calamity. The Dodd-Frank Act was passed in the U.S.A. to enforce stricter regulation of banks, mitigate hazardous lending practices, and enhance transparency in financial markets (Türk 2025). Stress tests were required to determine that banks could withstand economic shocks, and new regulations were implemented to restrict speculative trading that could jeopardise the entire economy. Comparable measures have been implemented in Europe and Asia, indicating a worldwide effort to curtail financial excess.

However, the restrictions are insufficient. One lesson from historical disasters is that markets consistently discover novel methods for circumventing regulations. Wall Street is ever-changing, generating novel financial products, tactics, and loopholes that regulators find challenging to monitor. The difficulty lies not just in enacting legislation but in its effective enforcement. Regulators must remain vigilant, continually monitoring markets for signs of instability, and adjust regulations to mitigate emerging risks. Should they postpone action until the bubble has developed? It is often too late.

Transparency is the cornerstone of trust in the financial markets. When corporations provide transparent disclosures of their profits, risks, and liabilities, investors can make informed judgements. When governments impose disclosure mandates, truthful representation of financial goods mitigates market distortions. When financial institutions function under transparent and uniform rules, the risk of a systemic collapse is reduced.

Nonetheless, openness must extend beyond companies' financial statements and banking disclosures. This should include the policies and activities of the regulators themselves. Governments and central banks possess significant authority in influencing markets, including the establishment of interest rates and the formulation of monetary policy. Confusion ensues when choices are made in secrecy. Investors often respond emotionally by attempting to predict future outcomes, rather than grounding their judgements in robust evidence. Conversely, when regulatory authorities function with transparency and accountability, market stability increases, and the likelihood of irrational speculation diminishes.

The objective of the regulation is not to eradicate risk, as it would be unfeasible. Markets flourish on risk; without it, innovation, economic progress, and rewards for those who undertake calculated risks are non-existent. The objective is to achieve equilibrium, enabling markets to operate effectively while avoiding the excess that can result in a financial calamity.

Financial markets will always remain unpredictable, and no regulation will eradicate human greed, fear, or the propensity for herd behaviour. By enforcing transparency, maintaining rigorous oversight, and holding accountable those who engage in excessive risk-taking, policymakers can cultivate an environment conducive to more rational market operations, enhanced investor protection, and the prevention of future financial catastrophes before they occur.

3.5 Conclusion

Financial history is replete with instances of devastating losses caused by herd behaviour. From the Dutch Tulip Mania to the 2008 financial crisis, markets have demonstrated a remarkable propensity to abandon rationality in favour of collective euphoria, ultimately succumbing to the consequences of their excesses. This chapter has examined the processes by which herd behaviour elevates asset prices above their fundamental values, results in speculative bubbles, and precipitates catastrophic market collapse. The financial repercussions of uncritically conforming to popular opinion are indisputable, as seen by the housing bubble driven by imprudent lending and the dot-com boom spurred by excessive enthusiasm.

The fundamental problem with herding is that it undermines market efficiency. Investors forsake an independent analysis of social evidence, believing that the market's collective knowledge is infallible. History has consistently shown that the majority are often erroneous on pivotal occasions. As asset prices diverge from fundamental values, speculative manias perpetuate themselves, fostering the illusion of infinite profit. However, when opinion changes and panic ensues, the decline may be as severe as the rise. The group that previously pursued profits is now rushing for the exit, resulting in economic destruction.

The essential insight for investors is the significance of logical decision-making. Successful market participants are those who see the psychological pitfalls of herd behaviour and refrain from conforming to the mob without a thorough analysis. Autonomous evaluation, rigorous risk management, and a contrarian perspective can help investors navigate through volatile markets while avoiding the dangers of collective panic. Rather than pursuing speculative bubbles, discerning investors focus on fundamentals, long-term trends, and strategic decision-making, rather than responding emotionally to market volatility.

References

Cividino D, Westphal R, Sornette D (2023) Multiasset financial bubbles in an agent-based model with noise traders' herding described by an n-vector Ising model. Phys Rev Res 5(1):013009

Danial K (2023) Cryptocurrency investing for dummies. Wiley, Hoboken

Delossantos C (2023) From hype to bust: investigating the underlying factors of the dot-com bubble and developing regression models for future market predictions. Open J Business Manage 11(5):2161–2174

Gordon C (2023) Many possible worlds: an interdisciplinary history of the world economy since 1800. Springer, Singapore, pp 495–529

Harju L (2024) Dynamics of crypto mining

Kinari Y (2016) Properties of expectation biases: optimism and overconfidence. J Behav Exp Financ 9:1–14

Kumar J, Prince N (2022) Overconfidence bias in the Indian stock market in diverse market situations: an empirical study. J Syst Assurance Eng Manage 13(3):762–774

Limongi Concetto C, Ravazzolo F (2019) Optimism in financial markets: stock market returns and investor sentiments. J Risk Financ Manag 12(2):85–102

Loang OK (2025a) Financial stability at risk: evidence from market overreaction and herding behaviour in developed and emerging markets. China Financ Rev Int 15(1):67–92

Loang OK (2025b) From tweets to trades: the dynamic dance of investor sentiment, attention, and news sentiment in ESG stocks. China Financ Econ Rev 14(1):70–91

Loang OK, Ahmad Z (2022) Market overreaction, firm-specific information and macroeconomic variables in US and Chinese markets during COVID-19. J Econ Stud 49(8):1548–1565

Ooi KL (2024a) Analyst forecasting and market liquidity dynamics: a comparative analysis of US and Chinese markets pre and post COVID-19. J Gen Manag. https://doi.org/10.1177/03063070231225603

Ooi KL (2024b) Demystifying behavioural finance. Springer, Cham

Öztürk A (2022) Dutch tulip mania: tulip crisis. In: Black swan: economic crises, vol I. Springer, Singapore, pp 13–31

Riaz T, Iqbal H (2015) Impact of overconfidence, illusion of control, self control and optimism bias on investors decision making; evidence from developing markets. Res J Financ Account 6(14):222–232

Sutton CV (2025) Navigating financial turbulence with confidence: preparing for future market challenges, crashes & crises. NuovoNova Ltd, Rehovot

Tuckman B, Serrat A (2022) Fixed income securities: tools for today's markets. Wiley, Hoboken

Türk MM (2025) 2008 global financial crisis and the Dodd-Frank act. Asya Stud 9(31):291–306

Zahera SA, Bansal R (2018) Do investors exhibit behavioural biases in investment decision making? A systematic review. Qual Res Financ Mark 10(2):210–251

Chapter 4
Psychological Drivers of Herding

4.1 Introduction

Herding behaviour in financial markets is a potent yet enigmatic phenomenon in economic decision-making. This psychological impetus has propelled some of history's most significant financial surges and declines, ranging from the seventeenth-century Tulip Mania to the 2008 global financial catastrophe. Herding fundamentally occurs when investors forgo independent analysis to conform to the majority, frequently assuming incorrectly that collective behaviour ensures financial safety. What causes people, especially astute institutional investors, to succumb consistently to this pitfall? The solution resides profoundly in the human mind. Herding is not just a financial misjudgement; it is an instinctive reaction influenced by evolutionary, social, and emotional elements that surpass logical reasoning.

Comprehending herding necessitates acknowledging that markets are not exclusively regulated by logic, evidence, or economic reality. Instead, they are influenced by the emotions and biases of participants, who often act out of fear, greed, and a fear of missing out (FOMO), rather than relying on objective financial evaluations. Investors, like all individuals, are predisposed to want security in the collectively. During times of uncertainty, the behaviours of others function as unspoken guidance, alleviating the apprehension associated with autonomous decision-making. When surrounding individuals purchase a particular stock, it seems prudent to participate. In the event of widespread market panic, it is prudent to divest the fruit before it is adversely affected. This innate inclination towards conformity elucidates why bubbles expand excessively beyond justifiable values and why markets plummet with astonishing rapidity when the mood changes.

Thus, the influence of mass psychology on finance is significant. Financial markets serve as a prominent arena for human behaviour, where optimism and pessimism proliferate like contagions. Social impact significantly enhances herding behaviour as investors seek validation for their decisions through the activities of

K. L. Ooi et al., *Following the Crowd: Psychological Drivers of Herding and Market Overreaction*, https://doi.org/10.1007/978-981-95-0792-4_4

other analysts, media pundits, successful traders, and even peers on social media. This phenomenon has intensified in the digital era, where news disseminates rapidly, and social media sites such as Twitter, Reddit, and TikTok can transform regular equities into speculative manias in a matter of hours. A single viral message may prompt thousands of investors to rush into a stock they barely understand, driven not by sound financial rationale but by the overwhelming force of collective enthusiasm.

However, the irony of herding behaviour often results in collective errors. Financial bubbles arise from widespread beliefs in the illusion of perpetual expansion, whereas markets collapse when a significant number perceive that all hope is extinguished (Loang et al. 2024). The cyclical characteristics of mass psychology in markets guarantee the recurrence of these historical patterns. This explains why investors persist in pursuing speculative manias, why frantic selling precipitates market collapse, and why even seasoned experts succumb to the biases they endeavour to avoid. The psychological factors that influence herding are universal, affecting both hedge fund managers and novice retail investors. Identifying these factors is not only an academic endeavour; anybody must traverse the volatile fluctuations of financial markets with lucidity and assurance.

Behind every market surge and every catastrophic crash lies not just data or policy but a beating human heart pulsing with fear, greed, and longing. As Table 4.1 reveals, herding behaviour is not merely a glitch in financial thinking; it is a profound reflection of who we are as social and emotional beings. Fear, the oldest survival mechanism in our psychological repertoire, emerges when uncertainty or negative signals cloud the market. It does not whisper; it screams. Investors gripped by anxiety begin fleeing their positions not based on logic but on the primal urge to escape the pain. Just as our ancestors ran from predators at the first crack of a branch, modern investors sold at the first sign of red, turning routine downturns into self-fulfilling spirals. But fear isn't alone in steering the herd. Greed, its deceptive twin, entices us with the promise of an unlimited gain. It fuels irrational confidence, convincing us to chase bubbles and double down on high-risk bets, seduced by the thrill of winning. This emotional high is addictive and even blinds the most experienced traders to reality.

Then comes the invisible accelerant of modern markets: FOMO, or the fear of missing out. In an era where gains are flaunted in real-time across news tickers and social media feeds, FOMO is not just a feeling; it is a contagion. Investors no longer want to profit; they want to benefit *now*, just like everyone else. It does not matter whether the asset is a tech stock, a meme coin, or a commodity; if it surges, people want in. The crowd then becomes a compass. Social influence amplifies this dynamic as the opinions of influencers, analysts, and digital communities begin to substitute for personal conviction. At that moment, the line between the research and the retweet blurs. Underneath, it is a deeper, quieter driver: evolutionary instinct. Long before Wall Street, survival depended on sticking to the tribe. Now, that instinct has followed us into boardrooms and brokerage apps. When panic spreads or euphoria takes hold, investors respond not as economists but as humans, seeking validation, safety, and a sense of belonging. Understanding these drivers is not just the key to becoming a better investor; it is the key to understanding ourselves.

Table 4.1 Psychological drivers of herding behaviour

Driver	Definition	Core emotion	Investor impact
Fear	Fear emerges when markets turn volatile or when negative news signals potential loss. It is the primal emotion that urges us to act swiftly to avoid pain even at the cost of rational judgement	Anxiety, panic	Investors respond to uncertainty by selling en masse, often dumping valuable assets out of sheer dread of watching values fall further. This reactive fear transforms downturns into full-blown crashes
Greed	Greed tempts investors to chase extraordinary gains without properly assessing the risks involved. It is the seductive voice whispering that 'this time is different', luring even seasoned professionals	Euphoria, overconfidence	When driven by greed, investors disregard fundamentals and pour money into overheated assets, inflating bubbles and setting the stage for future corrections
Fear of missing out (FOMO)	FOMO is the emotional cocktail of envy, regret, and urgency created when others appear to be gaining, and you are not. It feeds off the illusion that opportunity is slipping away forever	Social pressure, envy	Investors buy into rapidly rising assets not because of solid research but because 'everyone else is doing it'. This accelerates herd movements and inflates valuations beyond reason
Social influence	Social influence is the psychological pull to conform with others be it friends, analysts, influencers, or online communities especially when one lacks confidence in their own decisions	Desire for belonging	Investors mimic popular trends and expert opinions, abandoning their independent analysis in favour of perceived consensus. This amplifies market direction and dampens contrarian thinking
Evolutionary instinct	Herding is hardwired into human nature from our earliest days as hunter-gatherers. In times of threat, following the group ensured survival. That ancient reflex still shapes our reactions	Instinctive fear	During crises, investors subconsciously fall back on this inherited mechanism 'if everyone is running, I should run too' which spreads panic and accelerates market contagion

Source: Authors' work

4.2 Fear and Panic in Financial Markets

Fear is the most fundamental and infectious emotion in the financial markets (Naeem et al. 2024). It disseminates rapidly, traversing trading floors, broking offices, and investment portfolios with power capable of annihilating riches in a single night. In times of economic uncertainty, rationality is often the primary casualty. Investors, both individual and institutional, seek refuge and are eager to avoid entrapment in the devastation. Regardless of whether fear is warranted or overstated, once it manifests, it transforms into a self-fulfilling prophecy. Prices fall not due to an overnight devaluation of enterprises but because widespread fear necessitates it. Markets unravel via an emotional chain reaction, in which anxiety generates more fear, compelling investors to engage in irrational, herd-driven decision-making.

The psychological origins of the financial panic are profound (Kahneman 2003). One of the most potent influences is loss aversion, the concept that individuals perceive the anguish of financial losses far more acutely than the satisfaction derived from similar profits. The pain of losing $10,000 on the stock market far outweighs the gratification of earning the same sum. This excessive fear of loss prompts investors to behave rashly at the first indication of difficulty, forsaking even prudent assets because the appearance of negative figures on a screen evokes an almost instinctive feeling of peril. Rather than seeing a transient market decline as an opportunity, investors yield to fear, divesting assets at significant discounts and cementing losses that might have been averted.

Loss aversion is the first concept of this kind. The negativity bias exacerbates this situation. Humans are predisposed to prioritise insufficient information over pleasant news, an evolutionary advantage that historically aided our ancestors in surviving perilous circumstances (Brown and Lala 2024). In financial markets, even small losses may overshadow investor confidence, eclipsing years of consistent expansion. An unfavourable earnings report may reverberate across the entire sector. A transient decline in GDP may obliterate billions of stock market valuations. Even ambiguous rumours, hints of a possible recession, or conjecture about an interest rate increase can induce fear within financial institutions. Investors concentrate on pessimistic outcomes, disregarding long-term patterns in favour of current anxieties.

Additionally, a status quo bias exists, which is the inclination to resist change and seek reassurance of stability (Thaler 1999). During economic prosperity, investors delude themselves into believing that favourable conditions would last indefinitely (Bradley et al., 2021). However, this illusion is dispelled when markets begin to decline. Suddenly, the desire to safeguard remaining assets prevails, prompting individuals to liquidate their investments hastily, sure they can avert more losses by withdrawing from the market. This enormous migration exacerbates a dismal trajectory. The same herd that inflated prices now depresses them, penalising those who delay their actions and rewarding just those who maintain composure among widespread fear.

The incessant barrage of financial news and media conjectures intensifies anxiety in financial markets. In an era of continuous news cycles and social media-driven trade, adverse headlines, market declines, and analyst downgrades are amplified into a significant catastrophe (Ricciardi 2004). A solitary tweet from a central banker, an inadequately articulated earnings report, or a misleading media interpretation of economic data may precipitate a sudden decline in global markets. The media is aware that panic generates sales. A more dramatic tale yields greater engagement. This creates a feedback loop: investors see alarming headlines and respond by selling, their actions precipitate more market declines, and media reports on the downturn exacerbate worry.

Fear-driven herding is most apparent in currency crises and sovereign debt breakdowns. In these circumstances, terror transcends mere emotional reactions and evolves into systemic danger. Investors seeing economic instability in a nation hastened their withdrawal of cash, instigated capital flight, and precipitated a currency collapse (Loang 2024). Governments try to stabilise their economies, often resorting to drastic measures, such as increasing interest rates, implementing capital restrictions, or pursuing international bailouts. However, once trust diminishes, restoration becomes very difficult. Fear-based marketing perpetuates itself, engendering a downward cycle that may lead to economic devastation in all countries.

The 1997 Asian Financial Crisis exemplifies this phenomenon (Souvannaseng 2022). The initial currency depreciation in Thailand escalated rapidly into a comprehensive economic catastrophe across Asia. As investors saw the decline of the Thai baht, they experienced panic and were apprehensive of similar outcomes in other developing economies (Subash 2012). They withdrew funds from South Korea, Indonesia, Malaysia, and the Philippines, initiating a domino effect that obliterated billions of dollars in market value and devastated economies. Governments were compelled to intervene, raise interest rates to untenable levels, and arrange emergency loans with the International Monetary Fund (IMF) to avert a complete economic catastrophe. What is the most critical aspect of this study? The basic conditions of several economies were not as grave as panic implied. However, as terror ensued, perception transformed into reality, and even the most robust financial institutions succumbed to frenzy.

The message is unequivocal: fear is an inexorable force in financial markets (Walsh 2021). It is disseminated through whispers, headlines, and innate human intuition. It supersedes rationality, incites collective behaviour, and propels markets into disarray. Individuals who discern their patterns and see that fear often poses a greater risk than the actual economic peril can strategically position themselves to not only survive but also prosper. The capacity to maintain composure during chaos has consistently distinguished exceptional investors. It is the distinction between individuals who liquidate assets at the nadir and those who acquire them when fear pervades the market. Fear always exists in financial markets. The study is: Will it dominate you, or will you see it for what it really is transient illusion that obscures the perception of the majority while presenting possibilities for those who resist conformity?

4.3 Greed and the Illusion of Endless Gains

Greed is a counterpart to fear in financial markets, similarly potent, infectious, and equally detrimental (Johnston 2024). It entices investors with the allure of easy affluence, drawing them into a speculative frenzy that obscures their perceptions of reality. When avarice prevails, the reason is forsaken for a perilous delusion: the conviction that prices will perpetually rise, that market fundamentals are irrelevant, and that this time, unlike previous occurrences, the bubble will remain intact. This idea of perpetual profits has driven some of history's most remarkable financial catastrophes, including the South Sea Bubble and the dot-com crash. Consistently, the story remains unchanged: investors delude themselves into believing that they have discovered a new paradigm in which risk has been eliminated and that those who hesitate are only forfeiting certain wealth. In each instance, reality reaffirms itself with harsh intensity, revealing the absurdity of unbridled hope.

Overconfidence propels speculative bubbles. Investors often develop a sense of invincibility under bullish market conditions. They ascribe their successes not to chance or overarching economic factors but to their intellect and insight. This exemplifies self-serving bias, the tendency to attribute success to oneself while attributing failure to others in similar circumstances. A trader who doubles his capital in a bull market commends his exceptional investment acumen. Still, if he then loses all his funds in the accompanying collapse, he attributes the failure to the Federal Reserve, the government, or some unpredictable market occurrence. This biased thinking enables unbridled greed to thrive as investors constantly affirm the notion that they are invulnerable to failure.

Greed does not exist in isolation; it flourishes within a financial system that incentivises risk-taking and stimulates speculation. Accessible credit and leverage serve as catalysts, transforming a moderate rise into an unsustainable bubble. When borrowing is cheap and readily available, investors assume excessive risk by leveraging their portfolios to acquire assets that exceed their means, thereby enhancing their returns (Loang 2025). Banks and financial institutions, motivated by profit from the surge, promote this conduct by lending to ineligible borrowers and developing complex financial instruments that obscure inherent risks. A recurring pattern emerges: cheap capital fuels imprudent speculation, leading to asset values exceeding their actual worth. Ultimately, leverage becomes unsustainable, leading to the collapse of the system.

Confirmation bias significantly influences this loop, guaranteeing that investors see only what aligns with their desires. During market upswings, individuals aggressively seek information that corroborates their conviction that the rally will continue. They adhere to optimistic experts, consume publications that bolster their positivity, and disregard any facts that indicate an impending decline. During the early 2000s, commodity markets experienced an extraordinary surge, with oil, metals, and agricultural items reaching historic prices (Umar et al. 2021). Analysts contended that a new era of global demand had begun, driven by growing economies that would generate an insatiable need for raw commodities, resulting in perpetually escalating prices. Investors embraced this story, overlooking the inherent volatility of commodity cycles and the historical tendency of previous booms to culminate in severe declines.

Perception of control exacerbates speculative excess. Investors are confident in their ability to navigate the market more effectively than others, anticipating the optimal moment to exit before the bubble collapses (Ricciardi 2008). Bubbles do not deflate gradually; they implode abruptly and obliterate wealth before individuals respond. When the commodities bubble of 2007–2008 ultimately collapsed, oil prices plummeted from $147 per barrel to below $40 within a few months. Investors who had previously been elated are now attempting to divest, only to discover a lack of remaining buyers. The same hedge funds and traders who had propelled prices to exorbitant heights were compelled to sell their holdings at substantial losses. Their conviction that they could manipulate the market was abruptly dismantled.

Greed-fuelled booms are especially common in developing nations, where rapid economic growth and an influx of foreign investment can inspire a frenzy of speculation. Countries with elevated GDP growth and increasing consumer demand attract global capital, as investors seek to capitalise on momentum (George 2023). However, the factors that propel these markets forward may also restrain them equally. As hope diminishes and international investors begin to retract their capital, the ensuing catastrophe may be catastrophic. The history of developing market bubbles is replete with instances of economies that rose due to speculative investment, only to descend into devastation when the mood shifts.

Greed is perilous because it obscures investors' perceptions of the new stability of cycles. Each market rally is driven by the conviction that this instance is distinct, that established principles no longer hold, and that innovation or economic transformations have made conventional valuation measurements irrelevant. However, history is unrelenting. Every bubble, regardless of the allure of its foundational myth, ultimately collapsed. The message is unequivocal: greed-fuelled herding may provide temporary exhilaration; however, it always culminates in a catastrophe. Individuals who pursue the mirage of perpetual profits ultimately become ensnared in the downfall, while those who heed cautionary indicators and withdraw are the ones who save their assets. This study does not consider whether the subsequent bubble will materialise. The fundamental research is as follows: Will you be the individual directing the herd or the observer at a safe distance, poised to exploit the moment when excitement devolves into chaos?

4.4 FOMO and Social Influence on Investing

The anxiety of being left behind is one of the most potent psychological drivers of today's financial markets. The unsettling murmur suggests that investors are missing out and that others are reaping the rewards while they remain inactive (Martaningrat and Kurniawan 2024). This drives illogical choices, urges individuals to pursue soaring stocks, and obscures their awareness of potential dangers. In a landscape dominated by social media, rapid news cycles, and trending investment fads, the fear of missing out has become a widespread phenomenon, fuelling a novel form of collective behaviour that is quicker, more intense, and more erratic than anything we have seen before.

The realm of finance was dominated by analysts, economists, and institutional investors, who produced meticulously prepared reports and comprehensive market analyses. Today, the reigning authorities in the world of investing are influencers dominating platforms such as Twitter, TikTok, Reddit, and YouTube, often lacking formal financial training yet amassing millions of devoted followers. A single tweet, viral post, or meme can trigger a frenzy among investors, prompting them to rush into buying a stock without conducting a thorough analysis of its fundamentals. Online communities such as Reddit's WallStreetBets, Twitter's FinTwit, and Telegram crypto groups have fostered a financial landscape in which speculation transforms into fact, and the shared conviction in a stock's ascent frequently outweighs its true worth.

This is the moment when excitement begins. When individuals observe others investing, they tend to believe that there must be a compelling rationale behind it. The reasoning is straightforward: when a multitude of individuals rush into a stock, IPO, or cryptocurrency, it stands to reason that they possess some significant insight. However, in truth, many individuals are just going along with the crowd, making choices driven not by careful analysis but by the exhilarating feeling of belonging to something significant. The greater the number of participants, the more influential the illusion. Collective enthusiasm surges, and before long, all are certain they are on an inevitable path to fortune.

The surge in meme stocks and cryptocurrency trading has clarified this. The rise in retail investment, driven by commission-free platforms such as Robinhood and eToro, has transformed the market into a fierce arena of excitement and speculation. Currently, a stock's success hinges less on robust earnings or a viable business strategy and more on an engaging narrative, a trending moment, or the support of a captivating figure. GameStop, AMC, Dogecoin, and Shiba Inu are more than mere financial instruments; they represent a cultural phenomenon fuelled by the conviction that the underdog can challenge the giants of Wall Street and emerge victorious.

Initial public offerings (IPOs) create an exciting atmosphere that often fuels a sense of urgency among investors (Ooi 2025). Each year, new enterprises make their public debut, generating a whirlwind of media excitement and anticipation. The narrative remains unchanged: Here comes the next big thing, the next groundbreaking innovation, and the subsequent extraordinary chance that comes around only once in a generation. Enthusiastic backers are keen to claim their share of a remarkable legacy. They are eager to seize the next significant opportunity, so they purchase it without hesitation. However, historical evidence suggests that numerous highly publicised IPOs often experience dramatic declines following their initial surge. The thrill diminishes, the truth emerges, and those who invest at the height find themselves with nothing to show for it.

4.5 Consequences for Investors and Financial Markets

The phenomenon of herding behaviour in financial markets transcends mere theory, as it carries tangible and frequently catastrophic outcomes (Cervellati et al. 2024). The shared actions of investors, driven more by emotions than logical assessment, lead to extreme misvaluations, market surges, and inevitable downturns. It skews the worth of assets, jeopardises financial security, and fosters an environment in which wealth can be gained or lost in an instant. The irony lies in the fact that, although each investor thinks they are making their own decisions, the truth is that the majority are merely following the crowd, caught up in the thrill of a booming market or the fear of a declining one. What unfolds when this collective behaviour goes beyond its limits? The solution lies within a recurring pattern of prosperity and decline in markets that challenge fundamental economic principles, as well as within a financial framework that becomes increasingly susceptible to the influence of institutions and technology.

The initial and most pressing outcome of emotional herding is the widespread inflation of asset values. When investors flock to a stock, commodity, or the entire market sector, prices can become utterly disconnected from reality. A prime illustration of this phenomenon is the dot-com bubble that occurred in the late 1990s (Fari 2023). Tech firms lacking profits, clear business strategies, and occasionally even a functioning product experienced a surge in their valuations solely due to their association with the 'new economy'. Investors were less concerned with a company's merit for a billion-dollar valuation and focused more on the upward trajectory of its stock. This is the process of overvaluation through collective illusion, where individuals persuade themselves that conventional valuation standards are no longer relevant. However, they consistently managed to find a way to do so. When the facade shatters, the market tumbles and frequently erases years of progress in just a few months.

The initial signs of overvaluation are merely the tip of the iceberg. The dynamics of emotional herding drive the formation of cycles characterised by dramatic peaks and devastating troughs in the market. As you ascend, descent becomes increasingly challenging. As the decline begins, a wave of anxiety washes over everyone. Once filled with excitement, investors are now hastily seeking the door and anxious to offload their assets before values plummet. This unexpected change in mood impacts not only single stocks but can also shake the foundations of all economies.

However, the most deceptive element of emotion-driven herding is frequently influenced by manipulation. Institutional investors, hedge funds, proprietary trading desks, and market makers recognise that retail investors often make decisions based on emotions. It is clear that when emotions such as fear and greed dominate, rational thought is usually set aside. They leverage this understanding for their benefit. When a stock is skyrocketing due to excitement, major investors frequently take the opportunity to cash out at a high point, reaping substantial gains before the inevitable downturn. On the other hand, when the market is engulfed in panic selling, they seize the opportunity to acquire assets at drastically reduced prices, being fully aware that fear has pushed valuations well below their actual value. This is why individual investors often find themselves at a disadvantage during these cycles: they tend to respond to the emotional fluctuations of the market, whereas experts tactically position themselves in opposition to them.

The emergence of algorithmic and high-frequency trading introduces an additional layer of intricacy. Although advancements in technology have enhanced market efficiency in numerous respects, they have simultaneously increased the susceptibility of markets to emotional intensification. Automated trading models lack the capacity for thought; they respond. As prices rise, algorithms tend to purchase more, further strengthening the upward movement. As prices drop, they move quickly to sell, further accelerating a downward trend. This establishes a perilous cycle in which market fluctuations that previously unfolded over months occur within minutes (Kaufman and Sicilia 2021). Flash crashes dramatic moments when markets dive and then bounce back almost instantly often stem from algorithms reacting to one another in a whirlwind of automated anxiety. The once-human-centric cycle of avarice and anxiety is now being mirrored at lightning speed by machines, resulting in markets that are more unstable and erratic than ever before.

The sole safeguard against these patterns of overindulgence and downfall is consciousness. Behavioural finance the exploration of how our minds influence investment choices has emerged as a vital resource for anyone seeking to navigate the financial landscape while avoiding its typical pitfalls. Recognising biases, such as overconfidence, loss aversion, and the bandwagon effect, enables investors to identify instances when emotions overtake rational thinking. It encourages them to challenge dominant narratives, resist the temptation to conform, and adopt a more structured approach to investing. In the ever-changing landscape of markets, individuals can maintain perspective, recognise broader trends, and make thoughtful choices amidst the chaos, ultimately finding success.

The impact of emotional herding on financial markets can be drastic (Chen et al. 2021). This situation results in inflated asset values, ignites perilous boom-bust cycles, enables institutional investors to profit at the public's expense, and fosters a market atmosphere in which technology exacerbates volatility. Nevertheless, despite everything, the cycle continues to unfold. What's the reason? This is because the essence of humanity has remained constant. The real test for investors lies not in eradicating emotion but in identifying when it influences their choices and having the self-control to respond differently. Financial markets transcend mere numbers and data, revolving around human emotions, psychology, and the timeless struggle between fear and greed. Individuals who grasp this dynamic not only endure the market but also flourish.

4.6 Conclusion

The dynamics of collective behaviour in financial markets uncover a crucial insight: emotions such as fear, greed, and the anxiety of being left behind shape the choices made by investors. The powerful sway of these emotions propels markets to irrational heights and depths, creating cycles of prosperity and decline that may seem illogical yet are remarkably predictable. Fear, the most fundamental human emotion, manifests in financial markets through panic selling, triggering a chain reaction of sell-offs that erases billions in wealth. On the other hand, avarice drives speculative bubbles, as investors persuade themselves that assets will continue to rise without end. The fear of missing out, intensified by social media and online trading platforms, drives hasty choices, causing investors to purchase not for intrinsic worth but out of anxiety about being excluded. The interplay between these elements forms a cycle in which emotional choices influence market trends, reinforcing the anxieties or excitement that propel them forward.

The essence of emotional herding is that it amplifies its effect. When anxiety grips the market, observing others offloading their assets prompts even more to follow suit. Investors caught in a web of fear and pessimism often jump to conclusions and prioritise security above all else. In thriving markets, the perception of limitless profits fosters overconfidence, impulsive investments, and, ultimately, the formation of a bubble. Institutional investors, keenly attuned to these patterns, frequently exploit retail investors' emotional vulnerabilities, steering market sentiment to enhance their gains. Amid this evolving landscape, the emergence of algorithmic trading introduces a fresh layer to the dynamics at play. Automated models designed to respond to price fluctuations have the potential to amplify market volatility in ways that human investors cannot replicate.

Understanding these psychological dynamics is essential for investors, regulators, and financial institutions. Investors need to develop emotional resilience, avoid the temptation to conform to the crowd, and concentrate instead on fundamental analysis and strategies that stand the test of time. Regulators need to establish protective measures to curb rampant speculation and alleviate the risk of market crashes fuelled by panic. Financial institutions must find a way to harmonise their quest for profit with a strong sense of ethical duty, ensuring that their actions do not worsen market instability. Ultimately, the key to overcoming emotional herding lies in awareness recognising that markets are more than mere figures on display; they embody the intricate dynamics of human psychology as a whole. Individuals who can transcend emotional chaos will not only safeguard their assets but also acquire the insight necessary to manoeuvre through financial markets with assurance.

References

Bradley D, Hanousek Jr J, Jame R, Xiao Z (2021) Place your bets? The market consequences of investment research on Reddit's Wallstreetbets The Market Consequences of Investment Research on Reddit's Wallstreetbets (March 15, 2021)

Brown GR, Lala KN (2024) Sense and nonsense: evolutionary perspectives on human behaviour. Oxford University Press, Oxford

Cervellati EM, Angelini N, Stella GP (2024) Behavioural finance and wealth management: market anomalies, investors' behaviour, and the role of financial advisors

Chen Y, Zhu S, He H (2021) The influence of investor emotion on the stock market: evidence from an infectious disease model. Discret Dyn Nat Soc 1:5520276

Fari S (2023) The 1990s crisis during the globalisation. In: The age of global economic crises. Routledge, London, pp 105–126

George AS (2023) Evaluating India's economic growth: challenges and opportunities on the path to 5 trillion dollars. Partners Univ Int Innov J 1(6):85–109

Johnston A (2024) Infinite greed: the inhuman selfishness of capital. Columbia University Press, New York

Kahneman D (2003) A perspective on judgment and choice: mapping bounded rationality. Am Econ Rev 93(5):1449–1475

Kaufman H, Sicilia DB (2021) The day the markets roared: how a 1982 forecast sparked a global bull market. BenBella Books, Dallas

Loang OK (2024) Stability of Shariah-compliant stocks in Indonesia, Malaysia, and Gcc: the roles of monetary and fiscal policies and contagion. J Islamic Monet Econ Financ 10(1):155–176

Loang OK (2025) Can machine learning surpass human investors? Evidence from adaptive herding behaviour in US, China and India. J Appl Econ 28(1):2435796

Loang OK, Candra S, Naveenan RV (2024) Stability in chaos: impact of monetary, fiscal, and firm characteristics on investor sentiment in Asian emerging markets. Int J Business Soc 25(3):1145–1164

Martaningrat NWS, Kurniawan Y (2024) The impact of financial influencers, social influencers, and FOMO economy on the decision-making of investment on millennial generation and gen Z of Indonesia. J Ecohuman 3(3):1319–1335

Naeem MA, Senthilkumar A, Arfaoui N, Mohnot R (2024) Mapping fear in financial markets: insights from dynamic networks and centrality measures. Pac Basin Financ J 85:102368

Ooi KL (2025) Behavioural anomalies and market inefficiencies. In: Demystifying behavioural finance: foundational theories to contemporary applications and future directions. Springer, Singapore, pp 23–38

Ricciardi V (2004) A risk perception primer: a narrative research review of the risk perception literature in behavioural accounting and behavioural finance

Ricciardi V (2008) The psychology of risk: the behavioural finance perspective. Wiley, Hoboken

Souvannaseng P (2022) Liquidated: US/Japan-Chinese rivalry, financial crises, and explaining shifts in hydropower finance regimes in the Mekong. Asian Perspect 46(1):49–75

Subash R (2012) Role of behavioural finance in portfolio investment decisions: evidence from India. Charles University DSpace Dissertation

Thaler RH (1999) Mental accounting matters. J Behav Decis Making 12(3):183–206

Umar Z, Jareño F, Escribano A (2021) Agricultural commodity markets and oil prices: an analysis of the dynamic return and volatility connectedness. Resour Policy 73:102147

Walsh J (2021) Investing with Keynes: how the world's greatest economist overturned conventional wisdom and made a fortune on the stock market. Wiley, Hoboken

Chapter 5
Types of Herding Behaviour

5.1 Introduction

The phenomenon of collective behaviour in financial markets has a compelling and contradictory influence on how investors make choices. In essence, herding occurs when investors, instead of trusting their analysis, mimic the behaviour of others, frequently magnifying market trends beyond what the underlying valuations would support. The urge to fit in extends beyond a mere mental shortcut; it is deeply ingrained in human nature, stemming from evolutionary traits that once enabled our ancestors to thrive in unpredictable environments. This behaviour does not guarantee survival in financial markets; instead, it frequently results in mispriced assets, speculative bubbles, and devastating market crashes.

What compels investors, even those among the most astute in the financial realm, to relinquish their decision-making to the collective? This solution is found in the nuanced yet impactful influence of external cues. The contemporary financial scene is overflowing with data stock tickers, analyst insights, algorithmic trading suggestions, and, increasingly, the deluge of perspectives pouring in from social media channels. In principle, an abundance of information ought to enhance decision-making, but the actual situation tells a different story. The overwhelming amount and intricacy of financial information lead people to choose a more straightforward path: instead of sifting through chaos, they watch the actions of others and believe that the market's collective insight is accurate (Loang 2024). The irony lies in the fact that when countless investors act on this shared impulse, the market loses its ability to discern wisdom. It transforms into a mere echo chamber of speculation and self-perpetuating illusions.

Herding behaviour is not just one thing; it is a combination of mechanisms that manifest in various forms based on the market situation. Confident investors participate in a phenomenon where they mimic the price movements or investment decisions of their peers, believing that the wisdom of the crowd offers superior insights. Some individuals fall prey to the powerful influence of reputational herding,

K. L. Ooi et al., *Following the Crowd: Psychological Drivers of Herding and Market Overreaction*, https://doi.org/10.1007/978-981-95-0792-4_5

particularly among fund managers and institutional investors who fear that straying from widely accepted opinions might jeopardise their professional futures. The era of digital innovation has unveiled a fresh landscape, one dominated by social media dynamics, where viral phenomena, influencer-led stories, and virtual collectives can send stock prices soaring to incredible heights or plummeting to shocking depths in the blink of an eye.

The impact of collective behaviour is significant, influencing not only personal investment results but also the overall stability of financial markets. Herding can ignite speculative bubbles, reminiscent of the dot-com era when a shared conviction in Internet stocks drove valuations to unsustainable heights that ultimately crumbled under pressure. It can also intensify market declines, as seen during the 2008 financial crisis, when rampant panic selling transformed the housing market adjustment into a worldwide economic catastrophe. Amid daily market shifts, collective behaviour skews prices, generates false momentum, and results in the misdirection of capital, impacting a wide range of sectors from stock markets to real estate and digital currencies.

As shown in Table 5.1, not all herding in financial markets stems from emotion or panic; some instances are strategic, deliberate, or even coldly rational. Informational herding occurs when investors assume that others possess superior insight. When uncertainty looms, and the fog of incomplete data clouds one's judgement, the crowd feels the safest path. 'Surely the majority can't all be wrong', one might reason (Loang 2025). However, the irony is haunting: if every investor is watching everyone else, and no one is actually leading based on sound information, the crowd becomes a self-reinforcing loop of misplaced trust. The appearance of momentum is mistaken for wisdom. Stocks surge not because they deserve to, but because enough people believe others know better. In this echo chamber of assumptions, prices inflate far beyond the fundamentals, setting the stage for inevitable corrections.

However, the desire to follow does not always stem from ignorance; it can arise from self-preservation. Reputational herding, as highlighted in Table 5.1, reveals how professionals, analysts, fund managers, and portfolio strategists often follow the crowd not because they agree with it but because going against it is too risky. In a performance-driven world, where one bad quarter can tarnish a career, being wrong in a group feels safer than being right alone. The logic is brutal but honest: If the herd fails, no single person falls. Then, there is compensatory herding, perhaps the most cynical of all. Here, decisions are not based on belief or insight but on incentive structures. Quarterly targets, peer comparisons, and bonus benchmarks prompt managers to make decisions that they know are not ideal in the long term, in order to meet short-term goals. In this world, the herd is not a weakness; it is a pay check. Together, these three forces demonstrate that herding is not always irrational. Sometimes, it is the most 'rational' way to survive in a system that rewards conformity over conviction.

This chapter explores the various herding mechanisms that influence financial markets, examining the psychological and structural factors that lead investors to conform to the majority. It examines the interplay between information-driven

Table 5.1 Types of herding in financial markets

Type of herding	Definition	Core motivation	Narrative insight
Informational herding	Occurs when investors mimic the decisions of others based on the belief that the crowd possesses superior or hidden information	Uncertainty, lack of confidence in personal knowledge or interpretation	This form of herding plays out like a financial version of 'follow the leader'. When investors don't trust their own judgement, they look to the crowd for guidance. But the crowd might be just as lost following others who are also guessing
Reputational herding	Arises when decision-makers, especially professionals, follow the crowd to avoid personal blame if things go wrong	Fear of career damage, embarrassment, or being judged for independent failure	Fund managers and analysts often feel pressure to conform. If they take a contrarian stance and lose, they risk their reputation. But if they follow the herd and lose, they're just one of many. It's a case of reputation taking precedence over actual fund performance, with safety in numbers serving as the cover
Compensational herding	Happens when investors or professionals make choices that align with short-term performance metrics or incentive systems	Financial incentives that prioritise quarterly gains or peer comparison	Compensation schemes often reward short-term gains, not long-term wisdom. This encourages herding for the sake of performance parity. Professionals don't necessarily believe in what they're doing but they do what's rewarded. It's strategy dictated by the pay check, not the market outlook

Source: Authors' work

dynamics, reputation, and the impact of the digital era on shaping market trends, often amplifying both unfounded optimism and unjustified negativity (Ooi 2024). This engaging exploration will showcase real-world examples, revealing how group dynamics influence choices at both personal and organisational levels while offering valuable perspectives on the ongoing effects of collective behaviour in today's financial environment. Ultimately, grasping these dynamics transcends mere academic interest; it is a crucial ability for investors aiming to manoeuvre through markets with insight, discipline, and a unique perspective in a landscape increasingly shaped by collective emotions rather than logical reasoning.

5.2 Information-Based Herding

Investors often fancy themselves as logical, methodical, and self-reliant decision-makers (Ali et al. 2021). However, the truth is much more complex. In the fast-paced realm of financial markets, where fortunes can change in the blink of an eye, the majority of investors lack the time, expertise, or patience to meticulously analyse every financial statement or evaluate every risk with exacting detail. Instead, they opted for an easy way. They observed shifts in the market, heeded the advice of experts, and frequently responded to the most recent news stories without considering whether the collective they were following was on the correct path. This captures the core of information-driven herding, in which investors forgo independent thoughts and turn to external cues to shape their choices.

The reasoning behind this action is surprisingly straightforward: If the crowd is investing in a specific stock, they must have some critical insight (Shiller 2000). When a prominent analyst elevates a company's rating to 'strong buy', it indeed suggests that the stock is poised for significant potential, would you not agree? When financial news outlets are abuzz with chatter about a sector poised for growth, is it not the perfect moment to dive before the opportunity slips away? This inclination to depend on group indicators instead of individual assessment stems from a concept known as rational ignorance, suggesting that since collecting and scrutinising financial data requires significant time and effort, investors sensibly opt to forgo it. Instead, they depend on the actions and choices of others, presuming that the more extensive market makes correct judgements. However, the flaw in this logic lies in the fact that when individuals act in this manner, markets cease to function efficiently and transform into speculative echo chambers.

One of the most striking instances of information-driven herding can be observed in initial public offerings (IPOs) (Aghamolla and Thakor 2022). The excitement surrounding a company's initial public offering (IPO) on the stock market is often palpable. Investors flock to seize their opportunities, primarily driven by the sight of others also taking the plunge. The company's early supporters and financial backers inundated the media with positive stories, bolstering the perception that this new stock is an essential addition to any portfolio. However, truth frequently diverges significantly. Research has repeatedly indicated that initial public offerings often see inflated prices at their debut, primarily due to demand driven by collective behaviour. The outcome? A phenomenon referred to as IPO overpricing is characterised by stocks skyrocketing on their debut day, only to lag significantly in performance in the subsequent months. Those who dive in at the start often catch up in the excitement of the market and frequently end up with stocks that swiftly decline in value as the initial buzz subsides.

The same trend emerges in movements following earnings announcements, showcasing yet another example of herding driven by information. When a company reveals earnings that exceed expectations, investors rush to buy the stock, believing that others possess better insight into its future potential. Research indicates that stock prices often exhibit exaggerated reactions in the short term, eventually revealing a more precise evaluation of a company's fundamentals. When earnings fall short, a similar dynamic unfolds: investors react with alarms, offloading their shares in droves, frequently pushing prices well beneath what is warranted by the actual situation. The audience responds to the prompt without reflecting on the broader economic landscape, leading to imbalances that savvy investors, especially hedge funds and large-scale traders, capitalise on for gain.

However, the phenomenon of information-driven herding is most clearly illustrated in the inflated valuations of tech startups in private equity markets. Over the last 20 years, investors in venture capital and private equity have consistently increased the value of tech firms, relying solely on a shared sense of optimism. A notable example is the dot-com bubble of the late 1990s, during which investors poured billions into Internet startups, many of which lacked revenue, a viable business model, and occasionally even a functioning product (Peters 2024). What is the rationale for this? If savvy investors place significant bets on these companies, there is likely a compelling reason for it. The bubble ultimately collapsed, erasing significant wealth and driving numerous so-called 'innovators' into financial ruin.

Indeed, the past has been echoing over time. During the 2010s, a familiar pattern emerged, characterised by the tech giants of Silicon Valley private companies boasting valuations exceeding a billion dollars, despite doubts about their profitability. Firms such as WeWork, initially celebrated as the next big thing in commercial real estate, experienced a meteoric rise in their valuations, fuelled solely by investors' fervour. In 2019, WeWork was poised for an IPO, boasting a remarkable valuation of US $47 billion. However, as investors began to scrutinise their financials, filled with losses, dubious governance, and unsustainable growth, the façade crumbled. In a matter of weeks, the public offering was called off, the valuation dropped by more than 80%, and the company's highly regarded founder had to resign. The WeWork debacle serves as a classic illustration of how collective behaviour can drive asset valuations to unsustainable heights, only for the truth to emerge when the group's faith begins to falter.

5.3 Reputational Herding among Institutional Investors

Institutional investors often portray themselves as logical guardians of financial markets, methodical experts who, in contrast to retail traders, base their decisions on extensive research and advanced models (Lu and Li 2023). However, in truth, even the most prominent figures in finance cannot escape the compelling influence of collective behaviour. In many cases, they tend to be more susceptible to these conditions. Investment professionals, monetary authorities, speculative investors, and collective investment schemes are interconnected in their operations. They operate in a realm in which every move is meticulously evaluated, examined, and contrasted. In this landscape, the anxiety of lagging behind rivals often overshadows the quest for a genuine understanding of investment (Pérez and Santos 2018). This captures the core of reputational herding, a compelling influence that compels even the most experienced individuals to follow one another's trades, not out of genuine conviction, but because straying from the majority feels far too perilous.

At the core of this vibrant landscape lies a pervasive anxiety that plagues every fund manager: the dread of falling short compared with its competitors (Guo et al. 2024). In a field where achievement is frequently measured by comparison, an investor who adopts a unique perspective and miscalculates faces consequences that extend beyond mere monetary setbacks: they jeopardise their professional future. A fund manager who adheres to traditional investments, even when they lag, can defend their choices by claiming, 'It's what everyone else was doing'. However, what about those who go against the crowd and come up short? They find themselves in the limelight, addressing furious clients and sceptical boards. This illustrates why numerous fund managers adopt trend-following strategies, aligning their actions with the overall market rather than taking daring or contrarian approaches. It is not just about what makes the most sense; it is about ensuring the most remarkable career stability.

The weight of quarterly earnings expectations and the influx of investor capital into funds add to this pressure. Institutional investors have limitations in terms of patience (Sahoo et al. 2023). Investment vehicles, such as hedge funds, pension funds, and mutual funds, are evaluated based on their performance over brief periods, typically every 3 months. When a fund fails to meet expectations in a particular quarter, investors may decide to withdraw their investments and shift their capital to a rival. Relentless pressure to achieve quick results compels fund managers to focus on short-term profits rather than sustainable growth (Canterbery 1999). Even when a manager spots a potentially rewarding long-term opportunity, they might hold back from taking action if this means falling behind their colleagues in the upcoming reporting period. Short-term thinking dominates, and the tendency to follow the crowd intensifies as investors rush to the same stocks, prioritising momentum over genuine value.

However, the phenomenon of reputational herding extends beyond fund managers; it also influences the largest financial institutions globally, encompassing central banks, hedge funds, and mutual funds. These organisations often group their transactions, indicating that they acquire and dispose of identical assets simultaneously. This establishes a continuous loop in which price changes are influenced not by underlying fundamentals but rather by the strategies of major institutions. When a prominent hedge fund begins to invest heavily in a specific asset, it often triggers a ripple effect, as other funds rush in, anxious not to lose their chance to capitalise on the opportunity. This illustrates how markets can become closely linked as major institutions act in unison, intensifying trends in either direction, driving prices well beyond their actual worth during prosperous periods and sending them spiralling into undervaluation when sentiment changes.

The phenomenon of being too large to fail stems directly from the influence of reputational herding. When organisations converge on similar investments, they create a systemic risk situation in which the failure of a handful of key players can destabilise the entire market. Financial crises are profoundly destructive because they stem not merely from a handful of individuals making misguided choices, but from a sector as a whole advancing together, blind to looming threats.

What can we learn from this? Reputational herding transcends mere academic theory; it is a powerful influence that has moulded some of the most pivotal financial moments in history. This explains the tendency of fund managers to pursue identical trades, the way hedge funds often replicate one another's strategies, and the cautious and synchronised movements of central banks. The outcome is a financial system that appears less autonomous, less logical, and more susceptible to dramatic fluctuations than we often assume. Understanding the dynamics of reputational herding is essential for investors (Zhao 2022). It delves into the reasons behind the irrational pricing of certain assets, the occasional disconnection of markets from reality, and the surprising irrationality of even the most powerful financial institutions, which often contradict their claims of rationality. Individuals who can detach from the crowd, assess the core principles, and engage in independent thought will consistently hold an edge because, ultimately, the markets favour those brave enough to look beyond the false sense of security that comes from conformity.

5.4 Compensational Herding

There is a certain romance that people often associate with the idea of a fund manager. This brilliant financial mind sees what others miss, navigates chaos with incredible precision, and calls the market's next big move while others are still trying to understand the last (Liu et al. 2024). However, peel back the curtain of that polished mythology, and you will often find something much more conflicted. Behind the Bloomberg terminals and beneath the tailored suits sit men and women whose decisions are driven less by conviction and more by compensation. This is the quiet force of compensation herding, a strategic yet deeply systemic form of conformity in which investment choices are made not necessarily to maximise returns but to meet the performance incentives that dictate one's next promotion, bonus, or even job security.

At its core, compensational herding is not about fear or ignorance; it is about rational career survival. Unlike emotional herding, which stems from panic or greed, compensational herding is driven by structured reward systems baked into the DNA of modern finance. Fund managers, portfolio advisors, and analysts many operate under intense pressure to deliver quarterly results. Their value, in the eyes of superiors and clients, was measured against benchmarks and peers. Underperforming the market even temporarily can be seen as incompetence, while losing money with everyone else might be forgiven as 'just part of the cycle'. The message becomes clear: If you want to stay afloat and stay with the pack.

Imagine managing a large mutual fund. You have performed your analysis and believe that a particular stock is grossly overvalued, a classic bubble waiting to burst (Mohacsy and Lefer 2007). However, your competitors piled into it, and your firm's compensation model was tied to its relative performance. If you stay out and the stock continues to rise, you will lag behind your peers and may lose clients. If you join in, ride the wave, and the bubble bursts later, well, everyone gets hurt. At that moment, the rational move is not to do what is right for the portfolio in the long term; it is to do what is safe for your career in the short term. You buy the stock. You join the herd. You pray that the music does not stop before your performance review.

This is the paradox of professional investing, which often rewards short-term conformity over long-term courage (Kalpathy et al. 2021). In such an environment, outperformance is not always prioritised; alignment is. Compensation schemes based on quarterly targets, performance rankings, and peer group benchmarking create a gravitational pull toward consensus. Managers are not just trying to beat the market; they are trying to avoid underperforming their competitors. Even if they believe the herd is heading off a cliff, they may follow, knowing that standing apart means standing alone and being financially exposed.

The ripple effects of this dynamic were significant. Compensational herding inflates asset bubbles, distorts price discovery, and increases volatility. When too many investors move in lockstep, market diversity disappears. Everyone is positioned in the same way, the moment sentiment shifts, and the stampede begins in the opposite direction. What started as a rational response to incentive structures could quickly escalate into an irrational market panic. A clear example of this is the dot-com bubble of the late 1990s. Despite widespread scepticism among veteran investors, many fund managers loaded up on tech stocks because that was where the benchmark gains were. To resist this, the risk was labelled as out of touch. When the crash came, the pain was shared, as was the justification. 'We were all in it together'.

Compensational herding is so insidious that it is often invisible to the outside world. Unlike emotional herding, which is usually characterised by panicked sell-offs or frenzied buying, compensational herding typically appears composed, calculated, and professional. Decisions appear sophisticated from a distance. Analysts publish glowing reports. Fund managers make confident appearances on financial television. However, beneath the surface, many make decisions not because they believe in the assets, but because they prioritise self-preservation. They manage not only portfolios but also perceptions. In such a setting, true contrarianism is a luxury that can be afforded.

However, in the long term, compensational herding is a dangerous game. While it may protect a manager's bonus in the short term, it often sacrifices the investor's interest (Ricciardi 2004). Herding into trendy sectors, overhyped IPOs, or fashionable strategies might deliver quarterly outperformance, but at the cost of long-term risk. For the average investor entrusting retirement savings to these professionals, this is the hidden cost they rarely see. The portfolio may appear diversified, and the strategy may sound intelligent; however, if bonus targets and peer comparisons influence the core decisions, the integrity of the investment process is already compromised.

Breaking the cycle of compensational herding requires more than individual awareness, which demands systemic reform. Incentive structures must evolve to reward long-term thinking, risk-adjusted performance, and strategic discipline, as well as short-term returns and relative performance. Some firms have begun experimenting with multiyear compensation models, clawbacks, and delayed bonuses (Liu et al. 2025). These steps are in the right direction, but cultural change is equally important. We must stop glorifying quarterly winners and start celebrating consistency, patience and contrarian courage. The truth is, great investors are not the ones who perform best in bull markets; they are the ones who resist the temptation to follow, especially when the rewards for doing so are most significant.

5.5 Digital-Age Herding and Social Media Influence

The era of digital innovation has transformed financial markets into a fiercely competitive arena where information travels at lightning speed, emotions fluctuate instantaneously, and market dynamics are increasingly influenced by social media buzz rather than traditional fundamentals (Thakkar 2024). Social media platforms, such as Twitter, Reddit, and TikTok, have evolved into modern trading arenas where everyday investors, influencers, and even anonymous meme accounts wield a remarkable influence over stock valuations. In today's landscape, investing transcends mere numbers; it revolves around compelling stories, trends that capture attention, and the skill of seizing opportunities before they slip away.

This transformation has led to a modern type of collective behaviour in the digital era, where countless traders move together, not because they analyse an asset but because they observe the crowd heading in a unified direction. In a world where the latest stock on r/WallStreetBets can capture attention, a TikTok sensation can promise untold riches, and a mysterious tweet from a tech mogul can skyrocket digital currency. The rapid pace and vast reach of these phenomena foster an atmosphere in which thoughtful investing frequently yields the thrill of fear-of-missing-out-driven speculation.

The dangers of this collective mindset in the digital age are significant. False information proliferates rapidly and frequently overshadows credible assessment. A solitary, unconfirmed update regarding a company 'heading to the moon' can trigger a stampede of traders, causing prices to soar in mere hours. Coordinated retail trading, though empowering for individual investors, can lead to market distortions in which assets are assessed not by their actual value but by the overwhelming power of collective conviction. When conviction falters, as it often does, downturns can be just as intense as upswings.

Few occurrences capture this essence, similar to the surge in short squeezes and the explosive nature of viral stock movements. One of the most notable instances occurred with GameStop (GME) in early 2021 when retail investors on Reddit's r/WallStreetBets executed a remarkably short squeeze, compelling hedge funds that had wagered against the stock to close their positions with significant losses (Baig 2024). The stock, which had previously hovered around $4 per share just months ago, soared to over $400 in just a few days. It was not due to any fundamental shift in the company but rather because the online community willed it to happen. A blend of savvy financial tactics, the defiance of Wall Street power players, and the vibrant energy of the meme culture drove the surge. However, as swiftly as it surged, GameStop plummeted, resulting in significant losses for those who entered the market at its highest point.

The Dogecoin narrative is a prime illustration of market-driven fluctuations. A light-hearted idea turned into a phenomenon as its value skyrocketed, fuelled by Elon Musk's frequent tweets. Retail investors, driven by social media buzz, poured billions into Dogecoin, elevating its market value above that of major Fortune 500 companies. However, as excitement dwindled, the truth began to emerge. The value plummeted, leaving countless individuals who thought they were on the fast track to wealth watching their investments vanish into thin air.

However, no phenomenon of the digital age has captured the essence of social media-fuelled speculation, similar to the Special Purpose Acquisition Company (SPAC) frenzy of 2021. SPACs, which are essentially shell companies created to merge with private firms and take them public without the conventional initial public offering (IPO) process, have gained rapid prominence in the financial world (Rodrigues and Stegemoller 2022). People from all walks of life, including prominent investors and social media finance experts, rallied around the notion that SPACs were the ultimate pathway to wealth. Firms lacking revenue, a defined business strategy, and often even tangible operations were inexplicably soaring in market value, propelled solely by the frenzy of online buzz.

Enthusiastic investors keen to seize the opportunity rushed into SPAC stocks. Among the notable names were Nikola, an electric truck company that had yet to deliver a single operational vehicle; Lordstown Motors; and Clover Health. These companies experienced a meteoric rise fuelled by speculation, only to plummet when investors came to the stark realisation that social media hype couldn't conjure profits from anything. As 2021 came to a close, the SPAC phenomenon deflated, resulting in a landscape littered with exaggerated disappointments and significant financial setbacks for those who had invested at the height of the frenzy.

The takeaway from the phenomenon of digital-age conformity is unmistakable: what social media provides can swiftly retract (Klinger et al. 2023). Excitement can drive costs to unreasonable heights, but it cannot maintain them forever. The audience has immense influence, yet their loyalty can be unpredictable. As online platforms have opened the doors to investing for everyone and shaken up the old financial hierarchies, they have also fostered a landscape in which wild enthusiasm can take hold at lightning speed.

For individuals navigating this evolving financial landscape, the crucial insight lies in discerning when the masses are accurate and when they are merely caught up in their repetitive discourse. Those who unthinkingly chase after the latest fads frequently become examples of what they do not do. However, individuals who grasp the mindset driving modern trends, who can distinguish between mere excitement and real value, and who recognise the right moment to withdraw before the tide turns will consistently maintain an advantage in a landscape dominated by online influence.

5.6 Empirical Experiment: Rational Vs. Irrational Herding

The experiment was carefully structured to create conditions under which both rational and irrational herding behaviours could be observed, manipulated, and measured. Conducted at a university in Malaysia, the study involved 80 undergraduate students from business, finance, psychology, and economics programmes. The participants were invited into a controlled, lab-based simulation that mimicked a high-stakes, fast-paced trading environment. The design of the experiment integrated elements from behavioural finance, game theory, and social psychology, with the objective of discerning when herding behaviour is motivated by logical, information-based strategy versus when it stems from psychological conformity and emotional volatility.

To create distinct psychological and cognitive environments, participants were randomly divided into four groups, each exposed to different types of decision stimuli. Each group interacted with the same base simulation software, which displayed three fictional assets TechCoin, AgroChain, and BioToken. These assets were designed to resemble speculative digital currencies with fluctuating prices. Students engaged in five trading rounds, each simulating a short market session. They were tasked with making investment decisions to hold or sell each asset in every round. Their goal was to maximise a virtual portfolio throughout the experiment, with leader boards and rewards introduced to simulate reputation, pressure, and incentive structures.

In the first rational herding condition, participants were told that some players in their group would receive access to more accurate or advanced information. In reality, two students per group were privately given correct directional signals about which asset was likely to increase in value. These signals were accurate 70% of the time and were randomly reassigned each round. Other participants were aware that someone in the group might have better information, but were not told who. Throughout the five rounds, behavioural patterns began to emerge. Participants without private signals started to mimic the decisions of those who had been correct in earlier rounds. The third round particularly pronounced this behaviour, as students began expressing confidence in 'leaders' based on observed performance. Exit surveys and in-game chat logs confirmed that participants made these choices not out of fear or emotion, but rather through rational inference, believing that others likely had superior insight. This condition successfully captured the logic behind rational herding: individuals making seemingly imitative decisions that are, in fact, grounded in Bayesian reasoning and strategic trust.

The second rational herding condition introduced a cost function into the decision-making environment. Participants were informed that any deviation from the group's average position, when coupled with a portfolio loss, would result in a deduction from their final performance score. This was designed to simulate institutional constraints in which investors are incentivised to conform in order to avoid being individually blamed for poor outcomes. Unlike the first condition, where informational inference drove imitation, this condition produced herding behaviour that was more passive and driven by risk aversion. Most participants chose to align with the group, even when they believed the group was wrong. Qualitative responses after the sessions revealed that many students prioritised 'not standing out' or 'not being the only one wrong' and justified their conformity as a protective measure. Although still rational, this form of herding revealed a different driver, one rooted not in trust in others' information, but in a desire to minimise social or reputational costs.

The first irrational herding group was placed in a high-pressure, emotionally manipulated environment. Unlike the rational conditions, all students had access to the same data and asset information. However, each round included simulated social indicators that showed exaggerated, pre-programmed trends. These included real-time popularity meters showing statements such as ‘84% of players are buying TechCoin’ or ‘Market buzz: BioToken expected to surge’. These cues were unrelated to the actual fundamentals of the assets. Additionally, a visible leader board displayed the top earners, with all students aware that rewards would be given to those with the highest cumulative returns. These elements were introduced to simulate the emotional conditions often found in social investing platforms, where crowd excitement, fear of missing out, and perceived majority opinion can influence decision-making.

Under these conditions, student behaviour shifted dramatically. Rather than using available data, most participants began following perceived crowd behaviour, especially when it appeared to be associated with prior success. Many abandoned their strategies to mimic top performers or align with the majority indicator. Interestingly, decision logs showed that these behaviours became more reactive and less consistent over time, reflecting a detachment from underlying logic. Post-session reflections revealed emotional reasoning such as ‘I didn’t want to miss out’, ‘Everyone was buying so it must be going up’, and ‘I got nervous when I saw the trend’. This behaviour reflected a classic form of irrational herding, in which participants relied on external social cues rather than internal analysis, driven by emotional contagion and the psychological safety of following the crowd.

The final group was exposed to a panic catalyst scenario, a deliberately engineered crash condition in the fourth round. After three stable trading rounds, the simulation introduced a sudden, unexplained drop in all asset values. This was paired with fabricated headlines such as ‘Market-wide collapse hits all tokens’ and ‘Traders panic-sell across the board’. Participants had only 30 s to react. Despite the absence of real causative data, the majority of participants liquidated their holdings almost immediately after the crash began. Panic-driven behaviour overtook prior strategies, and nearly 80% of the group conformed to the initial wave of selling. When the market rebounded in the final round, many expressed regret. During the debriefing, students admitted they had not evaluated the situation logically, with responses such as ‘I panicked because everyone else was selling’, and ‘I didn’t want to be the last one holding’. This confirmed that under time pressure and emotional shock, even previously independent students succumbed to herd dynamics. The irrationality here was not rooted in low intelligence or carelessness, but in emotional vulnerability, fear of loss, and the need to act in the face of uncertainty.

The results of this study highlight that herding is a multifaceted behaviour with both cognitive and emotional dimensions (Loang, 2023). In rational conditions, students followed others because it made strategic sense, because others had demonstrated informational credibility or because aligning with the group was safer. In irrational conditions, however, the drivers shifted. Social pressure, visual cues, time stress, and emotional arousal can lead to conformity even when no logical basis exists. The distinction between rational and irrational herding was not merely academic; it was observable in how students justified their choices, in the consistency of their strategies, and in the degree to which their decisions aligned with or detached from available information.

5.7 Conclusion

Exploring the dynamics of collective behaviour in financial markets has a significant influence on investment choices, frequently resulting in substantial market fluctuations, inefficiencies, and economic turmoil. In this chapter, we delved into various forms of herding behaviour. We examined information-based herding, in which investors follow trends without conducting their analysis; reputational herding, where institutional fund managers prioritise career safety over independent thought; and digital-age herding, where social media rapidly escalates speculative bubbles like never before. Every mechanism showcases how group behaviour influences market trends, occasionally bolstering irrational enthusiasm and, at other times, hastening panic-induced sell-offs.

A key insight from this conversation is that investors should exercise caution regarding trading patterns lacking fundamental support. When market prices, asset values, or whole sectors are influenced more by collective sentiment than by the underlying financial realities, they become susceptible to significant downturns. Markets have consistently demonstrated that although momentum can fuel irrational growth for a period, unsustainable trends are ultimately bound to fall apart. Similarly, the GameStop short squeeze of 2021 highlighted the impact of modern digital communities, where individual investors, united through social media, drove stock prices to unprecedented levels before the inevitable correction occurred.

Strategic policy measures are essential to address the challenges presented by collective behaviour. Regulatory authorities must take decisive action to minimise the chances of widespread market bubbles and subsequent crashes. This involves improving clarity in financial markets, ensuring that rating agencies and financial analysts deliver impartial evaluations, and establishing protections such as circuit breakers to avert crashes driven by panic. Furthermore, social media platforms have become significant financial influencers, highlighting the need for increased oversight to prevent misinformation, which could trigger drastic market fluctuations. Authorities and monetary institutions need to remain alert to systemic dangers that can arise from collective behaviour among institutional investors, reminiscent of previous financial upheavals.

References

Aghamolla C, Thakor RT (2022) IPO peer effects. J Financ Econ 144(1):206–226

Ali M, Amir DH, Shamsi DA (2021) Consumer herding behaviour in online buying: a literature review. Int Rev Manag Business Res 10(1):345–360

Baig MW (2024) The influence of r/wallstreetbets on gamestop stock price: a behavioural finance perspective

Canterbery ER (1999) Irrational exuberance and rational speculative bubbles. Int Trade J 13(4):389–412

Guo X, Gu C, Zebedee AA, Chiu LT (2024) The effect of institutional herding on stock prices: the differentiating role of credit ratings. J Bank Financ 163:107186

Kalpathy SL, Nanda VK, Zhao Y (2021) Herding on stars in CEO compensation

Klinger U, Kreiss D, Mutsvairo B (2023) Platforms, power, and politics: an introduction to political communication in the digital age. Wiley, Hoboken

Liu Y, Zhang X, Deng H (2024) Construction and influencing factors of voluntary compensation subjects for herdersfrom the perspective of sustainable utilization of grassland resources. Sustainability 16(6):2576

Liu H, Hou L, Nan Z, Huang J, Su L (2025) Herders' willingness to accept compensation for grassland grazing ban in Northwest China. J Integr Agric 24(1):366–379

Loang OK (2023) Sustainable development goals, herding, and risk-averse behavior in Muslim countries. J Islam Monet Econ Financ 9(2):313–336

Loang OK (2024) Stability of Shariah-compliant stocks in Indonesia, Malaysia, and Gcc: the roles of monetary and fiscal policies and contagion. J Islam Monet Econ Financ 10(1):155–176

Loang OK (2025) Can machine learning surpass human investors? Evidence from adaptive herding behaviour in US, China and India. J Appl Econ 28(1):2435796

Lu S, Li S (2023) Is institutional herding efficient? Evidence from an investment efficiency and informational network perspective. J Behav Exp Financ 39:100828

Mohacsy I, Lefer H (2007) Money and sentiment: a psychodynamic approach to behavioural finance. J Am Acad Psychoanal Dyn Psychiatry 35(3):455–471

Ooi KL (2024) Analyst forecasting and market liquidity dynamics: a comparative analysis of US and Chinese markets pre and post COVID-19. J Gen Manag. https://doi.org/10.1177/03063070231225603

Pérez CJ, Santos MS (2018) Speculation, bubbles, and manias. Work Paper Ser 1(1):1–30

Peters N (2024) Solving the problem of abundance: venture capital and the making of asset-driven inequalities. Rev Int Polit Econ 32:287–309

Ricciardi V (2004) A risk perception primer: a narrative research review of the risk perception literature in behavioural accounting and behavioural finance. SSRN Electron J 1(1):1–42

Rodrigues UR, Stegemoller M (2022) Redeeming SPACs. Fla St UL Rev 50:667

Sahoo GS, Rajvanshi V, Syamala SR (2023) Herding behaviour of institutional investors: evidence from an emerging market. In Presentation at JAAF symposium, IIM-K, India

Shiller RJ (2000) Irrational exuberance, 1st edn. Princeton University Press, Princeton

Thakkar N (2024) Harnessing the power of herding for real (estate); factors influencing herd mentality, driven by social media in the real estate market. Open J Business Manag 12(5):2983–3003

Zhao Y (2022) Institutional investors herding behaviour under analysts rating. Acad J Business Manage 4(6):47–52

Chapter 6
Digital Herding and Technology's Role

6.1 Introduction

The digital revolution has completely transformed financial markets, altering how investors approach decision-making, engage with information, and respond to market trends. The era when investment was limited to the bustling trading floors of Wall Street, ruled by experts with extensive market insight and years of experience, is now a thing of the past (Loang 2024a, b). Today, a fresh wave of investors, armed with smartphones, social media updates, and AI-powered trading strategies, has emerged, frequently acting as a unified entity. The emergence of tech-driven financial choices has ushered in an era where market shifts are influenced not only by economic fundamentals but also by the impact of online sentiments, trending phenomena, and automated reactions.

A remarkable change in accessibility has driven this transformation. In the past, the world of investing was reserved for big players, institutional titans and hedge fund moguls. However, the rise of online trading platforms has completely transformed the landscape, breaking down the long-standing barriers to entry. Every day, investors can now tap into live-market insights, trade without commissions, and utilise sophisticated algorithms that were previously reserved for top-tier companies. Platforms such as Robinhood, eToro, and WeBull have transformed investing into games, allowing users to buy, sell, and hold with just a simple tap, much like swiping on a dating app. The simplicity of entry has sparked a fresh surge of market players, a significant number of whom lean more on the insights of digital communities than conventional financial frameworks.

These online communities have emerged as contemporary financial sages, shaping trends and influencing markets in ways that were previously unimaginable. Social media platforms, such as Reddit, Twitter, and TikTok, have evolved into arenas where individual investors come together, formulate strategies, and take collective action. The 2021 GameStop short squeeze marked a pivotal chapter in financial history, demonstrating how unified online efforts could challenge even the most

K. L. Ooi et al., *Following the Crowd: Psychological Drivers of Herding and Market Overreaction*, https://doi.org/10.1007/978-981-95-0792-4_6

advanced hedge funds. What began as a small conversation on Reddit's r/WallStreetBets transformed into a financial uprising, highlighting the remarkable impact of collective online actions. The effect of these digital movements is not merely a concept; it is a reality, shifting billions of dollars in capital within days and, at times, even hours.

However, the opening up of finance brings about some unexpected outcomes. Technology that fuels investor confidence can also intensify irrational enthusiasm, heighten volatility, and exacerbate systemic risks. Algorithmic trading, intended to enhance efficiency, can descend into an automated disorder when trends are pursued without human oversight. Flash crashes, sudden and severe declines in the market caused by high-frequency trading algorithms, serve as powerful reminders of the consequences when machines dominate decision-making devoid of human emotion. Every millisecond can shape destinies, and the world of finance has transformed into a digital arena where collective behaviour transcends mere psychology and evolves into a coded reaction (De Bondt and Thaler 1994).

This chapter explores the complex dynamics of digital herding, examining how technology has transformed financial markets, empowered retail investors, and introduced new risks into an already volatile system. Through a close look at trading platforms, online communities, and algorithmic trading, we reveal the significant impact of technology on reshaping market dynamics. We examine case studies of financial events that illustrate the effects of digitally driven herding, ranging from meme stock surges to disastrous flash crashes.

6.2 Social Media and Herding Acceleration

In today's digital landscape, financial markets are increasingly interconnected and influenced by factors beyond corporate earnings, economic indicators, and shifts in interest rates (Yoon and Oh 2022). Instead, they flow with the rhythm of social media. A single tweet, a viral post, or a trending hashtag can spark a buying frenzy, causing stock prices to skyrocket beyond logical valuation, only to plummet days later when the mood changes. The dynamics of digital herding have been intensified by the algorithms driving our online interactions, establishing a feedback loop that rapidly escalates market surges and declines as never before.

Social media is a powerhouse of virality, which is particularly clear in the realm of investment trends. Online spaces, such as Reddit, Twitter, TikTok, and YouTube, have evolved into bustling hubs where numerous retail investors converge, share stock insights, discover new trends, and collectively determine which assets are poised to capture the spotlight (Sprecher and Stevens 2023). In contrast to conventional investment approaches that rely on fundamental or technical analysis, these online communities operate on a fundamentally different principle: momentum. The more buzz surrounding a stock, cryptocurrency, or NFT, the higher its perceived value. The greater the number of shares or tokens purchased, the higher the price increases, strengthening the conviction that this is a successful investment.

The pattern persists, drawing on more participants, until the truth inevitably surfaces, frequently resulting in devastating losses for those who entered the fray too late.

Algorithmic suggestions drive this phenomenon, ensuring that the most captivating and emotionally resonant content reaches the most significant number of people. When a post about investing captures widespread attention, it not only impacts those actively seeking financial guidance but also reaches numerous individuals who may have never considered trading before. Short clips on social media hint at instant wealth, online discussions forecast the next big thing, and influencers on various platforms promote niche digital currencies, all in an environment that values hype over genuine value. The algorithms do not care about accuracy; they thrive on engagement, regardless of whether that engagement stems from thrill, fear, or impulsive speculation.

The rise of this online collective mindset has led to some of the most remarkable financial shifts ever witnessed (Murphy 2024). The surge in meme stocks, spearheaded by GameStop and AMC in early 2021, demonstrated that unified efforts on social media could disrupt Wall Street's most entrenched establishments. What started as a light-hearted jest on Reddit's r/WallStreetBets rapidly evolved into a monumental financial upheaval as retail traders united to challenge hedge funds that aggressively shorted these companies. The outcome was an unprecedented market spectacle, stocks soared by hundreds of per cent within days, not due to enhanced fundamentals, but because a digital community wielded the ability to influence billions through sheer collective strength.

While social media has the potential to empower investors, it also exposes them to significant risks, including misinformation and manipulation. The online landscape is filled with individuals claiming to be 'financial gurus' who dispense stock recommendations without any accountability, influencers who are compensated for endorsing investments they covertly sell off, and blatant con artists running complex schemes to inflate and then deflate asset values (Kemp 2023). Rapid dissemination of misinformation can lead to disastrous consequences. A single deceptive tweet implying that a company has landed a significant agreement can cause its stock to skyrocket, only to crash down when the reality comes to light. The realm of cryptocurrency has become a hotbed for such trickery, with notorious 'rug pulls' leading numerous investors to financial devastation.

A striking example of social media's power to both inflate and deflate financial bubbles is the dramatic rise and subsequent collapse of the NFT market in 2021 and 2022. Once celebrated as the next big thing in digital ownership, NFTs (non-fungible tokens) skyrocketed in popularity seemingly in an instant, fuelled by an unyielding wave of social media excitement. Stars, tech guys, and big-name companies have embraced this phenomenon, showcasing high-value digital art pieces and unique virtual collectables. Twitter and Discord emerged as the epicentres of NFT speculation, where influencers claimed that specific projects would be 'the next big thing'. Prices soared as individuals rushed to purchase, convinced that they were securing a piece of digital legacy.

Then, just as swiftly as it surged, the NFT market plummeted. The excitement that had propelled prices to unprecedented levels began to fade as critics highlighted the absence of actual value in numerous digital assets (Kahneman 2003). Accounts surfaced of con artists disappearing with vast sums from investors, initiatives left in the lurch by their creators, and purchasers coming to grips with the fact that they had invested six figures in a digital image without real-world application. Social media, initially the catalyst for the NFT surge, evolved into a platform where investors expressed their discontent, cautioning others about the market's instability. The excitement faded, and by the middle of 2022, NFT sales dropped by more than 90%, resulting in a significant financial fallout (Dalton 2023).

The swift ascent and decline of digital investment trends highlight the complex nature of trading influenced by social media. On the one hand, it has opened up investing to everyone, empowering individuals and demonstrating that everyday traders can have a significant impact on markets, just like large financial institutions (Loang 2025). Conversely, it has brought about intense fluctuations, where excitement can propel values to ridiculous heights, only for them to plummet swiftly. In today's landscape, where social media trends and algorithmic suggestions significantly influence financial markets, understanding the psychology behind digital herding has become increasingly crucial. Those who overlook its dangers are destined to become another victim of the upcoming speculative frenzy.

Figure 6.1 captures a moment in financial history that reads more like a modern fable than a market chart does. In January 2021, the stock price of GameStop (GME), a struggling brick-and-mortar video game retailer, began a trajectory that defied logic, gravity, and the foundations of fundamental analysis. For years, Wall Street had a bet against the company's future. Hedge funds held enormous short positions, wagering that GameStop's outdated business model and declining revenue would drive its stock to zero. However, the institutional giants did not account for a new force in the financial arena: the digitally connected retail investor,

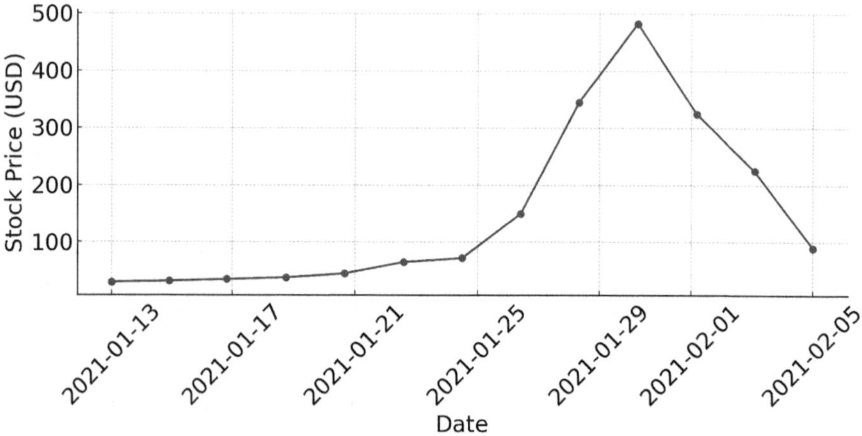

Fig. 6.1 GameStop (GME) stock price during the short squeeze. Source: Authors' work

emboldened by memes, Reddit threads, and the powerful psychological draw of a collective mission. As seen in the figure, the stock surged from just over $30 in mid-January to an all-time intraday high of $483 within 2 weeks, representing an astronomical increase of over 1400% that shocked the world.

The movement was not born in boardrooms or bank towers; it was incubated in the chaotic, irreversible world of Reddit's r/WallStreetBets. What began as jokes and banter quickly evolved into a digitally orchestrated short squeeze, a deliberate attempt to corner hedge funds that had overextended their bearish bets. Armed with commission-free trading apps, stimulus checks, and a sense of camaraderie, tens of thousands of retail investors piled into GameStop not just to make money but to make a statement. They were not just buying stock; they were buying into a rebellion. Each green candlestick on the chart in Fig. 6.1 was more than a price action; it was an act of defiance. The spike on January 27 and 28 represents the pinnacle of this movement, where financial activism, social virality, and raw human emotions merged into a market-shaking crescendo.

However, euphoria is rarely eternal in financial markets, especially when built on sentiment rather than substance. As shown in Fig. 6.1, the fall was as breathtaking as the rise. From the $483 peak, the stock plummeted first to $325, then to $225, and eventually to double digits within days. The sudden collapse was fuelled by a mix of panic, trading restrictions (notably from platforms such as Robinhood), and the realisation that momentum cannot suspend reality forever. While some early participants exited with fortune, many latecomers who caught the tailwind of FOMO were left with massive losses (Morovati 2020). What felt like a revolution was devolved into regret for thousands. However, even in the fall, the legacy of GameStop was etched in the market lore: a David vs. Goliath saga, where retail investors briefly turned the tables on institutional power.

Beyond these numbers, Fig. 6.1 tells a deeper story about the nature of digital herding in the age of social media. This was not simply a stock chart; it was a social movement with a ticker symbol (Ricciardi 2008). This finding demonstrates that markets today are no longer moved solely by quarterly reports and economic indicators. In the era of virality, trading is influenced by likes and retweets as it is by earnings and forecasts. The GameStop saga compelled regulators, analysts, and investors to confront a new financial reality: a meme can trigger a billion-dollar movement, market psychology is amplified by algorithms, and ordinary people, united through screens, can become a powerful force on Wall Street (Guan 2022). The echoes of this event are still felt today, reminding us that in the digital age, the herd moves faster, louder, and often more unpredictably than ever before.

6.3 The Risks of Algorithmic Trading and AI-Driven Herding

In the current financial market landscape, human intuition has taken a backseat to other driving forces behind decision-making (Guntuka 2024). On the trading floor, algorithms dominate, executing countless trades in mere fractions of a second, far surpassing human reaction time. What used to be a contest of strategy, patience, and thorough analysis has transformed into a race of speed, where high-frequency trading firms, hedge funds, and financial institutions utilise advanced AI-driven systems that adhere to one straightforward principle: tracking the trend and doing it quicker than the competition. However, this unyielding automation brings about an unforeseen outcome: a marketplace that has ceased to think and merely responds. When countless machines respond identically, catastrophes are simply a heartbeat away.

At the heart of this evolution lies high-frequency trading, a cutting-edge technology designed to capitalise on microsecond advantages. These algorithms analyse market data, identify trends, and execute trades with incredible speed, taking advantage of the slight shifts in stock prices. At first glance, high-frequency trading appears to enhance efficiency, inject liquidity into markets, and narrow bid-ask spreads. However, hidden beneath this facade of calm is a much more perilous reality: high-frequency trading not only reacts to trends but also intensifies them. As a stock starts to climb, automated systems quickly jump into purchase, intensifying the upward momentum. As the sell-off begins, high-frequency trading amplifies the decline and executes trades with robotic accuracy. The outcome? Market instability escalates rapidly, transforming a simple shift into a chaotic frenzy of trading activity.

The emergence of AI-powered sentiment analysis further solidified this trend. In today's world, financial algorithms go beyond mere number tracking; they analyse the vast expanse of the Internet. Advanced AI systems are currently analysing earnings reports, news articles, financial blogs, and Twitter feeds to assess investor mood (Sahani 2024). When an AI system identifies an abundance of favourable languages regarding a stock, it activates buy orders. When anxiety takes the central stage in the news, it captures attention. This cycle is when real risks emerge. When numerous AI systems simultaneously consume identical information, they interpret it uniformly, resulting in a coordinated surge in trade. Of course, the mood of the market has shifted from natural to artificial; it is now driven by algorithms, responding instantly to news and social platforms, amplifying collective behaviour as we have never seen.

The fallout from this technological competition has resulted in some of the most dramatic market collapses ever (Johnsson et al. 2002). The most notorious of these events was the 2010 Flash Crash, a rapid market collapse that wiped out nearly a trillion dollars in value in just 36 min. It started with a seemingly harmless sell order, one that, under typical circumstances, would have caused little to no disruption. In a landscape ruled by trading algorithms, it felt akin to igniting a flame in a space brimmed with flammable fuel.

On May 6, 2010, an institutional investor executed a significant sell order on S&P 500 futures contracts (Smales 2016). Typically, this type of trade is taken in stride by those on the market. However, high-frequency trading algorithms designed to identify momentum changes interpret the substantial order as a red flag. In reaction, they started to unload their holdings, further intensifying the decline. As algorithms detected the trend, the whirlwind of buying and selling erupted in mere moments.

A remarkable aspect of the flash crash was not only its astonishing speed but also the immense magnitude of the event. The Dow Jones Industrial Average, a cornerstone of international finance, fell by almost 1000 points, marking the most significant single-day point decline ever recorded. Prominent stocks, such as Procter & Gamble, experienced a temporary 35% decrease in value. At the same time, Accenture, a major consulting firm, saw its stock price drop bizarrely to just one cent before quickly recovering shortly thereafter (Loang 2025). It was a whirlwind of financial turmoil, escalating at a pace that left human traders struggling to grasp and respond.

Then, just as abruptly as it started, the downfall occurred. Trading algorithms, identifying oversold conditions, reversed their strategy, igniting a rapid buying frenzy that brought most prices back to their initial levels in just minutes. However, this harm had already been inflicted. In an instant, investors saw their fortunes evaporate, trust was obliterated, and regulators found themselves in a frenzy, trying to make sense of how the pinnacle of financial ingenuity briefly went awry.

The 2010 Flash Crash served as a crucial reminder. Yet, it was merely one event among many that have been haunted by similar algorithm-driven anomalies, such as the Knight Capital disaster in 2012, where a malfunctioning trading algorithm resulted in a staggering loss of $440 million in just 45 min. Additionally, the Bitcoin flash crashes of 2021 triggered automated liquidations, resulting in dramatic declines in digital assets that plummeted by double-digit percentages within a few hours. The message is unmistakable: when algorithms take the reins of the markets, the assurance of rationality fades away.

The emergence of AI and algorithmic trading has transformed the essence of financial markets, enhanced their speed and efficiency, while simultaneously introducing a new level of fragility (Ameye et al. 2023). The debate has shifted; it is no longer about whether machines can surpass human capabilities in trading, the contest has already been decided. This crucial study examines the capacity of financial markets to withstand the consequences of a world where human decision-making has been superseded by rapid automation.

Based on experience, this conclusion is disconcerting. Markets operating at lightning speeds allow minimal opportunities for human involvement when issues arise (Hoffman and Yeh 2018). In moments of panic, the absence of a seasoned trader means a relentless march of algorithms executing orders, adhering to patterns, and intensifying chaos. History has shown that the outcomes can be disastrous when a multitude of machines experience panic simultaneously.

The rise of the digital era has brought numerous benefits to financial markets, yet it has also revealed new weaknesses (Taskinsoy 2019). In an era where trading choices are influenced by artificial intelligence, social media, and rapid-fire algorithms, impending financial turmoil may not stem from a housing crisis or banking failure. It could just be a glitch in the system, a lone error that triggers an unstoppable chain reaction. When that moment arrives, it will be a slow decline. This will be a rapid, algorithm-driven plunge, with vast sums of money disappearing instantaneously.

6.4 How Did Digital Herding Unfold?

It began as a light-hearted joke on Reddit, shared among a small group of retail traders who exchanged memes, stock tips, and a shared dislike for Wall Street. At first, few people took it seriously. Almost overnight, the joke turned into a movement. A mix of everyday investors, armed only with commission-free trading apps and a viral idea, set out to challenge some of the biggest hedge funds in the world. Their target was GameStop, a struggling video game retailer that many large investors had already dismissed as a relic of the past. What followed was a remarkable financial spectacle, a digital uprising that exposed the weaknesses of modern markets, shook Wall Street, and left behind stories of big wins, painful losses, and ongoing debates about the power of online communities in shaping markets.

6.4.1 Phase 1: Discovery and Coordination a Digital Uprising Begins

It began in the most unexpected setting: a Reddit forum known as r/WallStreetBets, a digital space where everyday traders gathered to discuss bold, high-stakes stock investments. Renowned for its bold humour and rejection of traditional financial norms, the online community was populated by traders who viewed themselves not as conventional investors but as risk-takers, mavericks, and often, self-identified outlaws who welcomed uncertainty with enthusiasm. Amid the turmoil, a fresh story unfolded: hedge funds took a bold stance against GameStop, and if individual investors united, they could trigger a rare and extraordinarily short squeeze.

A short squeeze occurs when short sellers, who have wagered against a stock, are compelled to repurchase shares at soaring prices to mitigate their losses (Feldstein 2021). In the case of GameStop, prominent hedge funds, such as Melvin Capital, engaged in substantial short selling, wagering that the company's stock value would continue to decline. However, Reddit traders recognised a chance: by banding together to elevate the stock price, they could inflict significant losses on hedge funds.

6.4.2 *Phase 2: Mass Participation and Media Frenzy the Stock that Defied Gravity*

Initially, the financial district regarded the GameStop surge as a nonsensical online-driven spectacle. Suddenly, these figures began to rise. What started as a stock priced below $20 in early January 2021 skyrocketed beyond $100, then $200, and continued its upward trajectory (Cheng and Lin 2023). Once it reached $480 per share, laughter from financial institutions faded. Countless fortunes were on the line, and investment firms lost cash at an alarming pace.

The media, captivated by the unfolding drama, focused intently on the turmoil. CNBC anchors engaged in a lively discussion about whether this situation represented a financial uprising or a perilous phenomenon of groupthink. Social media was ablaze with humorous takes on the turmoil faced by Wall Street leaders. Elon Musk, always ready to stir the pot in the digital realm, ignited the frenzy with a straightforward tweet: 'Gamestonk'!! A link to the Reddit discussion board accompanied this. Everyone, from university students to rideshare drivers, was eager to get involved.

What separated this movement was the unwavering determination of those involved. In contrast to conventional investors, who aim to purchase at a low price and sell at a high price, GameStop traders are driven by a spirit of rebellion. Numerous individuals stood firm, regardless of how high the offers were. They referred to themselves as 'diamond hands', a phrase that represented their unwavering commitment to holding onto their shares, regardless of the substantial profits at stake. They aimed to extract every last drop from Wall Street. For an instant of fleeting, they triumphed.

6.4.3 *Phase 3: Market Instability and the Great Betrayal*

Suddenly, the momentum abruptly stopped. On January 28, 2021, Robinhood, the trading platform that enabled countless retail investors to join the surge, abruptly limited the purchase of GameStop shares. Investors had the option to sell, yet the opportunity to buy was no longer available to them. This decision has far-reaching implications for the financial landscape.

For numerous traders, this felt like an outright betrayal (Cleather 2022). The platform that once claimed to empower the masses in finance appeared to align with the interests of hedge funds. Allegations of market manipulation surged across social media, accompanied by a whirlwind of conspiracy theories, suggesting that influential Wall Street figures had coerced Robinhood to thwart the squeeze. In truth, the broking firm found itself ensnared in a liquidity crisis, overwhelming volume of trade was being executed, leaving it with insufficient cash reserves to satisfy regulatory demands. However, for GameStop traders, this rationale is irrelevant.

This was a profound unfairness and manipulation of the system designed to shield the influential party.

Restrictions on purchasing led to a significant decline in momentum. Once the stock reached incredible heights, it started its descent back to reality. Those who jumped in at the last moment, lured by the rapid ascent, found themselves grappling with significant loss. While a few pioneers reaped incredible fortunes, countless others faced devastating losses.

Following the events, congressional hearings and lawsuits emerged, and regulators rushed to tackle the consequences of what had occurred. The GameStop saga transcended a mere stock market event; it became a defining cultural phenomenon, embodying the escalating conflict between everyday investors and financial establishments. It reveals the weaknesses of a system that is increasingly influenced by online emotions, automated trading, and trending market shifts.

It also acts as a powerful cautionary tale. Digital herding possesses immense power yet is marked by unpredictability and instability, with the potential to disrupt financial systems at an extraordinary pace. The GameStop rally demonstrated that when individual investors come together, they can influence markets in ways previously considered unimaginable. However, it also revealed the rapidity with which a frenzy fuelled by digital forces could unravel, ensnaring countless traders in its aftermath. This marked the inception of a new phenomenon in the stock market. Although the GameStop phenomenon may have sparked the initial surge, it was certainly not the final chapter. The financial landscape has undergone a significant transformation, with the digital revolution bringing about substantial improvements.

6.5 Conclusion

Digital technology has significantly influenced the swift transformation of financial markets, revealing its advantages and potential dangers more clearly than ever. As algorithmic trading, AI-driven sentiment analysis, and social media platforms have made financial markets more accessible and efficient, they have simultaneously intensified herding behaviour, increased market volatility, and heightened systemic risk. Instruments that facilitate immediate decision-making and accessible investing can likewise fuel unchecked enthusiasm, leading to significant market surges and downturns. The GameStop saga, NFT boom, and historical flash crashes all highlight the complex and often contradictory role of technology in today's financial landscape.

For those in the investment and regulatory spheres, the task is to navigate these risks while still fostering creativity and progress. Oversight of AI-driven trading and algorithmic market-making is essential to mitigate the dangers of excessive volatility and unforeseen outcomes. Regulatory authorities need to enhance their supervision of automated trading systems, implement circuit breakers, and protect themselves against severe market upheavals. Similarly, the spread of false information and manipulative trading tactics driven by social media highlights the urgent need for greater transparency and rigorous oversight of financial content.

To address the challenges of digital herding, it is essential to emphasise the importance of financial literacy and the cultivation of independent thought. Investors should adopt a healthy dose of scepticism regarding trending market phenomena, ensure their portfolios are well-diversified, and steer clear of the allure of hype driven by social media. Authorities and financial entities must allocate resources to developing regulatory structures that address the issues arising from AI-driven trading and the dissemination of financial misinformation. By striking a proper balance between creativity and reliability, markets can harness the benefits of technology while mitigating the risks of disruption. When social media posts, popular trends, and automated trading systems sway financial decisions, maintaining a level-headed approach amidst a crowd mentality is increasingly vital.

References

Ameye N, Bughin J, van Zeebroeck N (2023) How uncertainty shapes herding in the corporate use of artificial intelligence technology. Technovation 127:102846

Cheng Z, Lin S (2023) Defying gravity: the determinants of China's outbound mergers and acquisitions. Contemp Econ Policy 41(4):714–732

Cleather AL (2022) HP blavatsky; a great betrayal. DigiCat, Hyderabad

Dalton K (2023) The rise and fall of the NFT empire: the social phenomenon of non-fungible tokens (Doctoral dissertation, Dalhousie University)

De Bondt W, Thaler RH (1994) Financial decision-making in markets and firms: a behavioural perspective. Handb Oper Res Manag Sci 9:385–410

Feldstein S (2021) The rise of digital repression: how technology is reshaping power, politics, and resistance. Oxford University Press, Oxford

Guan SS (2022) Meme investors and retail risk. BCL Rev 63:2051

Guntuka S (2024) AI-driven algorithmic trading: advanced techniques reshaping financial markets. Int J Comput Eng Technol 15(5):564–571

Hoffman R, Yeh C (2018) Blitzscaling: the lightning-fast path to building massively valuable companies. Crown Currency

Johnsson M, Lindblom H, Platan P (2002) Behavioural finance and the change of investor behaviour during and after the speculative bubble at the end of the 1990s. Lund Univ Stud Pap 1(1):1–60

Kahneman D (2003) Maps of bounded rationality: psychology for behavioural economics. Am Econ Rev 93(5):1449–1475

Kemp M (2023) The Ulysses contract: how to never worry about the share market again. Major Street Publishing, Elsternwick

Loang OK (2024a) Risk avoidance, macroeconomic indicators and bank performances in developing economies. Ann Financ Econ 19(4):2450018

Loang OK (2024b) Stability of Shariah-compliant stocks in Indonesia, Malaysia, and Gcc: the roles of monetary and fiscal policies and contagion. J Islam Monet Econ Financ 10(1):155–176

Loang OK (2025) Can machine learning surpass human investors? Evidence from adaptive herding behaviour in US, China and India. J Appl Econ 28(1):2435796

Morovati F (2020) Economic analysis of the airplane industry (Doctoral dissertation, Politecnico di Torino)

Murphy MC (2024) Cultures of growth: how the new science of mindset can transform individuals, teams, and organizations. Simon and Schuster, New York
Ricciardi V (2008) The psychology of risk: the behavioural finance perspective. SSRN Electron J 1(1):1–36
Sahani T (2024) Decoding market emotions: the synergy of sentiment analysis and AI in stock market predictions. J Next-Gener Res 1:47
Smales LA (2016) Trading behaviour in S&P 500 index futures. Rev Financ Econ 28:46–55
Sprecher A, Stevens A (2023) 21st-century narrative change with focus on social media
Taskinsoy J (2019) The famous new bubbles of the 21st century: cases of irrational exuberance. SSRN Electron J 1(1):1–25
Yoon J, Oh G (2022) Investor herding behaviour in social media sentiment. Front Phys 10:1023071

Chapter 7
Rational Vs. Irrational Herding

7.1 Introduction

The movement of individuals in the financial market due to collective behaviour is an interesting and complex phenomenon. Investors, whether retail traders or institutional giants, typically tend to follow the crowd, buying when others do and selling when others do. This primal instinct, known as herding, is psychologically embedded in human beings and is driven by a combination of fear, greed, and an inherent desire for social validation. Although herding is frequently dismissed as an irrational act of blind conformity, it is not always a case of judgement error. In some situations, the act of crowd-following becomes an entirely logical decision that minimises the cost of information, diminishes uncertainty, and, in some cases, even leads to higher market efficiency. Nevertheless, behaviour that can lead to making the best decision can also result in ruinous repercussions if emotions are uncontrolled and speculation prevails.

The crux of financial herding is the interaction among market efficiency, risk aversion, and information asymmetry. In a perfect world, the market functions efficiently, and prices reflect all available information. In such a situation, investors without direct access to crucial insights may rationally decide to follow the actions of those presumed to be more informed. This method of herding, which aligns with the collective psyche, serves the purpose of aligning prices with their actual levels. However, markets are far from perfect. Information is sometimes unevenly distributed, placing investors in a precarious position (Loang et al. 2024). The fear of missing out (FOMO) or anxiety of being left out triggers traders to follow the crowd, even if the reasoning behind such moves is not well-formed. Risk aversion is yet another leading factor: when the general atmosphere is tempestuous, potential actors tend to seek the wall of safety, holding the line that if they are wrong, they will not be alone in the fault.

However, what will we do if it is a flock that leads sheep astray? When market sentiment takes precedence over fundamentals, herding shifts from a rational

K. L. Ooi et al., *Following the Crowd: Psychological Drivers of Herding and Market Overreaction*, https://doi.org/10.1007/978-981-95-0792-4_7

strategy to a completely misguided stampede. Speculative bubbles inflate as investors become involved, not because the assets are fundamentally strong, but because they believe that prices will continue to rise as long as the masses invest. As soon as trust is undermined, hysteria begins, and the factor that previously raised prices now works in the opposite direction, causing a steep decline in prices. The 2015 Chinese Stock Market Crash stands up as a striking case in point for this kind of behaviour; millions of investors made their way to this platform only to be attracted by momentum, no matter what logic dictated, yet they were cast out and faced with a severe downturn of the markets, resulting in trillions of dollars in losses.

Table 7.1 shows herding, one of the most misunderstood phenomena in the financial markets. At first glance, the term often carries a negative connotation, evoking images of panicked investors rushing for the exits or piling into the latest market fad without thinking. However, this table elegantly draws a bold line between two dramatically different forms of crowd behaviour: rational herding, driven by strategic alignment and information efficiency, and irrational herding, fuelled by emotion, speculation, and fear. Rational herding is not about thoughtless conformity; it is a calculated move to surf waves of macroeconomic momentum. When investors track signals from central banks, major fund movements, or GDP data, they do not surrender their judgement; they are optimising them. It is a deliberate act of outsourcing heavy analysis to those with informational advantages, thereby conserving resources and reducing exposure to idiosyncratic risk.

In contrast, irrational herding thrives in the chaotic noise of social media, rumour mills, and panic-driven sell-offs. It is a spark that lights bubbles and an avalanche that triggers crashes. Think of meme stock manias and crypto frenzies as strategies, but consider them stampedes.

What makes rational herding so powerful and underrated is its grounding in economic reality. Imagine an investor during a tech boom: the data support it, demographic trends are shifting, innovation is accelerating, and institutional funds are reallocated to technology-intensive ETFs. Following the herd in this context is not sheepish, it is bright. Rational herding works exceptionally well in high-liquidity, transparent markets, where prices reflect available information and aligning with trends can actually *reduce* risk. Millions of investors are not chasing hype, but instead trusting decades of evidence that shows markets, in the long run, tend to rise. They leverage the wisdom of the crowd rather than surrendering it. They avoid costly mistakes in stock picking, minimise fees, and achieve broad diversification. It is not giving up control; it is evolving as an innovative player in a complex system.

However, once rationality gives way and emotions take the reins, the story undergoes a dramatic change. Irrational herding is seductive in its simplicity: everyone is doing it, so it must be correct. It creates echo chambers in which scepticism is drowned out, and fundamentals are forgotten. Whether it's retail traders jumping on viral TikTok 'stock tips' or panic-driven mass withdrawals during a market dip, this behaviour feeds volatility and disrupts price discovery. At these moments, markets cease to function as mechanisms of capital allocation and become casinos of collective anxiety. The challenge and brilliance lie in understanding these differences (Ooi 2024). Table 7.1 presents multiple comparisons, offering a lens to decode market

Table 7.1 Rational vs. irrational herding

Aspect	Rational herding	Irrational herding
Definition and nature	Rational herding refers to investors deliberately aligning with market trends based on informed reasoning, economic signals, and cost-benefit analysis. It is a strategic behaviour, not emotional	Irrational herding occurs when investors follow the crowd without logical analysis, often driven by panic, speculation, or cognitive biases like FOMO (fear of missing out)
Decision-making drivers	Decisions are grounded in macroeconomic indicators (e.g. interest rates, inflation, GDP), expert opinions, and observed actions of informed agents such as institutional investors or central banks	Decisions are based on emotional contagion, social proof, hype, or behavioural biases (e.g. overconfidence, loss aversion), often without checking fundamentals
Cost and efficiency	Saves time, reduces analytical costs, and improves efficiency by piggybacking on expert analysis (e.g. fund managers following central bank policies). Particularly common when analysis is too costly or complex	No cost-efficiency advantage. Instead, the investor may act impulsively, react to rumours or crowd noise, and end up duplicating losses or misallocating capital
Information use	Heavily relies on credible information channels (e.g. policy announcements, earnings reports, macro data). Investors act only after validating the trend's logic	Based on limited, selective, or misinterpreted information (e.g. viral tweets, herd panic). The crowd's actions often stray far from the underlying reality
Market impact	Can promote price discovery, liquidity, and alignment with fundamentals. When informed agents herd, prices tend to reflect economic reality	Distorts market signals, leads to bubbles or crashes, and fuels volatility (e.g. meme stock frenzies like GameStop, speculative crypto booms)
Examples in practice	Surge in tech stock investments during digital transformation trends backed by data Passive investing in S&P 500, MSCI index Institutional reallocation after fed interest rate decisions	Panic selling during market downturns without assessing fundamentals Retail investors rushing into hype stocks due to social media (e.g. Reddit rallies) Herd-driven property bubbles
Outcome and risk profile	Generally, leads to long-term gains, enhanced diversification, reduced idiosyncratic risk, and better alignment with structural trends	Leads to poor timing, herd-induced losses, exaggerated market corrections, and higher exposure to systemic risks due to uninformed mass actions

Source: Authors' work

psychology, distinguishing the wisdom of collective logic from the madness of emotional contagion. It invites the reader not only to observe the herd but also to understand it and, most importantly, to decide when it is wise to follow it and when it is better to step aside.

This chapter offers an overarching perspective on the complex dynamics of herding in financial markets. It presents a structural analysis of its emergence, the reasons behind its beneficial and destructive effects, and further implications for market stability. National herding is categorised into rational and irrational, the former leading to the complex mechanisms of collective decision-making and the latter to the visible world of profligate and irrational behaviour in the financial markets. Through this analysis, we aim to gain a clearer view of the psychology of investors, the limitations of market rationality, and the forces which actually create booms and busts.

7.2 Rational Herding: When Following the Crowd Makes Sense

Contrary to common assumptions, conforming to the majority is not necessarily an indication of thoughtless speculation or unfounded enthusiasm. In numerous instances, following the crowd is a deliberate and tactical choice that enables investors to reduce risks, enhance decision-making, and improve overall market effectiveness (Bikhchandani et al. 2000). This phenomenon is known as rational herding, a type of collective behaviour in which individuals or institutions decide to follow broader market trends based on logical reasoning rather than being swayed by emotions or speculation. Rational herding occurs when investors deliberately choose to align their actions with those of others, not out of fear or greed, but because it is the most logical financial decision.

The high cost of independent analysis is a significant factor that contributes to the widespread occurrence of rational herding in financial markets (Loang, 2023). Engaging in thorough market analysis, monitoring economic signals, and predicting upcoming trends requires considerable time, knowledge, and resources. Market players, including institutional investors, hedge funds, and individual traders, often recognise that leveraging insights from more knowledgeable participants is a more effective strategy than analysing every detail independently. For instance, when central banks announce adjustments in monetary policy, such as increasing interest rates or implementing quantitative easing, investors who closely monitor these indicators can make informed decisions. Instead, they strategically navigate the landscape by relying on macroeconomic fundamentals and fine-tuning their portfolios to resonate with the anticipated market shifts.

The inclination to synchronise with essential market movements is a prevalent factor behind rational herding. Investors recognise that the dynamics of markets are shaped by overarching economic factors such as GDP growth, inflation, and corporate earnings. When these essential elements align in a specific manner, it makes sense to follow the crowd. Explore investment options that dynamically shift holdings in response to enduring economic patterns. When an economy is witnessing swift advancements in technology, fund managers may pivot their investments towards tech stocks, not out of mere trend-following, but because analytical insights support this decision (Tian et al. 2024). In this way, they enhance their gains while mitigating the risks associated with excessive deviation from prevailing market views.

A compelling illustration of rational herding in contemporary finance is the widespread adoption of passive investment approaches, including index funds and exchange-traded funds (ETFs). In contrast to speculative trading, where investors pursue fleeting price changes, passive investors intentionally opt to track the market by investing their money in broad-based indices, such as the S&P 500 or the MSCI World Index (Loang 2025). This method is rooted in historical evidence, demonstrating that, over time, markets generally trend upward, even amid temporary fluctuations. Investing passively reduces expenses, eliminates the risks associated with poor stock choices, and offers benefits in diversification. In this context, aligning with the majority is not only sensible but also a strategy grounded in data that has consistently outperformed numerous actively managed funds over the years.

Rational herding thrives in markets characterised by high liquidity and abundant information accessibility. In well-functioning markets, where asset prices truly embody all accessible information, adhering to recognised trends is frequently the wisest strategy. For example, when a sector exhibits robust earnings growth and heightened investor enthusiasm, it is logical to consider investing in that area, provided the underlying fundamentals support this trend. Similarly, when large-scale investors react to shifts in the economy by adjusting their portfolios, they approach it with a calculated perspective, ensuring that their choices align with broader economic trends rather than relying on guesswork.

The main point to remember is that not every instance of following a crowd is thoughtless or unwise (Jacobsen and Lund 2024). At certain moments, aligning with the crowd proves to be the wisest strategy, enabling investors to enhance their gains, minimise risks, and manoeuvre through markets with greater ease. The real test involves discerning whether collective behaviour is based on sound reasoning and evidence or if it is simply a response fuelled by fleeting emotions in the chaos of the market. Understanding the dynamics of rational herding empowers investors to navigate market trends with greater insight, allowing them to capitalise on opportunities instead of being carried along by the tide.

7.3 Irrational Herding: Evidence of Bias-Driven Decision-Making

Herding is often a target painted with a broad brush and dismissed because it is considered a reckless and irrational force that distorts financial markets. However, what if sometimes, the smartest thing an investor can do is to follow the crowd? Essentially, herding is not about blindly following the masses, but rather it is strategically aligned with market forces. This is what we term rational herding calculated decision made to follow the majority of people involved, as it benefits the individual (Yi et al. 2024). In contrast to its chaotic and speculative counterpart, rational herding is based on data, logic, and economic fundamentals. It is an attitude that promotes market efficacy, with prices mirroring actual value, and investors navigate uncertainty without paralysis by analysis.

The fact that it saves time, effort, and resources is one of the most compelling reasons why investors engage in rational herding. Conducting independent research in financial markets is not only challenging but also expensive. It requires both significant expertise and access to premium resources to gather macroeconomic data, analyse it, interpret corporate earnings reports, and analyse geopolitical trends. Rather than reinventing the wheel, many investors consider the actions of well-informed market participants to be a shortcut to success. If large institutional investors, economists, and central banks signal a change in policy or market conditions, rational traders take note. They do not follow the herd unthinkingly; instead, they align their decisions with those who have higher informational rents. Therefore, they reduce their risk exposure and increase their probability of winning.

The phenomenon of rational herding is observable in how institutional investors respond to central bank policy decisions. When a central bank indicates a change in its interest rate, institutional traders immediately adjust their financial positions. Suppose the Federal Reserve proclaims the rate hike. In that case, the funds immediately shift from riskier assets into more secure bonds. They already know that the coming economic situation might be more complicated, with borrowing costs going up and the economy causing a slowdown (Sias 2004). This is not being done irrationally, but rather a rational move based on credible data. Even when they do obtain the correct information, mutual funds bear the weight of the trend towards adjustment by swapping portfolios in response to the influence of long-term economic variables, such as demographic patterns, inflation expectations, and technological improvements.

The peak example of rational herding that people generally recognise worldwide is the rise in passive investing through index and exchange-traded funds (ETFs). Instead of the majority trying to outsmart the market, millions have come to accept the idea that following the market as a whole is the most efficient way to succeed. Index funds track broad market indices, such as the S&P 500, thereby expanding the reach of investors with minimal effort required for ongoing decision-making. It is not only a money-saving technique but also a proven alternative to many long-standing actively managed funds (Escobar et al. 2023). The reasoning behind this is straightforward if we consider the long term: since the entire market progresses to the top, why bet on the wrong side of risk? The overall shift towards passive investing illustrates how rational herding works best by leveraging the collective wisdom of the market, not counteracting it.

Nonetheless, rational herding is not a universal method that suits all cases. It functions appropriately in liquid environments, where information is conveyed reasonably and is displayed in the prices of goods. At these times, trend-following based on a fundamental analysis can be very effective. Investors follow the economic directives and significantly adjust their portfolio allocations. However, even discussing rational herding is an oversimplification. In addition, the proper context involves not only keeping pace with trends but also understanding the reasons and causes behind crowd movement.

Rational herding is not about joining the crowd; instead, it involves making informed decisions based on credible signals and evidence. It is like art that helps you discern when it is wise to go with the flow instead of following the pack. In some cases, it becomes the best weapon in an investor's arsenal to navigate the challenges of the financial market with clarity, efficiency, and protection from the risk of acting irrationally.

7.4 The 2015 Chinese Stock Market Crash and Irrational Herding

7.4.1 Background

During the period spanning slightly over a year, from tmid-014 to tmid-015, the Chinese stock market was remarkably driven by one of the fastest bull runs globally in modern economic history (Li et al. 2023). The Shanghai Composite Index saw an increase of more than 150%, turning the entire stock market into a trending national topic. In every corner of China, people joined, particularly those without experience, such as when they invested their savings in stocks, or rather, the expected path to wealth. This particular surge did not stem from corporate returns, underlying economic health, or green tech. Still, it was driven by an alternate model: the excitement that comes from a rapidly rising market.

The central figure of remarkable development was the strong backing from the Chinese authorities for such involvement in the capital market. Politicians who were on a mission to create a financial system that was less rigid introduced measures that made it easier and more attractive to invest. The state-run press was actively disseminating a patriotic message about the stock market, portraying it not only as a means to create personal wealth but also as a way to contribute to the national economy. Margin lending, borrowing money to purchase new stocks, was extensively advertised, fostering the idea of speculation and lifting the veil of fog on the market's forward momentum. As the asset class, traditionally focused on houses and flats, had been immensely popular for years, stocks, which had become a new investment vehicle overnight, were attractive with promises of great and swift returns, and seemed to be a mandatory option.

Price hikes caused herding behaviour to be the only way to behave. The combination of fear, occupation, and management was so potent that it formed a mass psychology, generating the most powerful emotional state in the community a fear of missing out on the stock's rise. It was business as usual in the stock market; companies seemed to prioritise their share price over their profit margins, and if they had promising projects for the future, what mattered was that their shares were in an upward trend. It was the case that people were not spending their money on companies; instead, they were investing it in the growing economy. Meanwhile, a definite outer limit for the crowd's psychological state was fixed, leading to vague and unreliable investments.

This was not an isolated phenomenon in cities. In addition to urban regions, even towns and agrarian areas in China, where small-time investors and farmers demonstrated, often with no education, started stock trading through the opening of public brokerage accounts (Welch 2000). Stocks of companies were widely shared on social media, and people discussed them with others. Lo and behold, there was a brand-new group of first-time investors who had a vision of stock trading as a step beyond simply making money and becoming rich, but as a charter, a near guarantee of wealth. In fact, the good mood was so pervasive that some people raised loans to invest in the stock market, thinking that the market would remain bullish.

However, many weaknesses were uncovered beneath all that apparent prosperity. Prices were increasingly diverging from reality, debt continued to rise, and the market was becoming fixated on speculation rather than underlying fundamentals. However, in the current state of affairs, very few have considered these issues (Rahayu et al. 2021). The force of inertia swayed them, and the feeling of mass was too strong. It was as if the stock market had a fever; there were trading prices that did not move in either direction, and there were no tangible assets in the form of risk. Nevertheless, just as in the fairy tale world, markets were able to transform good dreams into nightmares. For the Chinese stock market, the reckoning day was imminent.

7.4.2 How Irrational Herding Led to the Market Crash

Phase 1: The Boom (2014–2015)

The terrifying rise of the Chinese stock market in 2014 and early 2015 was well calculated. It was, in many ways, a wonderfully staged show, one powered by government support, cheap loans, and the exuberant optimism of retail investors. The Chinese authorities were committed to the idea of economic stimulation and were the leading promoters of stock market investment as a means to achieve wealth. The state media portrayed the stock market as a new world where one could capitalise on the nation's wealth and make a fortune. The statement was distinct: entering the stock market was not only an investment but also a civic movement.

The turn of the event was unbelievable. The number of retail traders, many of whom had no prior trading experience, surged rapidly. Accounts were opened on brokerage sites at an alarming rate, and first-time traders made up the majority of the trades in the market. Euphoria is a contagious species. Taxi drivers, small shop owners, and factory workers have become newcomers to the stock market. Whole families put their money together and bought shares, firmly convinced that the perpetual rally of the market was only a one-way ticket to wealth.

The cherry on the cake was the widespread use of margin trading, borrowing money to buy stocks. Banks and brokers made it so simple for investors to leverage their holdings that they were practically in control of the situation. The effect was a barely intact market structure, where billions of yuan were borrowed. Every rise in the market brought about new optimism, which strengthened the illusion that stocks would only continue to rise. Company fundamentals no longer matter (Ayoub and Balawi 2022). Even businesses that were in debt, inexperienced in business ventures, or those that had not been earning at all, saw their value skyrocket merely due to the lack of supply for such high-demand stocks. Consumers wanted it, so the market moved upwards.

The investors who were burned by market volatility did not realise that they were not earning profit from the right investments; instead, they were part of a very lucrative speculative gambling game. This game, like any other game, could only be played as long as the illusion of eternal economic growth was preserved.

Phase 2: The Bubble Bursts (June–July 2015)

All bubbles explode at a certain point, the moment when joy begins to fracture and the truth takes hold. The Chinese bubble reached this point in June 2015. Setting investors, the leading players were often the first to catch on to a market that was overheated and began to pull their money out of the channels. The immeasurably overvalued increase rates, the precarious levels of margin debt, and a lack of fundamental quest behind the spectacular singularity all the traders saw. Initially, sales began slowly; yet, on a market defined almost entirely by emotion, it did not take long for fear to take hold.

As retail investors face a downward trend in the market, they are deterred by fear. Most had taken out bank loans to invest, which made them feel like they were on the edge of losing everything. The almost frantic exercise in fleeing gave rise to a new cycle: the more participants sold, the faster the prices fell; again, the quicker the prices fell, the more investors were unwilling to carry their weight and cashed out. In a matter of weeks, the market lost all its gains in the harsh downward spiral.

The Chinese government, being aware of the magnitude of the catastrophe, made bold attempts to intercede. It shut down trade on more than 1400 stocks, nearly half of the entire market, in the hope that this would halt the nosedive. The measure did not surprise the investing community, but was followed by the same act of broking houses with trading halts. Instead of restoring trust, it produces a different effect. It was seen as a panic move by the government; thus, investors lost faith in the market. The stock fell off the cliff. If people are unable to sell due to timing issues, their panic intensifies. Failure is unavoidable.

Phase 3: The Aftermath

Upon the arrival of peace, the crash caused the Chinese stock market to lose an unprecedented $3.5 trillion, which was more than the GDP of many of the world's most prosperous countries. The stock market was designed to generate profits with minimal effort; however, now it was on the walls of the casino, and the money went to the house. Nobody should discount the toll taken on the numerous retail traders who, in many cases, had borrowed extensively to participate in the stock market and ultimately suffered severe losses. Some ended up having no money. Others who could not pay their debts faced financial crises in their lives.

The damage was not confined to individuals; it was systemic in nature. The erosion of confidence in equity markets led to a slowdown in the economy. The government, faced with an economic calamity, took control of it by quelling excessive speculative activity and margin trading. Investor trust, which had once been easily gained, was now gravely violated, as was the trust of many people who were deeply hurt by the crash (Walsh 2021). Some people who had suffered as a result of the plunge rightfully doubted the market's ability to function as a fair enterprise, and some vowed to fold their cards and cut their losses.

The 2015 Chinese stock market crash was a significant financial event, and more importantly, it served as a valuable lesson about herding and the dangers it entails. It was a demonstration of the extent to which unbridled speculative optimism can degenerate into widespread panic, whether leverage is only concerned with gains, and whether markets based on market sentiment rather than substance are prone to failure. The mass, which had previously been responsible for the market's new height, became the primary liability for it. Once a crash occurs, no intervention can change the matter. It must be repaired anyway.

7.4.3 Lessons from the 2015 Chinese Stock Market Crash

The 2015 Chinese stock market crash was not merely a financial disaster; it was a perfect case study to demonstrate the hazards of unregulated speculation, government-driven market expansion, and investors' fragile psyche. It brought to light the harmful effects of irrational herd behaviour and explained how mood can switch from one extreme to another within the twinkling of an eye, from greed to fear. Economists, policymakers, and investors have learned crucial lessons from past market crashes about the tight relationship between market growth and financial soundness.

One of the most notable observations is that government intervention can act as a catalyst for the expansion of the market for wild mushrooms. The Chinese government, in its effort to boost the economy and increase financial market participation, inadvertently created fertile ground for speculative mania. State media, along with official policy, encouraged citizens to invest in the stock market, which was presented as a straightforward and almost guaranteed means of accumulating wealth.

Millions of retail investors, most of whom were novices, took the messages literally, convincing themselves that the government could solve stock market crashes (Dodaro 2023). However, the point is that government proclamations do not solely dictate markets, but rather are driven by real economic fundamentals, including investors' psychology and financial mechanics. Once the prices were misaligned with reality, no amount of state support could have avoided the crash.

Another vital conclusion is the scope of margin trading and excess leverage. The crash period revealed that leverage is not only a means of achieving twofold benefits but also a major driver of loss, leading to spiralling difficulties. The rapid rise in stock prices prompted many investors to borrow large amounts of money to invest, assuming the market would continue to grow. However, once the stocks began to decrease their positions based on the quoted financial time bombs. Pressurised margin calls sparked the release of even more sales, which rapidly hastened the market's downfall in a ruthless feedback loop. This self-programming movement highlights that speculative gain through borrowing is one of the worst financial decisions one can make. When the market turns, it does not simply lift off; it goes up in flames.

It is psychological to realise that retail investors are hurt the most by market fluctuations. Unlike institutional investors, who are equipped with better information, risk management tools, and diversified portfolios, retailers often trade on emotions rather than logic. In 2015, many retail traders were lured by flashy promises of easy money and were blinded by the fear of missing out (FOMO) when the party finally ended. When the downturn occurred, they lacked the skills and habits to behave rationally. Some panicked and sold at huge losses, while others were left with their money tied up as the government halted trading in about 50% of the market. Ultimately, the emotional and financial toll was high for many of them. The crash was the last straw, and they realised that trading without prior knowledge was akin to committing a bet.

Finally, it is reiterated that the crash was indeed a terrible and sad consequence of the fear-based market interventions by regulators, which will be discussed between the lines. In their attempt to address the constantly declining collapse, the Chinese government took several steps, including temporary trading and sales bans. However, the effort to restore the public's faith has failed. These measures had the opposite effect, sowing even more profound distrust in investors' minds. Investors realised that they were not free to sell their stocks, which caused them to be even more frantic. The loss of trust has an enduring quality: measure it in years, and it will slowly rebuild itself over time. The point is clear: markets operate on trust, and when that trust is broken, no amount of work can rapidly unblock the situation.

The 2015 crash was a severe shock to the Chinese financial system and a reality check on the strength of irrational herding. This proves that unrestrained speculation in bull markets can never last long, leverage can quickly turn optimistic views into disasters, and public sentiment, as a policy, plays a vital role in maintaining market stability. However, the most enduring lesson is that, in the stock market, as in life, following the crowd is often not a good approach, especially when the herd is rushing towards a cliff.

7.5 Implications for Long-Term Market Stability

The investor market is an ecosystem with active living organisms, comprising a single initiative involving millions of investors. When the market is at a fundamental level, informed analysis of decisions is made, leading to greater efficiency and effectiveness. However, at times when human emotions are the determining factor (e.g. greed inflating bubbles and fear that spurs crashes), the market is fragile at the threshold of chaos. One of the critical mistakes in the 2015 Chinese stock market was that the line between rational and irrational herding was very close. At one point, investors follow market recommendations based on statistics, which are generally aligned with the economic trend. However, after they unthinkingly pursue the market trend, the risk increases, and the same investor who initially invested may pull out. The challenge for policymakers, investors, and regulators is to identify the transition of herding from the stabiliser to the destabiliser before the harm occurs.

This is the meaning of policymakers closely surveilling herding tendencies to maintain excessive speculation. Speculative bubbles seldom appear on their own; they typically spread across multiple asset classes, including individual small-scale and institutional investors who are confident that they will exit the market before the turning point is reached. Government bodies and central banks must closely monitor the market, identifying the initial warning signs of asset prices being too high in relation to the actual state of the economy, such as soaring trading volumes or an unsustainable level of borrowed money for speculative investments. The most effective tool for addressing these risks is promoting investor education. When people realise the perils of speculation, the implications of leverage, and the psychological biases that motivate herding, they can avoid taking the reckless step of investing in an inexperienced manner (Qin et al. 2023). Financial education is more than just an instrument for managing wealth. This bulwark against the widespread loss of market value.

Another area where one reads between the lines is the regulation of margin lending and leverage ratios. Examining the 2015 situation reveals that excessive leverage can transform a minor correction into a genuine crisis (Sun et al. 2022). Regulators can prevent immaturely expansive speculative bubbles by applying stricter rules that state the amount investors and institutions can borrow in the stock market. It is the areas where retail investors are highly involved, and financial regulations are still underdeveloped compared to those in developed countries, making this issue even more relevant. Although restraining leverage will not eliminate market cycles, it will undoubtedly slow the pace at which speculation turns into a market crash.

However, classical policy measures cannot suffice in isolation. The introduction of artificial intelligence (AI) and machine learning in the field of finance is no less than a revolution in identifying and managing herding behaviour. These machines can handle modern data revolving in a circular and real-time process, leading to profitable business patterns that human analysts often miss. AI can identify rare conditions in market trends that are not sustained by fundamental reasons and provide forecasts of speculative asset bubbles. Machine learning expertise can integrate data sources such as social media, financial press, and trading metrics to anticipate which sectors will be most affected by capricious investor attitudes.

For instance, in 2017 and 2021, during the enormous crypto booms, AI models experienced a significant surge in retail trading volume, which garnered the most visibility in the mass media and exhibited the most extreme price fluctuations, characteristic of a speculative mania. Should instruments be used in conjunction with traditional stock markets, which often lack resources, the authorities and individuals could address these issues in advance by adjusting the course of monetary policy or financial regulation before a crisis arises. The fact of combining AI in the monitoring phase of the markets is not to eliminate risk, the risk goes hand in hand with investing, but to identify the moment when market dynamics shift from rational to irrational. Thus, pre-emptive actions can be taken, as opposed to damage control, at an earlier stage.

In general, for sound and stable financial markets, it is essential to maintain a delicate equilibrium between the freedom of the market and the speculative potential of small investors or the risk of exposed inflation historical defaults, such as Com bubble, the 2008 financial debacle, and the 2015 Chinese stock market, including the undercurrent perception, convey that the market is not influenced by mere documents but by the human psyche. Fear and greed will remain in the investor's psyche as long as human beings exist; for this reason, there will always be a tendency towards herding. The foundation of balance lies in the wisdom of the collective state, when the herd is moving correctly and heading toward a disaster.

7.6 Conclusion

In financial markets, herding behaviour is a significant force, thus playing a role in both upward and downward movements. Criticised as reckless and irrational by many, the situation bears a much richer truth. Herding is not always a bad thing; at times, it can be a rational move to follow markets under certain conditions. Collective behaviour supports market functions well when investors react to reliable economic data, fundamental changes, or the directives of a central bank. Actual prices are the result of market deliberations, and the wisdom of the crowd can enhance the decision-making processes. However, when the crowd becomes intoxicated, when speculation is replaced with reason, and when investors chase momentum without understanding it, herding, which was previously a stabilising force, turns into a destructive force.

The 2015 Chinese stock market crash, similar to many other financial crises that have occurred before, is representative of the immense costs that come with emotional decision-making and excessive speculative behaviour. During these periods of irrational exuberance, the fear of missing out (FOMO) blinds investors to fundamental risks. Margin trading, leverage, and the illusion of unstoppable growth amplify the gains until the market's rollover sends it into freefall. The same herd that recently hoisted prices above the cloud now, in the opposite direction, triggered panic selling, thus causing a market-wide collapse. These cycles are not random occurrences but rather recurrent phenomena in financial history, which are produced by cognitive biases deeply ingrained in human behaviour.

For investors, the main recipe for survival is to identify rational market windfalls rather than irrational speculation. This includes the ability to perceive a situation in which the value of assets increases due to solid fundamental conditions, as well as the case in which the value of the same assets rises only because everybody else is purchasing them. It seeks to overcome the temptation to be carried away by the wave of an upsurging stock and to develop the ability to step back when the stock evaluation no longer makes sense. Those capable of explaining the difference between a fact-based trend and a hype-driven bubble emerge from market downturn periods with their portfolios intact.

Financial markets will always be a mixture of rationality and irrationality, some of which may be due to data, analysis, and right investment decisions, but also due to fear, greed, and the power of the crowd. Bearish sentiment is not the absence of herding behaviour; instead, it is the realisation of when the herding behaviour is for your benefit and when it is your demise. The distinction between financial prosperity and disillusionment is usually just a single decision away: Will you stick with the crowd, or will you have the courage to think for yourself?

References

Ayoub A, Balawi A (2022) Herd behaviour and its effect on the stock market: an economic perspective. CAL 23(188):285–289

Bikhchandani S, Hirshleifer D, Welch I (2000) Learning from the behaviour of others: conformity, fads, and informational cascades. J Econ Perspect 12(3):151–170

Dodaro JF (2023) Stop checking the Price! Lose money every time you look at the stock market? The simple investing strategy for beginners to pick winners by trading only 4 times a year! First Principles Publishing, Pune

Escobar JJ, Rodríguez F, Prieto B, Kimovski D, Ortiz A, Damas M (2023) A distributed and energy-efficient KNN for EEG classification with dynamic money-saving policy in heterogeneous clusters. Computing 105(11):2487–2510

Jacobsen MH, Lund PC (2024) Panic: fight or flight in a culture of fear? In: Dark emotions. Routledge, London, pp 134–155

Li T, Chen H, Liu W, Yu G, Yu Y (2023) Understanding the role of social media sentiment in identifying irrational herding behaviour in the stock market. Int Rev Econ Financ 87:163–179

Loang OK (2023) Sustainable development goals, herding, and risk-averse behavior in Muslim countries. J Islam Monet Econ Financ 9(2):313–336

Loang OK (2025) From tweets to trades: the dynamic dance of investor sentiment, attention, and news sentiment in ESG stocks. China Finance Econ Rev 14(1):70–91

Loang OK, Candra S, Naveenan RV (2024) Stability in chaos: impact of monetary, fiscal, and firm characteristics on investor sentiment in Asian emerging markets. Int J Business Soc 25(3):1145–1164

Ooi KL (2024) Analyst forecasting and market liquidity dynamics: a comparative analysis of US and Chinese markets pre and post COVID-19. J Gen Manag. https://doi.org/10.1177/03063070231225603

Qin M, Zhang X, Li Y, Badarcea RM (2023) Blockchain market and green finance: the enablers of carbon neutrality in China. Energy Econ 118:106501

Rahayu AD, Putra A, Oktaverina C, Ningtyas RA (2021) Herding behaviour in the stock market: a literature review. Int J Soc Sci Rev 1(2):8–25

Sias RW (2004) Institutional herding. Rev Financ Stud 17(1):165–206

Sun L, Fang S, Iqbal S, Bilal AR (2022) Financial stability role on climate risks, and climate change mitigation: implications for green economic recovery. Environ Sci Pollut Res 29(22):33063–33074

Tian H, Wang W, Yang M, Yilmaz A (2024) Investigating the profit performance of quantitative timing trading strategies in the Shanghai copper futures market, 2020–2022. Int Stud Econ 19(4):589–616

Walsh J (2021) Investing with Keynes: how the world's greatest economist overturned conventional wisdom and made a fortune on the stock market. Wiley, Hoboken

Welch I (2000) Herding among security analysts. J Financ Econ 58(3):369–396

Yi L, Shen N, Xie W, Liu Y (2024) Rational herding: evidence from equity crowdfunding. Manag Decis 62(3):1008–1029

Chapter 8
Herding's Hidden Risks and Rewards

8.1 Introduction

Financial markets are a mesmerising battleground where psychology and strategy meet, and few forces can be as powerful or as dangerous as herding behaviour. At its core, herding is the instinctual predisposition of investors to follow the crowd, often without conducting independent analysis or considering fundamental factors (Ooi 2024a, b). This phenomenon can be viewed as a double-edged sword. At times, walking hand in hand with the majority can make significant profits as momentum builds and asset prices reach new peaks. However, equally quickly, the same collective actions can cause dreadful collapses when feelings flip, thus revealing the risks of unthinking agreement. Grasping the push and pull of herding is a must-learning task for any trader who is keen on dancing through treacherous markets.

Herding is not limited to a single asset class; it is inherent in stocks, commodities, and, in particular, cryptocurrencies, which have become particularly evident in recent years. In ameliorating markets, herding boosts Bubbles of happiness as traders amp up a rising trend, regularly, under the belief that 'this time is different'. This can be the self-reinforcing cycle that creates prices detached from the intrinsic value and ultimately leads to the bursting of speculative bubbles. On the contrary, in the bear market, the same herd behaviour can trigger mass panic selling, extending downturns beyond the estimates of fundamentals alone. Knowing when to surf the wave and when to decline, or even to bet against the crowd, are signs of an actual investor.

The art of discerning the rational crowd's movement from irrational crowding is the token that divides voyagers from the mess. However, some gain from herding, and they are the people, while others are misled by their seductive charm. The focal point of this matter is timing: being able to discern when real fundamentals drive the wave of trader movement and when it is merely a matter of emotion and speculation. By separating past trends in the market and identifying subsequent recurring

K. L. Ooi et al., *Following the Crowd: Psychological Drivers of Herding and Market Overreaction*, https://doi.org/10.1007/978-981-95-0792-4_8

patterns, investors can strategically position themselves either by capitalising on the upswing or by taking a contrarian position ahead of the crowd turning back.

This chapter focuses on the varied markets in terms of herding, explaining its implications in different settings. We will examine a treatise on old-fashioned market trends, in which we will witness the breathless rise and fall of Bitcoin, revealing how mass psychology influences price movement. The chapter will provide practical tips for investors on when it is beneficial to follow the crowd and when it is prudent to stick with their path. By the end of the book, readers will gain a deeper understanding of how to leverage herding proclivities to their advantage while avoiding the pitfalls of inconsiderate crowding.

8.2 Risks of Crowd-Induced Market Bubbles

A speculative bubble is one of the most eye-catching and destructive spectacles in finance. The thrill of it, the skyrocketing prices, and the strong faith of almost everyone that 'this time is really different' all resulted in an overwhelmingly intoxicating atmosphere that attracted everyone from highly experienced traders to ordinary people just looking to earn a quick buck (Li 2015). It starts with a straightforward assumption: a positive attitude. Whether it is an amazing brand-new technology, a boom in a still-not-used commodity, or a promising brand-new investment vehicle that is just too good to be true. As investors enter the market, prices begin to ascend. They continue to rise, and in the process, an increasing number of people adopt the narrative. A self-reinforcing loop is constructed, whereby climbing valuations provide their justification by continuing to increase. Finally, a surprising turn of events, it falls apart. The bloom burst, and the market, which was once at the top, crashed down, leaving destruction in its wake.

The main component of the speculative bubble is a psychologically dangerous mix of both speculative elements, and speculation remains unchecked. The yellow light of this phenomenon is none other than confirmation bias: investors actively elaborate on their opinions by receiving information about the bullish economy, while ignoring meetings that indicate prices have deviated mainly from reality (Loang 2024). Arguments that would make the bubble seem dubious are overridden by mere negative or even fear-mongering tones (Lee and Phillips 2016). The second idea in this context is the Greater Fool Theory, which states that, for an investor, it is not essential whether an asset is overpriced if he can find a 'greater fool' willing to pay more for it. This reckless mentality prevails during the final and most severe period of the bubble, when no one is concerned with reality anymore, and the primary reason for buying is that prices continue to rise.

History books are filled with such tales, each boasting an individual theme despite the identical fate of extinction (Torres 2023). Let us say that the silver bubble of 2011, fuelled by investors driven by the economy's wrongdoing, bid silver up to a whopping $50 an ounce. Speculative leverage led to an influx of money that could not be sustained; however, once institutional owners withdrew, the tide turned quickly and severely, removing billions within weeks. Just the other day, the 2021 SPAC bubble exposed a modern variant of irrational exuberance. Blank-check companies, which actively seek investors to fund their acquisition plans, have become some of the most sought-after commodities in the market, despite not yet having operational activities, for reasons including celebrity endorsements, media hype, and the widespread belief that every SPAC would discover a lucrative acquisition. Reality struck when many companies were either grossly overpriced or had no genuine business prospects, the SPAC phenomenon vanished, and vast portions of investor wealth disappeared in a flash.

Retail investors are often the most severely affected in these speculative bubbles (Agarwal et al. 2024). Unlike institutional players, who have access to in-depth research, high-frequency trading advantages, and effective risk management strategies, everyday investors typically enter the market late, when prices are already inflated, and exit at the worst possible time, after the crash wipes out most of their capital. The mass media and financial news exacerbate any existing sentiment and contribute to a false perception that money can be easily made (Baissa et al. 2024). Family, friends, and even strangers on the Internet share examples of their success, turning it into a tempting opportunity that nobody should pass up. However, the truth is that by the time most retail investors are well-informed and decide to take the plunge, the institutional players who triggered the initial rally are already preparing for the inevitable decline.

Market bubbles are familiar acquaintances, but they continue to plague both those driven by greed and those fearful (Jennings 2023). The sanguine moral is to tell: when we see prices going unreasonably up, when endless optimism takes the place of rational judgement, and when happiness replaces common sense, we think twice. Bubbles are always burst, and those who are the first to see the signals will prosper through the years.

8.3 Opportunities for Contrarian Investors

In the finance sector, where emotions often take control and the crowd's mentality prevails, contrarians tend to invest their way to success by doing the opposite of the majority (Munir et al. 2022). When the market is filled with fear and everybody is selling in panic mode, contrarians spot an opportunity. When the market is euphoric, but companies' stocks reach levels that cannot be justified, they quietly exit or provide a sell order at the wrong price. Although this is difficult to do and requires considerable patience, it has become a wise investment principle (Yadav et al. 2024). Contrary to the traditional approach, contrarian investing is about believing that a crowd is wrong when it goes to extremes. To achieve this, they look for opportunities such as irrational enthusiasm and unwarranted fear, when they can buy assets at a discount. When they become aware of the truth, the market responds by selling them at a higher price accordingly.

The process of a herd mentality is responsible for distortions in financial markets, and these distortions also create opportunities for contrarian investors (Ooi 2024a, b). When the majority runs scared and sells mindlessly, as a result of wars, accidents, or any number of local or economic problems, property becomes available for purchase or is sold at a bargain price. A typical scenario of market collapse occurs when solid companies plummet to absurdly low prices, allowing those who think ahead to acquire valuable assets at bargain prices (Levis and Liodakis 2001). In contrast, death by speculation occurs when the market rate exceeds the actual value, allowing a bold investor to manipulate the game by betting short and profiting when the market takes a nosedive. It is during these decisive moments of price differences that the contrarians step in, doing the opposite of what others do to realise a profit.

There are many ways in which contrarians can execute their tactics, but they all require the same mindset as a professional (Shiller 2000). Value investing is the primary approach advocated by investors such as Benjamin Graham and Warren Buffett. It aims to acquire equities that are undervalued, thus mitigating the public's transitory mental pessimism and anchoring it to the company's long-term business success. In contrast, short selling, which allows investors to not only profit from overvalued assets but also bet that their inflated prices will eventually return to reality, is betting against the issuer. Notably, it involves precise timing and unwavering faith, as markets can behave irrationally for longer than the majority of traders involved in the game. Above all, contrarians are able to practice patience and concentrate on their investment objective by keeping their emotions in check and resisting the pressure to conform to the majority, even if it is substantial.

There is considerable evidence that contrarian investors have challenged the prevailing market belief with varying results (Ofek and Richardson 2003). Warren Buffett's most notable piece of advice can be summarised in just three words: 'Be fearful when greedy and greedy when scared'. During the 2008 financial crisis, as the panic sale drove down the prices of real estate and stocks to unprecedentedly low levels, savvy investors purchased assets that had been depreciated and turned out to be undervalued; hence, they set the stage for significant profits over the next decade (Cheah and Fry 2015). On the same note, those who sold and perpetrated scams wowed the market with high returns in the early 2000s.

8.4 Case Studies: Bitcoin's Boom and Bust Cycles

8.4.1 The 2017 Bitcoin Surge and Collapse

In modern history, several financial episodes have reflected the relentless power and risk of crowd psychology, as well as the rise and fall of Bitcoin in 2017 and 2018. Bitcoin was the first cryptocurrency to gain popularity, transitioning from being a technology-driven currency, primarily discussed in tech forums and among libertarian circles, to becoming the hottest investment on the planet. At the commencement of 2017, Bitcoin had a modest trading price of $1000, even though this price represented a massive increase in value from its early days. However, what happened next was a performance influenced by the financial industry. In a year, Bitcoin's value jumped from $1000 to $20,000, representing a 2000% increase, and its all-time high was unforgettable. The mania was undeniable. All the outlet libraries were publishing it. The Internet was swamped with stories of people becoming millionaires overnight. Everybody, from friends and relatives to people who had never invested a dollar in their whole life, was talking about Bitcoin. The fear of missing the bus was turning into a force of mass progression that enticed retail investors in the first-come, then-they-were-dead approach.

There were ubiquitous tokens of typical speculative damage, but few people were able to see them. News about people taking out loans, maxing out credit cards, and even selling their homes to cover their Bitcoin purchases was frighteningly familiar. The gossip media company incited the minds of the masses, bringing attention to the wild, lavish gains, yet for the most part, leaving the risks unmentioned (Loang 2025). Celebrities and influencers were among the first to jump on the bandwagon, while some even pretended to promote different cryptocurrencies that would soon be forgotten. Nothing can halt feelings of happiness. Investors did not accumulate Bitcoin due to their advanced understanding of blockchain science or adherence to long-held principles of trust in the instrument's capability for long-term returns; they were, by and large, buying the currency that was trading at the highest rates because they believed it would always be that way.

However, a complex and painful lesson is always the end of a musical piece, and bubbles in finance always explode. Bitcoin experienced a spectacular rise to fame, followed by a subsequent decline. Just 3 weeks after reaching an all-time high of $20,000, the price plummeted below $10,000, representing a 50% decline in value. The end of 2018 was marked by the fall of Bitcoin to just a little over $3000, another 80% historically low. The same investors were those who reached unimaginable heights and persuaded them to possess a superpower that would never be broken. They were now left horrified at the losses they had suffered on their portfolios. Those who were the most unfortunate were those who had gone to the bank to borrow money so that they could pursue their fortunes and were left all alone with huge debts, and their dreams were buried in oblivion.

Figure 8.1 shows one of the most electrifying and devastating episodes in recent financial history. It was not just a price chart; it was the emotional heartbeat of a generation of investors who were swept up in the cryptocurrency frenzy. As Bitcoin rocketed from $1000 to nearly $20,000 in 2017, it was not logical that fuelled the ascent; it was euphoria, FOMO, and the seductive allure of easy riches. New investors flooded in, many of whom had never invested in a stock before, let alone a blockchain. Conversations at dinner tables, offices, and gyms revolved around digital wallets and 'moonshots'. However, few studies have paused to understand what Bitcoin actually represented or questioned whether such exponential growth was sustainable. It was a textbook case of herd behaviour, with social media influencers, celebrity endorsements, and media hype fanning the flames of speculative mania.

However, as Fig. 8.1 shows, the climb was only half the story, and the crash served as a harsh reality check. Within weeks of reaching its historic high in December 2017, the price of Bitcoin plummeted by 50%. By the end of 2018, it had lost over 80% of its value, falling to just above $3000. The silence that followed was deafening. Investors who had borrowed money, emptied savings, or mortgaged homes to buy at the top were left with portfolios in ruins, and dreams turned to dust. It was not just a financial loss; it was a loss of confidence. The collapse revealed the true nature of economic bubbles: they are built on emotions, driven by psychology, and burst with punishing indifference. Figure 8.1 stands as a stark reminder that in financial markets, unchecked enthusiasm can inflate even the most promising innovations into unsustainable illusions. When the crowd finally sees the truth, the stampede is merciless.

The accident served as a wake-up call to the perils of blindly following the herd. When its actual value does not determine the prices of an asset and is instead set through speculation and mass hysteria, it essentially sets the stage for an inevitable crash (Kirsh 2020). The sale of Bitcoin skyrocketed and then crashed, revealing the primary psychological aspects behind the financial bubble: blind pretence, unrestrained greed, and the brutally harsh reality that immediately follows. Many years later, Bitcoin would recover, but a number of retail investors who had entered at the top would never do so again. The lesson is exceptionally vivid: the more people who are directly involved in an asset that is not reasonably worth it, the more time the juncture to buy it. When the mob discovers reality, the stampede occurs with no quarter given.

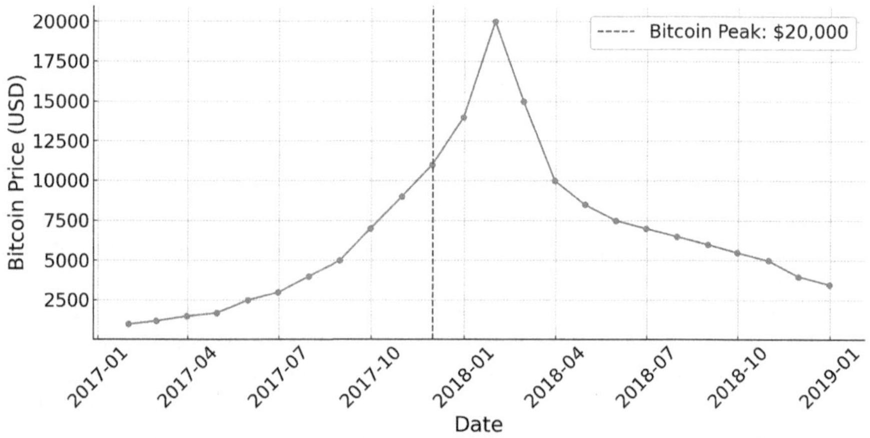

Fig. 8.1 Bitcoin's 2017 surge and 2018 collapse. Source: Authors' work

8.4.2 The 2020–2021 Bitcoin Rally and Correction

By the last few months of 2020, Bitcoin had become more than just a popular digital currency for tech lovers and libertarians; it had also emerged as a significant financial tool sought after by many institutional investors, hedge funds, and even listed companies (Shu et al. 2023). Bitcoin, once considered a fad by Wall Street, is now being purchased by some of the world's largest financial firms, including MicroStrategy and Tesla, in billions of dollars. Additionally, payment networks like PayPal and Square have begun integrating cryptocurrency into their platforms. The Ozarks gave birth to these ideas, and now they are reflected in widespread investment in Bitcoin.

The price of Bitcoin continued to climb, reaching a new record, driven by the surge in December 2020. The sector was boosted by institutional endorsements and relentless media coverage, which were in high demand. Influencers and analysts made bold predictions that Bitcoin would reach six figures. At the same time, retail investors, many of whom had previously had no chance but were now rushing to sell their assets, were expected to make huge profits from the price hikes.

Retail investors in Bitcoin were now of the opinion that things were panning out and thus took control of the game. The media reported that Bitcoin had stabilised, and consumers' questions about government decisions and power-related issues arose. The market was experiencing what is termed 'the bear market', and when all traders and investors were at a loss, the media went on to state, 'The bull run is over'.

The surge in Bitcoin in 2020–2021 and its subsequent decline confirmed the notable influence of herd mentality on the market (Isa 2023). However, when retailers arrive in droves, the market's excessive growth is not sustainable and eventually leads to inflated volatility and an inevitable crash. The lesson is always the same: at the moment when happiness is at its highest and when every single person believes only in positive changes for an asset, that is usually the right time to buy. The market appreciates the character attributes demonstrated by patience and self-discipline, while punishing those who follow the crowd without conscious questioning.

8.4.3 Lessons from Bitcoin's Market Cycles

If history could teach us anything about Bitcoin, it would be that it is never quiet; instead of what they say, its price changes are always dramatic. Unlike traditional assets, which are often driven by fundamentals, Bitcoin operates in an environment where speculation, hype, and mass psychology exert significant influence. The story of Bitcoin has always been the same: first, the early believers accumulate when no one cares about the results, then the trend is going to be positive when the big companies come in, and finally, the last act, the retail investors come in at the top, because of what we call FOMO (fear of missing out) and unreal expectations. What is usually left is the crowded fears, instead of the greed that was present earlier;

traders who were overleveraged are often demolished, as always, and prices are frequently lost by 50% or more. To the naked eye, what remains is just a growing pile of dreams that never came true, serving as a solid reminder of how herd behaviour can exacerbate volatility in the case of speculative assets.

Bitcoin's volatility is not solely a matter of financial speculation; it also has a direct impact on the psyche of the people. The allure of making easy money blinds investors to the dangers; thus, they buy at very high prices without having any actual understanding of the asset (Teitelbaum 2021). Making high-risk decisions based on emotional factors rather than careful analysis is the primary driving force behind many trades. When prices are on the rise, the belief in 'this time is different' spreads quickly, pushing valuation beyond rational thought. However, when the tides turn, emotions rise. People who previously swore that they would never sell Bitcoin suddenly rush to sell, cashing out forever on their losses and never looking back at crypto. Throughout every cycle, the pattern is repeated: it is the first-time users and disciplined traders who will walk away with substantial profits, whereas those who arrive late and let their emotions dictate their decisions will be left with massive losses.

Nevertheless, cryptocurrencies are among the most significant asset classes with the highest possible risks and uncertainties. Cryptos are more about the media, speculation, and macroeconomic trends. Bitcoin's price is subjective and not entirely tangible by market forces. Stocks or real estate, for instance, are more closely tied to earnings and fundamentals; accordingly, while adoption has increased and institutional backing has provided some assurance of legitimacy, the market is still significantly influenced by the public's behaviour. Regulatory news, social media sentiment, and these giant whale deals can make money go up or down in a split second. As far as I can see, those who grapple with these forces are the only ones who will profit. However, for the followers of the pack who jump into the market indiscriminately, Bitcoin is a financial field of landmines that might blow them up in a different direction at one time.

The most straightforward lesson to learn from the Bitcoin story of drastic fluctuations is that discipline is often better than emotion. Making good money in the market is for independent thinkers who take advantage of opportunities when others are overjoyed and buy low when fear prevails. The market is allowed to do as it wishes without consequence, yet without understanding its implications. Whether Bitcoin will continue its cycles indefinitely or, by some miracle, stabilise is the question to ask. However, one thing is sure: human mind psychology is regarded as constant, so the wheel of greed and fear will always define the future.

8.5 Conclusion

Herding behaviour is among the most dominant aspects of financial markets; it is a force capable of creating plenty of wealth but can quickly destroy it. It is this very aspect that propels bulls to high altitudes while being the discreet planner of devastating crashes. The simultaneous action of investors results in a breakneck pace of trends, enabling a small group of investors who surf the wave early to obtain the required profit. The same force responsible for the rapid increase in prices could reverse the trend and bring them down. The difference between financial gain and loss is often dependent on an irreplaceable skill deciding whether the driving force of the trend is solid fundamentals or simply speculation dressed up as an opportunity.

We have witnessed numerous cases where herd mentality has been the primary cause of the capital market exceeding its limits. Enchanted by tales of full potential, investors become convinced of the only possible uptrend in prices. In these situations, disbelief occurs, and the risk is neglected while emotions take precedence over reason. However, the brutal nature of the market throws people off the pedestal of irrational exuberance. At the instant when the crowd becomes aware of its action on an asset, extreme opposition is quick and merciless. People who were sidetracked by the flock, who bought the asset at high prices, were basically the same as those who were mistaken and stepped into the trap, that is, 'holding the bag'. The distinction is not about the lucky ones but rather about those capable of discerning the impending downtrodden phase of a trend and responding accordingly.

Contrarian investors understand this concept better than anyone else. They discover that the time for scepticism is when it is about the euphoria of the masses, and when growth translates to profitability, it is about the people panicking. Their profits depend less on conforming to the crowd but more on their ability to foresee when the crowd will turn. They maintain a distance when speculative bubbles are being created, waiting for reality to speak for itself. They then balance their portfolios, holding undervalued assets, driven by the fear that others are too scared to invest in them. Independent thinking, patience, and discipline are virtues that the course of action fosters. Nevertheless, the practice has yielded positive outcomes throughout all seasons and has proven to be a solid route to accumulating wealth.

The most important lesson for all types of investors is that fundamentals truly matter more than speculation. The financial world is a chaotic place, with a great deal of noise generated by social media trends, sensational headlines, and the so-called trendsetters selling their version of the next big thing. However, triumphant investors manage through clutter and consider the general outline. They realise that the fleeting emotions of the market do not determine true worth, but rather the enduring value of the asset. This principle applies regardless of whether one deals with stocks, commodities, or even cryptocurrencies. Those who invest in dependable and practical factors will stand the test of time, while those who merely seek fads will not.

Herding behaviour is unlikely to occur. It is a component deeply rooted in human nature that has been a constant presence and influence on financial markets for many years. However, individuals who attack the private sector will take both the dangers and the chances related to that phenomenon into account. The decision is relatively straightforward: go with the flow without thinking and end up at risk, or think independently and find a way to profit from the rush of the masses. The market handsomely rewards those willing to invest time, practice discipline, and question the methods used by the herd. The question for you is, when will the new wave of speculation occur? Are you going to be ready?

References

Agarwal V, Taffler RJ, Wang C (2024) Investor emotions and market bubbles. Rev Quant Finan Acc 64(1):339–369

Baissa B, Fuoli M, Grieve J (2024) The news values of fake news. Discourse Commun 19(3):418–440

Cheah ET, Fry J (2015) Speculative bubbles in bitcoin markets? An empirical investigation into the fundamental value of bitcoin. Econ Lett 130(1):32–36

Isa I (2023) AR, VR, and immersive technologies: the new mode of learning and the key enablers in enhancing library services

Jennings JM (2023) The uncertainty solution: how to invest with confidence in the face of the unknown. Greenleaf Book Group, Austin

Kirsh Y (2020). Crises in prosperous societies: are they inevitable?

Lee J, Phillips P (2016) Asset pricing with financial bubble risk. J Empir Financ 38:590–622

Levis M, Liodakis M (2001) Contrarian strategies and investor expectations: the U.K. Evid Financ Anal J 57:43–56

Li NJ (2015) Study on the influence of the crowding trade of securities investment funds on stock bubble. Oper Res Manag Sci 41(1):87–99

Loang OK (2024) Stability of Shariah-compliant stocks in Indonesia, Malaysia, and Gcc: the roles of monetary and fiscal policies and contagion. J Islam Monet Econ Financ 10(1):155–176

Loang OK (2025) Can machine learning surpass human investors? Evidence from adaptive herding behaviour in US, China and India. J Appl Econ 28(1):2435796

Munir A, Sukor M, Shaharuddin S (2022) Adaptive market hypothesis and time-varying contrarian effect: evidence from emerging stock markets of South Asia. SAGE Open 12:490

Ofek E, Richardson M (2003) DotCom mania: the rise and fall of internet stock prices. J Financ 58(3):1113–1137

Ooi KL (2024a) Analyst forecasting and market liquidity dynamics: a comparative analysis of US and Chinese markets pre and post COVID-19. J Gen Manag. https://doi.org/10.1177/03063070231225603

Ooi KL (2024b) Demystifying behavioural finance. Springer, Cham

Shiller RJ (2000) Measuring bubble expectations and investor confidence. J Psychol Financ Mark 1(1):49–60

Shu A, Cheng F, Han J, Liang Z, Pan Z (2023) Arbitrage across different Bitcoin exchange venues: Perspectives from investor base and market related events. Accounting & Finance, 63(5):5183–5210

Teitelbaum SH (2021) Smart money: a psychologist's guide to overcoming self-defeating patterns in stock market investing. Page Publishing, Conneaut Lake

Torres ÉP (2023) Human extinction: a history of the science and ethics of annihilation. Routledge, London

Yadav R, Patil A, Sarda K, Bapat MM (2024) Does contrarian investing beat the conventional strategies and the index? SocioEcon Challenges 8(2):2520

Chapter 9
Cognitive Biases and Market Reactions

9.1 Introduction

Financial markets, often regarded as a basis for rational decision-making, are frequently influenced by the human psyche and are marred by flaws and irrational trends. While classical economics expects investors to be logical, weighing risks and rewards accurately, the actual case is the opposite, particularly when emotions, cognitive shortcuts, and other psychological factors are involved. Excessive weight and cognitive biases, which are intricately woven into the fabric of human existence, are the two primary culprits behind people's tendency to underprice things (Loang et al. 2024). The matter of sticking to the assumption of an investor who remains stubbornly anchored at the previous price, without adapting to changes in market perception, or a trader who rides the news wave and compulsively makes deals, is no different. Biases, which often coexist with market efficiency, contribute to the creation of bubbles and crashes, leading to periods of extreme volatility.

Behavioural finance emerged as a fundamental window through which we can comprehend irrational human behaviour. In contrast to classical financial theories, which assume that all available knowledge is reflected in the market and that people act rationally and optimally without exception, behavioural finance acknowledges that aspects such as emotion and psychology are involved in decision-making. That is why companies are sometimes perceived on the market to be worth a lot more than they intrinsically are, or why we sometimes see an abnormality in a stock's price going down for no real reason. These illogical price movements, frequently considered mere market 'noise', are actually the direct result of the implementation of normative cognitive patterns. The bias that dominates decision-making processes is often influenced by cognitive biases, according to modern psychology of investment.

Clustering the market around standard deviations decreases in value is a central cognitive bias that dominates in the vicinity of short-term volatility. Overconfidence bias increases traders' belief that they possess better-than-expected judgement,

K. L. Ooi et al., *Following the Crowd: Psychological Drivers of Herding and Market Overreaction*, https://doi.org/10.1007/978-981-95-0792-4_9

leading them to trade excessively and make incorrect decisions (Loang 2024). Anchoring bias occurs when investors become overly focused on past prices, leading to flawed judgements, even when new information suggests a different price. The availability heuristic, which relies too heavily on recent experiences rather than rational analysis, is also a reason for decision-making under emotional pressure. These biases, often out of sight, create a negative feedback mechanism due to the collective irrationality they foster, which in turn leads to momentum-driven markets and their consequent euphoric surges or panicked collapses.

Behind every market boom and bust, behind every irrational rally or sudden crash, lies an invisible puppeteer: the human mind. Table 9.1 returns the surface of financial decision-making to reveal powerful cognitive biases silently steering investor behaviour. Overconfidence bias is one of the most significant disruptors, an internal whisper that convinces traders they have superior insights, better timing, and sharper instincts than their peers. This misplaced belief leads to reckless trade, inflated valuations, and euphoric bubbles that eventually pop (Frydman and Camerer 2016). Anchoring bias follows a subtle but persistent force that tethers investors to historical prices and familiar reference points. Even as new evidence emerges, they cling to outdated benchmarks, miss opportunities, and ignore critical red flags. Meanwhile, the availability heuristic operates as a deceptive spotlight, placing undue weight on the most recent or dramatic events. Investors guided by this shortcut often overreact to headlines, chase market noise, and ignore deeper fundamentals, fuelling swings driven more by emotion than by reason.

However, the psychological minefield has not ended. Herding bias infects the crowd, pushing individuals to surrender their judgement in favour of the majority's actions; after all, if everyone else is buying, surely they know something. This group fuels manias and crashes, turning rational markets into echo chambers of fear and greed. Loss aversion and the disposition effect form a tragic duo in which the pain of losing overrides the joy of gaining, causing investors to irrationally cling to underperforming stocks while prematurely selling winners (Sussman et al. 2023). Confirmation bias quietly poisons decision-making. Investors often surround themselves with data that validates their existing beliefs while rejecting anything that challenges their narrative. These cognitive traps do not just affect a few isolated actors; they ripple through the entire financial ecosystem, distorting prices, amplifying volatility, and reshaping the risk landscape. Table 9.1 is not just a catalogue of errors; it is a mirror held up to the collective investor psyche, showing that the most significant risk in markets may not be external; it lives within us.

This chapter aims to uncover the psychological foundations of market behaviour and provide a thorough explanation of the cognitive biases that fuel excessive price movements. The latter half will be dedicated to examining the world around us, revisiting the historic 2010 Flash Crash, as well as the current day, to assess how these biases manifest in the context of high-frequency trading and retail investment decisions. The investigation of so-called 'patterns' is a type of intellectual endeavour with no direct practical relevance; however, it can provide tools and knowledge to investors, policymakers, and financial professionals to navigate the intricacies of the market with greater comprehensibility (Filho et al. 2020). As we examine the

Table 9.1 Key types of cognitive biases in financial decision-making

Bias type	Definition	Investor behaviour	Market implication
Overconfidence bias	A cognitive distortion where individuals overestimate their own abilities, knowledge, or control over events	Investors trade excessively, underestimate risks, and rely too heavily on personal judgement	Leads to inflated asset prices, excessive trading volumes, and increased market volatility
Anchoring bias	Tendency to rely too heavily on the first piece of information (anchor) when making decisions	Investors fixate on past prices or outdated financial data, even when new data suggests otherwise	Distorted valuations, resistance to new information, and delayed market reactions
Availability heuristic	Judging the probability of events based on how easily examples come to mind, often recent or dramatic ones	Investors overreact to recent news, trends, or events, ignoring historical patterns or fundamentals	Can fuel herd behaviour, market bubbles, or flash crashes due to short-term sentiment swings
Herding bias	The tendency to mimic the actions of a larger group, assuming they are better informed	Investors follow market trends blindly, fearing missing out or isolation	Creates bubbles or crashes through momentum trading and synchronised reactions
Loss aversion	Psychological tendency to feel losses more intensely than gains of the same magnitude	Investors hold losing assets too long and sell winners too quickly, fearing regret	Results in inefficient portfolio allocation and suboptimal long-term returns
Confirmation bias	The tendency to search for, interpret, and recall information that confirms pre-existing beliefs	Investors selectively gather data supporting their strategies while ignoring contradictory evidence	Reinforces poor investment decisions and delays necessary corrections in portfolios
Disposition effect	A tendency to sell assets that have increased in value while keeping assets that have dropped	Driven by emotional discomfort with realising losses, even when logic suggests otherwise	Prevents rational rebalancing and contributes to price stickiness in declining assets

Source: Authors' work

psychological forces that influence financial decision-making, we aim to equip the audience with the knowledge needed to recognise, mitigate, and, in some cases, capitalise on them for profit.

9.2 Behavioural Triggers of Short-Term Volatility

Statistics does not just control financial markets. They are influenced by computational numbers, algorithms, and earnings reports, and powered by human emotions, herd instincts, and subconscious biases. Is this the solution to psychological triggers amplified by speculative bubbles and panic-driven sell-offs, even to create an environment where logic is subordinate to impulse and fear?

This inconsistency is primarily due to the complex interplay of cognitive biases in cloud investor judgement. When markets are soaring, the overconfidence bias holds, persuading traders to believe that their predictive powers are unmatched (Audrino et al. 2018). This leads to excessive risk-taking, with investors chasing gains under the illusion that they can perfectly time the market. The same bias fuels speculative bubbles, where optimism becomes self-reinforcing, higher prices attract more buyers, and the cycle repeats until reality strikes. On the other hand, when the market declines, the heuristics of availability make investors rigid in the face of historic losses and quick-suspended decisions, resulting in increased selling pressure. A single reactive, negative headline can create panic and promote exaggerated declines, as assets are sold without discrimination in the first place.

However, cognitive bias does not only account for the extraordinary speed and intensity of contemporary market volatility (Kirilenko et al. 2017). Algorithmic trading is a digital accelerator that amplifies human irrationality. High-frequency trading (HFT) algorithms, designed to capitalise on microsecond price movements, react to the same psychological patterns that drive investors. When the tide of sales comes in, algorithms read the momentum and amplify it, which can cause cascading sell cycles that could destroy the market by wiping out billions within minutes. This phenomenon was observable in the 2010 Flash Crash, which occurred when automated trading and emotional decision-making among bulls caused the Dow Jones index to plummet by almost a thousand points in a matter of minutes, only to rebound within the same timeframe. Such occurrences reflect how biases, previously confined to human choices, also contribute to volatility in an era when machines trade at speeds beyond human comprehension.

This volatile-inducing cognitive bias is also among the reasons why many sectors are at high risk for both substantial gains and significant losses. Technology stocks, which are sometimes evaluated based on the 'hype' scenario or the optimism of rational decision-makers, will fully demonstrate the high swings that precede price directional moves; for instance, when investors base their predictions on previous 'record breaker' scenarios rather than considering the present intrinsic value (Loang 2025). The cryptocurrency market, known for its speculative craze and cult-like enthusiasts, is the most exposed. Bitcoin, Ethereum, and numerous Altcoins previously experienced price spikes of thousands of per cent, then fell just as dramatically due to cycles of overconfidence, former highs anchoring, and panic selling prompted by news or regulatory bans. These two dynamic sectors, which have a more significant impact on moods than actual values in short-term price actions, are prime examples of cognitive biases that directly affect the ticker tape.

Grasping these psychological triggers is not merely a scholar's endeavour; it is key for anyone willing to journey through the current chaos of the markets. One can improve their investment strategy by becoming attentive to how biases increase market overreaction, understanding how algorithms amplify these patterns, or finally, realising in which sectors most volatility lurks. Alternatively, the cost of greed and the gain of fear write the book, and this is why The Key to a Survivor not only predicts the next significant movement but also explains the forces of invisibility behind the crowd's madness.

9.3 The Role of Heuristics in Market Distortions

9.3.1 Overconfidence Bias

In the realm of investing, a fine line exists between confidence and overconfidence, which is particularly true when it comes to financial losses (Barberis and Thaler 2003). Every trader, from the Wall Street elite to the weekend stock picker, believes that they possess a unique edge or advantage, particularly relevant to a specific idea. This extraordinary intuition leads to a superior understanding of the market (Gavrilakis and Floros 2022). The exceptional vision of the trader is often just that; it is an illusion. Overconfidence bias leads traders to overestimate their brilliance, competence, and knowledge, causing them to make unwise decisions, take on excessive risk, and ultimately suffer severe monetary losses.

What is the most dangerous aspect of the overconfidence bias? Its potential to mislead a risk reaction is the one that causes the most harm. Investors who are confident about their future predictions tend to underestimate their chances of failure. Therefore, they may take on more debt than they should, ignore warning signals, and bet the market aggressively. That is how speculative bubbles are born: traders begin to buy assets they believe will continue to grow without limit, driven by optimism and a strong faith in their success and the absolute correctness of their judgement. The more they win, the more confident they become, causing a loop in which risk becomes a secondary thing. This cycle can promote markets to unprecedented heights, as seen in the case of the dot-com bubble in the late 1990s, when investors poured money into tech startups with no earnings, believing they were driving a revolution that would never slow down.

The most notable instance of overconfidence bias occurred in the years leading up to the 2008 financial crisis. Hedge funds and investment banks, equipped with complex financial models and a solid faith that they could outsmart the market, borrowed at an unprecedented level. The housing market, which had been a safe and stable investment for a long time, became the core of the financial empire built on overconfidence (Ooi 2025). Investors, rating agencies, and policymakers repeatedly believed they understood the risk fully and that the models were correct, which said that housing prices could only go up. They ignored the warning signs, dismissed sceptics, and kept doubling down until reality crashed in on them. When the economy turned, the leverage that had grown them finally went against them, creating a catastrophic downfall that destroyed trillions of wealth globally and led to the collapse of many economies.

Overconfidence is not just a problem for institutional investors but also for retail traders. The emergence of commission-free trading and the ease of leverage have provided individual investors with unprecedented power, while also exposing them to the most significant risks associated with their own biases. Through limited knowledge about specific issues, people can be vulnerable to the problem of self-belief. Still, traders often find it most prevalent, making high-risk speculations when they fail to understand the distinction between luck and skill. They enjoy record-high win rates, growing in confidence, while neglecting the fact that economic conditions are unpredictable. Consequently, the losses become catastrophic as they retain the same overconfidence that guided their profitable times, affecting their perception of the risks that ultimately lead to their downfall.

Identifying and controlling the overconfidence bias is one of the most challenging and crucial skills in investing. This activity requires a high level of self-awareness, a willingness to challenge assumptions, and an understanding of the market's instability. The greatest investors are not those who think that they are gods who know everything about the future, but those who recognise the complexity of their knowledge and adapt their strategies. Ultimately, however, the markets do not reward arrogance; they punish it.

9.3.2 Anchoring Bias

Consider a situation in which you purchase a stock at a cost of $100 per share. The price drops to $80, but rather than re-evaluating the investment based on its current financial situation, you convince yourself that the stock is still 'worth' $100. You hold onto the thought that the price of management will surely return to it later (Ly et al. 2023). The addition of anchoring bias to the behavioural finance concept is a cognitive trap that prevents investors from seeing the bigger picture; instead, they choose to focus on old price points, even when the current market is in a state of complete chaos. The psychological influence of a reference price initially has the power to distort rational decision-making, thereby keeping traders in short sales, unexploited opportunities, and financial stagnation.

Anchoring bias is undesirable because it occurs unconsciously and can lead to inaccurate decisions. Investors establish mental reference points, such as the highest price a stock has reached, the price at which they bought a house, or the valuation of the broad market in the past, and then use these as reference points for the future (Benartzi and Thaler 2007). However, these markets are not sentimental. Prices do not 'owe' investors a return to previous levels, and past highs do not guarantee future performance. Yet, despite overwhelming evidence that adhering to old price levels is irrational, traders remain reluctant to accept it, haunted by a deeply rooted fear of regret. Selling at a price lower than what they originally paid feels like a loss, even when keeping it longer can result in even more significant losses.

This bias was glaringly present during the 2008 housing market crisis. As the real estate bubble burst, home prices plummeted, and sellers struggled to adjust to their outdated price expectations. For example, homeowners believed that their properties were still worth the peak valuations of 2006; thus, they did not lower their prices, even though few buyers were available. Many could not rid themselves of unrealistic quotes, being certain of a near-future market recovery, and unwilling to come to terms with the painful reality that things had changed. At the same time, banks and lenders, based on their risk models inflated by asset prices, were slow to realise their losses (Owusu and Laryea 2023). This collective refusal to accept the actual state of things, in turn, fuelled and spurred the crisis, which, instead of being a harsh but manageable downturn, transformed into a full-scale economic disaster.

Stock exchanges are not significantly different. After significant corrections and even crashes, investors are hesitant and cautious about purchasing assets that have experienced a considerable drop, as they fear that these may still be overvalued compared to the previously observed highs. In contrast, when a stock or asset reaches a historical peak, investors may assume that it is overvalued, although the fundamental variables suggest further growth potential. Anchoring bias clouds judgement, preventing the investor from adjusting to market changes with the flexibility and objectivity that a successful investor demands.

Avoiding anchoring bias involves learning to attribute value based on the current situation rather than relying on arbitrary reference points. A stock is not worth something because it once was; it is worth something based on future potential. A house is not what someone paid for it five years ago; it is worth what the market is willing to pay. The best investors, who are detached from past numbers, see not only the uncertainty but also the potential for growth and make decisions based not on where it has been, but where it is heading.

9.3.3 *Availability Heuristic*

The human brain was created to follow the most straightforward course of action. We are instinctively directed to take the most immediate information available: the titles of newspapers we recently read, the stock chart we examined this morning, or the most recent financial crisis that we can still remember plainly. The predetermined cognitive shortcut (recent events vs. overarching trends) drives this mechanism of investing, which invalidates broader time perceptions and gives an investor more significant weight to short-term data than to long-term historical trends. It blinds their vision, creates a false perception of market normalisation, and allows emotional logic to dominate over fundamental economic law.

Think about investor behaviour after a significant market crash. Most traders are mainly driven by their memory of a second meltdown lurking in the dark, which keeps implanting doubt about re-entering the market, even when conditions become favourable. Every downturn serves as a reminder of the past, and every recovery is taken with a surprising lack of confidence. Glen Cannon, a psychologist, said that this is not really about the numbers. Instead of relying on clinical analysis, these individuals often use the most emotionally charged memories of their financial crisis experiences as a basis for decision-making. For this reason, amidst the aftermath of the 2008 financial crisis, many traders stayed off the tracks, missing out on the most excellent bull market run of all time; the fear of an economic crash still overlapped with other memories.

The availability heuristic not only evokes fear and dread but also fuels a desire for financial gain. When the market experienced a significant advancement, what once worried the traders seemed to disappear, and the belief that the rise would continue indefinitely became firmly rooted (Suri et al. 2024). Recent increases give them the idea that past trends are evident, and then investments in highly speculative instruments absolutely follow without any cautiousness. Thus, the bubbles swelled up efficiently. The phenomenon of dot-com, where the movement was late in the 1990s, the cryptocurrency hype of 2017, and the meme stock craze of 2021, in addition to the above list, all took the same course: traders who rely on the rapid price increase as a sign to sell based on this time being different, when in fact it is just cyclic. Even though the economy is cyclical, humans do not usually perceive repetition of their actions in the way they wish. Those who adhere to the latest trend instead of adopting a broader outlook are the first to face a market downturn.

This bias poses a risk and adds cost to the investor because it makes them believe they are taking complete control and making informed decisions, when in fact they are merely following short-term noise. A bearish market crash is neither a deathblow nor a harbinger of doom; it is a regular part of a capitalistic market, and rallying does not guarantee an infinite recovery. However, investors still fall victim to such vagueness, which is evident at present, and, in turn, fail to see the big picture as a result.

However, the best investors, without a doubt, are superior to those screws that do not come loose from history (Kasoga 2021). They are unlikely to succumb emotionally to the recent market risk and instead encapsulate it within a broader context of market fundamentals, asset class diversification, and risk management. In the past, the market alternated between ups and downs; however, the key to being ahead in the long run is realising that you can learn from history, but it does not dictate how things will be in the future.

9.4 Case Study: The 2010 Flash Crash

On May 6, 2010, the U.S. stock market experienced one of the most significant and shocking declines in its history. In a matter of minutes, the Dow Jones Industrial Average dropped by almost 1000 points, erasing nearly a trillion dollars in market value, followed by a rapid recovery. It was a financial show unlike any other. No big news had started a crash. No catastrophic situation occurred after the global outburst. The market had visibly collapsed, thinking it could withstand the pressure exerted by new high-frequency trading (HFT), algorithmic overconfidence, and cognitive biases. It was a precise case in which it was demonstrated that financial markets do not operate continuously on perfectly rational choices in the contemporary age; instead, they are driven by psychological factors in both people and machines.

The central point in the flash crash was high-frequency trading. This advanced algorithmic trading model utilises ultrafast computers to execute thousands of trades in a fraction of the time. The firms that developed these algorithms were convinced that they had achieved ultimate market efficiency and created systems that targeted minor price discrepancies. However, this overconfidence, one of the significant cognitive biases in finance, ultimately led to their failure to acknowledge the potential risks associated with their inventions. Traders speculated that their schemes, which were assembled around historical trends and quotes from complicated mathematicians, would foresee and extensively dominate future financial phenomena. For a long time, they did not even comprehend that, at certain times, these algorithms, depending on the situation, might act disorderly against each other, thus causing a self-feeding cycle of panic selling.

However, in the realm of algorithmic trading, the act of one member was like a flare in a room filled with gasoline. As the price of the product began to decrease, the newly created HFTs responded with rapid reactions, exacerbating the situation by selling more. The result of this, the drop in the equity market, got out of hand and led to panic among traders who observed a sharp decrease and feared the worst outcomes. Investors susceptible to anchoring bias, who focused on previous prices, struggled to comprehend the unexpected turn of events, leading to indecision, confusion, and further selling. In a relatively short time, blue-chip stocks, once regarded as safe, suddenly lost their value, appearing to have no worth at all, with some dropping to fractions of a dollar before rebounding.

Additionally, the flash crash placed financial agencies and regulatory bodies under severe pressure. Moreover, the collision highlighted a marked improvement, yet one that was still insufficient, in algorithmic-driven weaknesses, rather than relying purely on human intuition. The authorities rushed to grasp the situation, realising that if no action were taken, such events might escalate. Hence, the Securities and Exchange Commission (SEC) took the initiative to launch circuit breakers, devices that function as a stop-loss switch to curtail trading during periods of extreme volatility. The plan was to replace panic-stricken selling with periodic market recalibrations, allowing them to expand their forces.

9.5 Conclusion

Regardless of whether financial markets continue to become sophisticated, one truth remains that human psychology will always shape market behaviour. Investors are not machines; they are made up of emotional, psychological, and instinctive forces that sometimes make them do things that, in many cases, look like irrational decisions. The traders' overconfidence is a blindfold that prevents them from seeing the risks; the anchoring bias is a valve that blocks their ability to use old valuations, and the availability heuristic distorts their view of market trends in their minds. Once again, these cognitive distortions are not an exception in finance; they are the norm. However, although biases are inevitable, they do not have to be fatal. Excellent investors are not those who feel they are immune to psychological warfare, but rather those who are honest with themselves and who recognise and then manage these risks.

Markets will always be subject to distortion due to the influence of human emotions and decisions. Booms and busts are not anomalies; they are inherent features of a system shaped by waves of optimism and fear. Investors, traders, and even policymakers often react to the world not as it is, but as they perceive it, coloured by the recent experiences they have gone through and the mental shortcuts their minds make. At the same time, behavioural finance has presented us with a better lens through which to examine these biases, but this is not sufficient. Controlling one's emotions, not by cutting off feelings but by regulating them, is key to rationality in investing. The distinction between successful investors who do not fall victim to market psychological traps and those who do is the capacity to rethink decisions that arise from instinctive reactions, to challenge one's own beliefs, and then to make choices based on reason rather than impulse.

That said, managing biases is not solely a personal issue but rather a structural one. The algorithmic trading boom has introduced a new dimension of complexity, as human biases also influence machine decisions, leading to a deterioration in their performance because attention to detail is lost. The 2010 Flash Crash was a clear indicator that, even though algorithms do not react to emotions, they can still exacerbate human irrationality by manipulating momentum, overconfidence, and panic at speeds that are beyond human control. Automated systems, if not controlled, can convert into minor market panic or complete market chaos. This fact has necessitated regulatory intervention in the market to establish protections, such as circuit breakers, transaction limits, and enhanced monitoring of automated trading strategies. Although these moves provide a certain degree of protection, they are certainly not perfect. The financial system remains in peril due to subjective-driven noise, necessitating ongoing adaptation to new risks and constantly evolving markets.

Financial markets are not solely numbers but people. Whether caused by individual investors' mistakes or systemic factors, market inefficiencies will always exist because people are inherently part of the market. Still, understanding this fact does not mean weakness; it signifies the presence of a competitive edge. Anyone who perceives the market as an emotional battleground in advance will be better at navigating volatility, will avoid making mistakes, and will, in fact, benefit from irrational behaviour from others. After all, the markets will always have errors, as long as there are people to correct them.

References

Audrino F, Sigrist F, Ballinari D (2018) The impact of sentiment and attention measures on stock market volatility. Capital Mark Asset Pricing Valuat eJournal 36:334–357

Barberis N, Thaler R (2003) A survey of behavioural finance. Handb Econ Financ 1:1053–1128

Benartzi S, Thaler RH (2007) Heuristics and biases in retirement savings behaviour. J Econ Perspect 21(3):81–104

Filho A, Silva D, Ferreira L (2020) Financial modelling with multiple criteria decision making: a systematic literature review. J Oper Res Soc 72:2161–2179

Frydman C, Camerer C (2016) The psychology and neuroscience of financial decision making. Trends Cogn Sci 20:661–675

Gavrilakis N, Floros C (2022) The impact of heuristic and herding biases on portfolio construction and performance: the case of Greece. Rev Behav Financ 14(3):436–462

Kasoga PS (2021) Heuristic biases and investment decisions: multiple mediation mechanisms of risk tolerance and financial literacy a survey at the Tanzania stock market. J Money Business 1(2):102–116

Kirilenko AA, Kyle AS, Samadi M, Tuzun T (2017) The flash crash: the impact of high-frequency trading on an electronic market. J Financ 72(3):967–998

Loang OK (2024) Risk avoidance, macroeconomic indicators and bank performances in developing economies. Ann Financ Econ 19(4):2450018

Loang OK (2025) Can machine learning surpass human investors? Evidence from adaptive herding behaviour in US, China and India. J Appl Econ 28(1):2435796

Loang OK, Candra S, Naveenan RV (2024) Stability in chaos: impact of monetary, fiscal, and firm characteristics on investor sentiment in Asian emerging markets. Int J Business Soc 25(3):1145–1164

Ly DP, Shekelle PG, Song Z (2023) Evidence for anchoring bias during physician decision-making. JAMA Intern Med 183(8):818–823

Ooi KL (2025) Behavioural finance and financial crises. In: Demystifying behavioural finance: foundational theories to contemporary applications and future directions. Springer, Singapore, pp 79–93

Owusu SP, Laryea E (2023) The impact of anchoring bias on investment decision-making: evidence from Ghana. Rev Behav Financ 15(5):729–749

Suri G, Slater LR, Ziaee A, Nguyen M (2024) Do large language models show decision heuristics similar to humans? A case study using GPT-3.5. J Exp Psychol Gen 153(4):1066

Sussman A, Hershfield H, Netzer O (2023) Consumer financial decision making: where we've been and where we're going. J Assoc Consum Res 8:365–372

Chapter 10
Emotions and Overreaction

10.1 Introduction

Financial markets have long been regarded as logical citadels, where market prices are determined primarily by data, earnings, and economic fundamentals. Nevertheless, similar to a broken record, the markets have once again proven that the key drivers are not only the numbers but also the individual sentiments of those involved. Investors, individuals, and their institutional counterparts do not reject the influence of fear, excess, and doubt. In times of trouble, these emotions take centre stage and drive the markets far from what is perceived as rational, through the ground of overreaction. In this chapter, we examine the primordial role of emotions in relation to finances, particularly fear, which can literally seize the markets and, through domino effects, result in extreme fluctuations.

Amplification of fear is one of the most remarkable aspects of a financial crisis. When markets decline, the initial reaction may be rational, as if investors recognise the need to rebalance their portfolios and make predictions about the forthcoming economic crisis. However, as more losses occur, there is a shift in psychology (Ooi 2024). The fear becomes self-reinforcing. Investors are in a panic, not due to a detailed study of the economy, but because they see others panicking. The newspapers are aghast with headlines about disasters, the stock market shows red signals, and all sudden, even top investors question their understanding. Indeed, during these moments, the markets no longer function as a rational price-discovery mechanism, and emotional warfare becomes a place where a chain reaction of sales occurs, some of which often lead to prices that are far below their actual value.

Investor sentiment, by its nature, is a fragile commodity. Confidence can be built over many years, but can be destroyed in just a few hours. This fragility of the markets is the reason for the contagion effect demo, which occurs when one investor fills the room with fear. Then, the fire of fear moves from one market to another and even from one country to another. A single bank failure, political crisis, or unexpected economic downturn in one region can send shockwaves across the globe,

K. L. Ooi et al., *Following the Crowd: Psychological Drivers of Herding and Market Overreaction*, https://doi.org/10.1007/978-981-95-0792-4_10

leading to widespread sell-offs driven more by emotion than by financial reality. The mechanisms of this contagion are deeply rooted in psychology: humans are wired to look to others for cues on how to behave, and in uncertain times, they often assume that if others are selling, they should be selling, too.

This chapter explores these dynamics in depth, dissecting the psychological and behavioural forces that drive irrational market reactions. We examine historical instances of emotional market behaviour, with a particular focus on the COVID-19 financial crisis one of the most dramatic demonstrations of mass panic in modern markets (Loang et al. 2024). Through this analysis, we aim to understand why these overreactions occur and how they shape economic realities long after the initial panic subsides. By the end of this chapter, it will become clear that emotions are not just a side effect of market movements; in many cases, they are the driving force behind them.

10.2 Emotional Contagion during Global Crises

Financial markets are not simply systems reliant solely on numbers and logic; instead, they are systems that are highly dependent on human emotions, and fear may be the most contagious of all emotions (Zhang et al. 2020). Emotional contagion refers to the transmission of emotions from one person to another. Its primary physical impact in social psychology is indirect, but it has a profound effect on financial markets. During times of global crisis, the fear of loss and uncertainty spreads from one investor to another, prompting widespread panic selling that can cause a market to lose billions of dollars in just a few hours. The concern does not stay just within those affected. Still, it crosses borders, asset classes, and economies, often leading to financial pitfalls that are significantly more severe than the one that caused it.

Doubt is the power that supplies emotional contagion to the market. In contrast to rational decision-making, which is based on accurate data and calculated risks, uncertainty keeps clients guessing in the dark. They are unsure whether they will be worse off, how long this will take, or what the right course of action is (Barsade et al. 2018). To address this obscurity, they rely, for the first time, on a single and only available indicator: the actions of other investors. If the market is declining and others are selling, it is reasonable to think that they may have information that you do not. This herd mentality is not only a weakness of beginners but also experienced professionals, and is likewise affected by this mass panic. In bouts of selling unrealistic assets, fear triggers the initiation of the loop mechanism, decision-making leads to other concerns, and the situation escalates to a critical point where properties are priced too low for rational thinking.

What could be the most effective factor that increases the rate of emotional contagion? The media. During crises, financial pages become like an overcharged, running machine; they speak of doom, announce falling prices in red, and present the worst-case scenarios to people's faces (Barsade 2002). Although the media has a primary duty to convey information, it also has a complementary effect of amplifying fear. The more the media highlighted the outrageously negative impacts, the more it spread anxiety among investors, making it seem that a market fall was inevitable. This was particularly obvious during the COVID-19 pandemic crash in March 2020, when markets worldwide, in a seemingly historic move, fell drastically. The news channels filled their programmes with visuals of deserted streets, sick people in hospitals, and bureaucrats and officials in disarray, reinforcing their conviction that they faced a cataclysmic economic crisis. Investors, who were operating in a state of high uncertainty and relying on outdated knowledge, became a factor in the cash cliff.

However, COVID-19 was not the only instance where emotional contagion triggered a mass market reaction. Again, in 2008, we witnessed a classic scenario in which Lehman Brothers' bankruptcy reverberated across the world's financial systems. Fear spread like wildfire, prompting the indiscriminate selling of stocks, even among those with solid fundamentals (Beerel 2025). Investors who could not determine where the market bottom was set preferred to sell their shares altogether rather than risk incurring more significant losses. The same set of events occurred in previous stock market panics, such as the dot-com bubble of 2000 and the Black Monday crash of 1987. Each of these situations arose not only from actual economic causes but also from the genuine, uncontrolled feelings experienced by investors in uncertain contexts.

Understanding emotional contagion is vital because it places itself in the context of an essential fact: markets are not irrational; they are untainted by human consideration. They are subject to the same logic as the human psyche, and during crisis periods, fear often prevails over common sense. Therefore, the problem for investors is to learn to recognise the times when they are caught up in the emotional tide and when they should withdraw for the time being, focusing on the bigger picture. The past has demonstrated that those who can stay grounded and focused, those who can recognise emotional contagion for what it is, often emerge in more substantial positions when the situation has cooled down.

10.3 Financial Impacts of Panic-Driven Decisions

10.3.1 Market Freefalls and Recovery Delays

The market drops are not the same. Some originate from central economics, including reductions in profits, increases in interest rates, or the fragility of the financial system (Ford 2010). However, other studies are mainly driven by trepidation. These fear-induced descents are activated with incredible speed as panic selling overcomes rational reasoning, causing asset prices to be significantly lower than their actual value. What sets these two apart is their effects on the following period: a fundamentally rooted price correction almost always touches its bottom when prices revert to the level of the real economy. A panic-driven dive, however, can plummet far below the appropriate price levels, leading to prolonged recovery times and severe economic effects that persist long after the initial wave of fear has passed.

When fear controls the market, it not only lowers prices but also triggers a chain reaction of unintended consequences (Kaplanski and Levy 2010). The value of assets falls considerably, and investors who previously borrowed money for trading, such as leveraged traders, hedge funds, and, in particular, large institutions, find themselves betting against the deal (Lleo and Ziemba 2016). All at once, margin calls flood in, forcing them to the point where they need to auction off their assets in a fire sale to obtain the required coverage for their trading positions. This wave of forced selling creates more momentum in the selling direction; thus, it has become a full-blown liquidity crisis. Banks and financial institutions, concerned about being further affected by this instability, limit their lending, making it even more difficult for both social actors and businesses to access loans. Out of the blue, what began as anxiety in the financial market was now choking the real economy.

Liquidity crises are always hidden in the resurrection of the market. A rational course of action would be that once the fear disappears, the rates would promptly revert to those that appropriately reflect the true worth of utilities and resources. However, once there is no liquidity left, companies with strong fundamentals will struggle to raise capital, which can ultimately lead to layoffs, bankruptcies, and prolonged economic downturns. On the other hand, it is believed that those who have been frightened and left the market may not be able to re-enter at reasonable prices, thereby missing the potential rebound. Delayed recovery does not occur because the economic fundamentals change because of the psychological and financial scars left behind by the crash itself.

Time and history have shown that markets tend to overreact, resulting in more pain than necessary. The 2008 financial crisis was not an exception; instead, it was more a matter of panic that was responsible for the credit markets freezing and the economy plummeting, rather than just bad mortgages. The COVID-19 crash, which hit markets at the beginning of 2020, followed the same trend. The assets were losing their value not just because of concerns about the economy, but also because investors were anxious about the future and rushed to exit the market, thereby draining liquidity. Both cases posed problems, with governments and central banks intervening with massive measures to restore confidence and unfreeze the markets.

The fundamental lesson drawn from these crisscrossed is that market freefalls tend to be more emotion-driven than reality-driven. While economic downturns are unavoidable, the degree of collapse and the pace of recovery depend solely on the extent to which investor behaviour is ruled by fear (Roubini and Mihm 2010). Those who perceive this dynamic well, that is, when they understand that panic rather than fundamentals fuels a market crash, are the most qualified to navigate turbulence, avoid troublesome losses, and reap benefits when the situation eventually becomes favourable.

10.3.2 Retail Vs. Institutional Investor Behaviour in Market Panics

Generally, market panic does not impact all investors. The distinction between retail investors and institutional investors, including hedge funds, mutual funds, pension funds, and other large-scale organisations, is not merely about the volume of their transactions; it is also about how they weigh fear and uncertainty (Tan et al. 2023). Retail investors tend to make emotional decisions, which leads them to sell at the most unfavourable times. In contrast, institutional investors, who are equipped with data, experience, and capital, tend to view these panic-driven sell-offs as great opportunities to acquire undervalued assets.

Retail investors' primary difficulties are psychological in nature. Fear becomes reason, and with the markets in free fall, the instinctive response is to get out while the price is still correct. This is a loss-driven reaction; it is a well-known behavioural finance bias (loss aversion) that argues that the emotional effect of losing money outweighs that of making money more than twice as much. The market declines, and the fear of additional losses grows, creating panic selling, where many retail investors sell at or near the bottom, thereby locking in their losses. Ironically, by the time they find their feet and the market starts to recover, they have already left and, therefore, missed the opportunity for a comeback. This has always been the case since the dot-com crisis of 2000, the Great Financial Crisis of 2008, and the COVID-19 crash in 2020.

By contrast, institutional players are in a different game to play. They are not killed by emotions but by data, probability, or long-term strategy (Tetlock 2007). They do not sell stock for fear, but seize the opportunity to buy the stocks of great companies at a lower price. When a few investors are shedding their stocks in fear, companies are quietly gathering them, frequently at a markedly low price. This method is based on the firm experiences of these entities, as they realise that panic is momentary and that the markets will remain healthy. Their ability to put large amounts of capital to work at the right time frequently allows them to reap terrific rewards when sentiment stabilises and prices align.

Warren Buffett basically contained this approach in one phrase: 'Be fearful when others are greedy, and greedy when others are fearful'. This mindset is what makes winners flourish amidst market panic (Loang 2025). On the one hand, retail investors let their emotions get the better of them, leading them to short-term thinking; on the other hand, institutions do the opposite, seizing the opportunity of fear-induced mispricing, of which they are well aware.

Differences in retail and institutional bchaviour during crises are not only about experience but also about the availability of resources. Institutional investors have the advantage of utilising comprehensive research and real-time data, as well as employing advanced risk management techniques that few others can match; hence, they make more informed and analytical decisions (Choi et al. 2016). They can hedge during downturns, deploy derivatives to manage risk and lean on a network of analysts and economists to provide deeper insights into market trends. Meanwhile, retail investors typically rely on news headlines, social media, and gut instinct, which are more likely to amplify fear than misinterpret it.

Understanding this distinction is crucial for individual investors seeking to navigate volatile markets. The secret to long-term success is controlling emotional outbursts and analysing institutions, such as recognising fear-induced sell-offs as an opportunity to accumulate quality assets at discounted prices, rather than as a reason to exit. People who manage their feelings well and adopt a considered, systematic approach will be on the side of the winners when the inevitable market downturn arrives.

10.3.3 Role of Algorithmic Trading in Amplifying Emotional Reactions

Algorithms are not just tools in the financial market today; they also rule the market (Lo 2012). The leading operators in this scenario are hedge funds, high-frequency trading (HFT) companies, and institutional investors that utilise highly complex AI-based models to buy and sell securities at a breakneck pace, sometimes making decisions in just a matter of milliseconds. This is possible because the algorithms are designed specifically to maximise the efficiency of operations and to clear up market opportunities. Still, they also introduce a side effect: what was originally market emotionality resulting from periods of high volatility is being further amplified due to the behaviour of the rocket algorithms.

Automated panic selling is a primary mechanism through which algorithmic trading contributes to market crashes. Most trading algorithms have been developed to react to price changes and movement indicators rather than through fundamental data analysis. In turn, when markets are in a downward trend, the algorithms perceive this as a selling signal, execute a fair number of orders, and initiate a chain of automated commands (Addy et al. 2024). This is how the feedback loop works: the lower the prices of the stocks, the more the algorithms sell, which leads to declining prices, accelerated by the machines' trades that humans would never have made in the first place. A slight decline in the market can quickly become a complete crash, simply because machines cannot reason and sell uncontrollably.

The famous Flash Crash incident in 2010 exemplifies such a scenario. On May 6, 2010, the Dow Jones suffered a 1000-point decline, only to quickly regain that loss in record time. Later, it was discovered that a highly sophisticated trading algorithm had identified some unusual sell volume figures. With no other option available, they decided to quickly unload their positions, which in turn created a massive dip that the humans were unable to correct quickly enough. This incident has shown that in a world of mechanical trading, the risk of panic-driven cycles can form self-reinforcing patterns which no longer serve as stabilisers but as enhancers of the volatile environment.

Another core problem is that models of trading driven by AI do not instinctively consider the influence of the mind phenomenon, unlike real human investors. Regular models run through historical data, sort and assess patterns, and take action accordingly. However, during crises, the market tends to act irrationally. The application of emotional contagion, fear-ridden overreactions, and a herd mindset creates outbreaks of unpredictable behaviours that are not explained by pure statistics alone. If AI systems overlook these behavioural issues, they can be misled into believing that panic selling by humans is a sign of a structural breakdown, which further exacerbates the negative implications and damages market stability.

To tackle these issues, a few hedge funds and financial institutions have incorporated behavioural finance theories into their algorithmic models (Lo 2012). These models move away from relying strictly on price changes; instead, they derive from investor sentiment, news trends, and social media to emotionally forecast the extreme fluctuations in the market. Hence, they consider the behavioural triggers and are thus able to avoid the mistakes of adhering to the trend momentum without reason and to anticipate the time when the panic has caused an abnormal market reaction, rather than one driven by fundamentals. This marks a shift in focus to the fact that the economic system is not based solely on integers but also possesses a unique personality.

Still, regardless of the progress made, the fact remains that trading algorithms, due to their nature of operating on predefined rules, will always be prone to increasing market movements, both in upward and downward directions. When crises occur, even the shortest time is counted (Shin 2023). The lack of human judgement in such automatic systems can quickly bring what could be a normal correction in the market into a situation in which the listed factors cannot find a common platform. The challenge in financial markets is to manage this duality, benefiting from the swiftness and efficiency of algorithmic trading while also ensuring that its actions do not lead to the inflation of drives, mainly due to emotions.

Ultimately, human traders may act irrationally due to fear, whereas machines appear to panic for numerical reasons. In addition, in an era when such machines command a trading worth of trillions of dollars, their reaction to stress is equally crucial as understanding human psychology.

10.4 Case Study: Investor Overreaction during the COVID-19 Pandemic

The COVID-19 pandemic was a crisis that modern financial history had never witnessed, and its effects on global markets were instantaneous and dismal. Amidst the scars of the crash, against the backdrop of fear and fabric, the world witnessed the wildest market crash in history as panic spread more quickly than the virus itself. Notably, the world's stock exchanges experienced the fastest and most severe crash in their history, with the S&P 500 plummeting by almost 34% in just 33 days. This collapse was unprecedented and primarily driven by overwhelming fear and complex economic fundamentals. Panic-stricken investors rushed to cash out their asset portfolios, anticipating a significant financial crisis of historic proportions.

Not only was the speed of the drop remarkable, but it was also notable for the level of uncertainty, given that COVID-19 was a relatively new issue. When it comes to past financial crises, people often mention tangible reasons, such as the subprime mortgage crisis in 2008 or the dot-com bubble in 2000. In contrast, COVID-19 presented an unusual and unpredictable threat. On one hand, the governments were terminating functioning economies like a light switch; businesses had to be shuttered, and there was a question mark throughout the crisis. Uncertainty in the situation can lead to negative feelings. Therefore, investors chose to bet on the worst-case scenario, hoping that the depression would be severe and last a long time. This wave of selling led to the mass liquidation of assets, with investors selling stocks, bonds, gold, and even Bitcoin across the board to convert their holdings into cash.

The speed of the fall was worsened not only by algorithmic trading but also by margin requirements. As stock prices fell, hedge funds and leveraged investors selling assets were forced to sell more assets to meet their margin calls, marking the inception of this cycle of forced liquidation, which in turn lowered prices. Even the usually regarded safe assets, such as U.S. Treasury securities, experienced volatility spikes as market participants sought to free up cash amid the deteriorating crisis. The extreme behaviour of the market in this situation testified that the market was terrified and that fear dominated investors' oversight of economic fundamentals.

Nevertheless, the recovery stage was unbelievable, as was the collapse. In March 2020, governments and central banks in every part of the world launched an unprecedented attack on economic maladies with a stimulus toolbox that set the financial markets in a liquidity frenzy to raise people's confidence in the U.S.A. The Federal Reserve lowered interest rates to historically low levels and implemented a series of eye-catching bond-buying programmes, while expanding the money market by trillions of dollars. In addition, countries sanctioned trillions of dollars in stimulus packages, including direct relief for businesses and families. These measures triggered what is now known as a V-shaped recovery, with the markets rising sharply from their lows. As of August 2020, the S&P 500 had already recouped all its losses, whereas by the end of the year, it was trading at a record high, undoubtedly something most people would have never expected at the panic's climax.

Figure 10.1 illustrates a story of whiplash-inducing despair and revival, a market crash that rewrote history, followed by a comeback no one dared to predict. In early 2020, as the world grappled with the threat of COVID-19, financial markets buckled under a tidal wave of fear. The S&P 500 plummeted by 34% in just over a month, marking the fastest and most violent crash in modern market history. What made this moment unique was not just the speed of the collapse, but the murky uncertainty driving it. This was not about bad loans or a popped tech bubble, but about the unknown. Businesses were shut down by government mandate, economies were brought to a halt overnight, and investors, unable to model the magnitude of the threat, fled to cash in an unprecedented stampede. Margin calls, algorithmic sell-offs, and a desire for liquidity triggered a cascade that no financial institution could fully contain. Even traditionally safe havens, such as gold and U.S. Treasuries, saw volatility as cash became king in a market driven by a survival instinct.

However, just as breathtaking was the ascent that followed, a sharp, almost defiant rally powered by the lifeblood of fiscal and monetary firepower. By the end of March, central banks and governments launched a blitzkrieg of stimulus measures, including zero interest rates, bond-buying bonanzas, and trillions of dollars in direct aid to households and businesses. This sparked a V-shaped recovery that even seasoned analysts found stunning. As Fig. 10.1 illustrates, the S&P 500 not only recaptured its pre-pandemic levels by August but also went on to close 2020 at record highs. The market, it seemed, had chosen to look beyond wreckage and pricing in the post-pandemic future, even as the world was still in lockdown. This extraordinary rebound became a master class in investor psychology: the difference between reacting emotionally and thinking strategically. Those who gave in to fear missed the rally; those who held on or even bought at depths were richly rewarded. The pandemic taught us that markets are not mirrors of the present; they are projections of what lies ahead for those who understand that volatility becomes not a threat but an opportunity.

The lesson carved in stone by the COVID-19 crisis is that emotional trading can be dangerous. Investors who were nervous and sold their assets at the lowest levels of the crash internally accepted huge losses; they then became casual observers of the market, which recovered in a few months. Those who stood by their guns or even used the fear of equity markets to purchase cheap stocks received significant dividends. The episode of the COVID-19 pandemic crisis has once again highlighted the importance of emotional control and the understanding that fear can sometimes cause markets to deviate from reality, which is only comprehended in hindsight.

The most important lesson from the Cartesian perspective on this epidemic is that markets are looking to the future, while people are reacting in the present. A

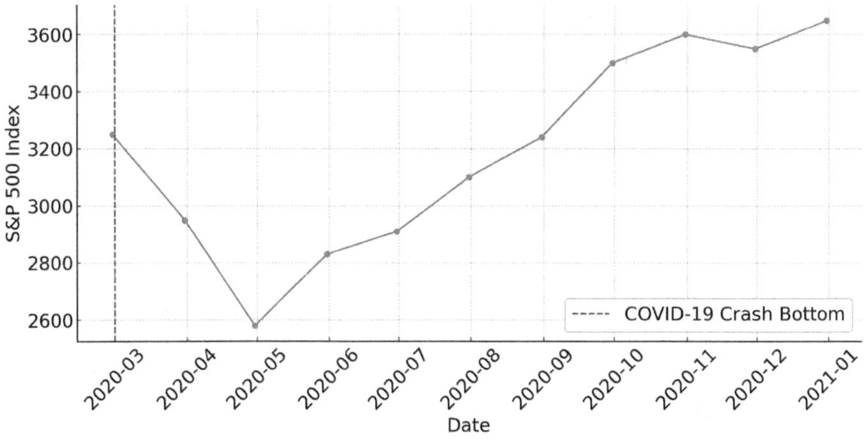

Fig. 10.1 S&P 500—COVID-19 crash and recovery (2020). Source: Authors' work

downturn in the economy marked the mid-2020s. Still, the stock market was moving in the opposite direction, and this was not a mistake of the year, but rather a sign that people had started to look ahead to the time when the economy would recover and thus decided to act. Decision-making must be based on a long-term view of fundamentals, not on temporary emotions. Hence, those who dominate a discipline will become capable not only of guarding against harsh financial times but also of moving a step ahead of them.

10.5 Lessons for Crisis Management

The uncanny nature of financial crises reveals the temperamental emotions that drive the forces that lead a person to make mistakes. The fear, panic, and uncertainty that joint troops evoke often cause investors' emotions to take over when making decisions. A decision made in haste can lead to more significant losses than savings. Nevertheless, the past has demonstrated that the majority of individuals who are able to identify and withstand emotional triggers during challenging times are those who, more frequently than not, become strong in the wake of market recovery. In some cases, learning from past crises can help investors devise strategies to navigate market turmoil without succumbing to the herd mentality and panic selling.

One of the most significant lessons that every investor should learn is to recognise their psychological biases. The automatic reaction to a down market is essential to eliminate the underlying assets; people who usually sell do so out of fear of additional losses. However, history is filled with examples in which panic selling has mainly produced negative rather than positive outcomes. Rather than making decisions based on fear, successful investors typically take a step back from the emotion, examine the fundamentals, and view their investments from a long-term perspective. Those who truly believed in their assets during the COVID-19 pandemic, the 2008 financial crisis, or even the dot-com bubble downturn turned out to be fortunate when the stock markets recovered. The acquisition of emotional commodities, such as media-induced fear or short-term volatility, may serve as a buffer against impulsive decisions that divert the accomplishment of long-term objectives.

Besides individual decision-making, central banks also stand at the centre stage of restoring market confidence during the crisis. When panic mode is activated, financial markets often experience liquidity freezes, a situation in which investors want to sell but few buyers appear in the market. The Federal Reserve (or the ECB) becomes the order of the day by injecting liquidity into the system and cutting interest rates to prevent a financial collapse. These actions, along with fewer emergency lending programmes, are just a couple of examples taken from the central bank's toolkit to help the system return to normal. Viewing this rapid intervention through the lens of the 2008 and 2020 beacons the sense of how transformative central banks can be in the quest to pacify the markets, securing the continued credit flow and the survival of financial institutions. This fundamental understanding can serve as a reliable anchor for investors during times of difficulty. As a consequence, one holds the conviction that global economic institutions are working hard to prevent destruction, which could mean reassurance, particularly in turbulent moments.

A tool that is often overlooked but has a significant influence in crisis management is behavioural finance, a branch of economics that examines the global impact of how psychological factors affect investments and personal finance. Such an approach is now being adopted by both the public and private sectors to prevent panic sales and to stabilise countries. For example, against the backdrop of customer concerns, halting trading alongside the setting of automatic circuit breakers can decrease mass panic selling and prompt investors to reconsider their intuitive reactions. Furthermore, policymakers' efforts to ensure coherent and straightforward communication, such as leaving no room for ambiguity, help contain fear spiralling out of control. Investors can also take the behavioural finance route through the introduction of things such as a predetermined investment plan, which in this case could be dollar-cost averaging, and removing emotions from decision-making.

The key to crisis management is the realisation that markets are cyclical, panic is only transitory, and rationality ultimately prevails in the long term. Regardless of whether for individual investors or policymakers, staying composed when navigating chaotic processes, trusting long-term fundamentals, and being aware of the psychological traps of crisis investing is the mantra for performing well. Those who are able to master these lessons will not only weather financial storms but also be appropriately positioned to thrive when order is restored.

10.6 Conclusion

In every aspect of trading, emotions are central; they have been so since the beginning and will always remain so. Market cycles, such as economic data and corporate earnings, are driven by fear and greed. Emotions, such as the fear of loss or the desire for profit, cannot merely be eliminated in the decision-making process of a financial adviser. In contrast, investors can utilise their awareness of these feelings' power to avoid extremes of their own, thereby avoiding unnecessary losses. By learning about the way fear spreads, uncovering behavioural biases, and adhering to a strict, self-disciplined investment strategy, a person can prevent the disorientation caused by emotional trading and maintain their focus on achieving their financial stability goal for a more extended period.

However, the situation is no longer the same. People are not the only cause of the transmission of emotions in markets. Modern mass media, artificial intelligence, and cutting-edge financial architectures have created a state in which fear can rapidly spiral out of control. Headlines that overly dramatise the situation make it difficult to see the whole picture. Computerised trading systems further depress the stock market, and social media promotes the herding of fears in the crowd, making it much easier for emotional transmission to take over the entire market. It is the understanding of these influences that empowers investors to assess the situation from a broader perspective and respond rationally, rather than succumbing to impulsive reactions to market noise.

In contrast, market conditions that cause panic in investors are typically triggered when the market fails to deliver what the trader has expected. Investors who aim to build strategies that withstand crises, such as diversified portfolios of stocks, automatic purchase plans, and pre-emptive risk management techniques, are those who endure market volatility the best. Investors who act out of fear and liquidate their positions during bear markets often miss the opportunity to buy into recovering companies. In contrast, their counterparts, who think strategically and rationally, make calculated moves to earn long-term profits. What you can learn from this conversation is basically the following: market panic attacks are predictable, and the fatal part is not giving in to them. By staying aware, being diplomatic, and resisting emotional impulses, investors can navigate the uncertainty with ease and emerge successfully when the market returns to normal.

References

Addy WA, Ajayi-Nifise AO, Bello BG, Tula ST, Odeyem O, Falaiye T (2024) Algorithmic trading and Ai: a review of strategies and market impact. World J Adv Eng Technol Sci 11(1):258–267

Barsade S (2002) The ripple effect: emotional contagion and its influence on group behaviour. Adm Sci Q 47:644–675

Barsade S, Coutifaris C, Pillemer J (2018) Emotional contagion in organizational life. Res Org Behav 38:137–151

Beerel A (2025) Courage: the heart of leadership. Taylor & Francis, Philadelphia

Choi TM, Chan HK, Yue X (2016) Recent development in big data analytics for business operations and risk management. IEEE Trans Cybernet 47(1):81–92

Ford C (2010) New governance in the teeth of human frailty: lessons from financial regulation. Wis Law Rev 2:441

Kaplanski G, Levy H (2010) Sentiment and stock prices: the case of aviation disasters. J Financ Econ 95(2):174–201

Lleo S, Ziemba WT (2016) How to lose money in derivatives: examples from hedge funds and bank trading departments. In: The world scientific handbook of futures markets. World Scientific, Singapore, pp 689–750

Lo AW (2012) Adaptive markets and the new world order. Financ Anal J 68(2):18–29

Loang OK (2025) From tweets to trades: the dynamic dance of investor sentiment, attention, and news sentiment in ESG stocks. China Financ Econ Rev 14(1):70–91

Loang OK, Candra S, Naveenan RV (2024) Stability in chaos: impact of monetary, fiscal, and firm characteristics on investor sentiment in Asian emerging markets. Int J Business Soc 25(3):1145–1164

Ooi KL (2024) Analyst forecasting and market liquidity dynamics: a comparative analysis of US and Chinese markets pre and post COVID-19. J Gen Manag. https://doi.org/10.1177/03063070231225603

Roubini N, Mihm S (2010) Crisis economics: a crash course in the future of finance. Penguin, London

Shin DD (2023) Algorithms, humans, and interactions: how do algorithms interact with people? Designing meaningful AI experiences. Taylor & Francis, Philadelphia

Tan L, Zhang X, Zhang X (2023) Retail and institutional investor trading behaviours: evidence from China. Annu Rev Financ Econ 16:459–483

Tetlock PC (2007) Giving content to investor sentiment: the role of media in the stock market. J Financ 62(3):1139–1168

Zhang G, Lu D, Liu H (2020) Strategies to utilize the positive emotional contagion optimally in crowd evacuation. IEEE Trans Affect Comput 11:708–721

Chapter 11
Identifying Overreaction in Markets

11.1 Introduction

Market overreaction is a key phenomenon in financial markets, where investors overreact to new information, leading to significant price swings that deviate from an asset's intrinsic value. In contrast to logical adjustments that bring prices in line with fundamental economic metrics, overreaction leads to temporary imbalances, resulting in inefficiency. These discrepancies frequently arise from psychological tendencies, market emotions, and collective actions, leading investors to make decisions about buying or selling assets that lack fundamental financial information. Exaggerated responses can be seen in both the optimistic and pessimistic market scenarios. During periods of rising markets, enthusiasm drives the creation of asset bubbles, causing prices to soar beyond their actual worth irrationally. Conversely, during bear markets, we frequently observe a surge in panic-induced selling. This fear can trigger steep drops, occasionally erasing substantial wealth in a matter of days.

The main factor behind market overreactions is rooted in investor psychology. Behavioural finance reveals that cognitive biases, including loss aversion, availability heuristics, and confirmation bias, influence decision-making and lead investors to respond impulsively rather than rationally. For instance, the tendency to avoid losses can cause people to dread losing more than they appreciate equivalent gains, which often triggers frantic selling during price drops. Similarly, the availability heuristic prompts investors to place undue weight on recent events, resulting in exaggerated responses to breaking news and temporary market fluctuations. The impact of media and social dynamics intensifies these biases, as eye-catching headlines and conjectural discussions stir emotions, fostering collective action that heightens market fluctuations.

Distinguishing between sensible adjustments and exaggerated fear is essential for investors looking to manoeuvre through financial markets. An analytical adjustment is a thoughtful recalibration of asset values influenced by critical

K. L. Ooi et al., *Following the Crowd: Psychological Drivers of Herding and Market Overreaction*, https://doi.org/10.1007/978-981-95-0792-4_11

developments, including changes in earnings forecasts, interest rate decisions, or broader economic indicators. These adjustments are crucial for maintaining market efficiency and ensuring that asset prices accurately reflect their intrinsic values. Conversely, overreaction occurs when emotions fuel price swings that far exceed what the fundamentals would support. For example, a business might announce a minor drop in quarterly profits, leading to an exaggerated sell-off even though it continues to show robust long-term growth potential. Those who are astute enough to notice these exaggerated responses can uncover hidden gems, setting themselves up for profits as prices align with their true worth.

An intriguing instance of market overreaction occurred in March 2020, coinciding with the onset of the COVID-19 pandemic. Global stock markets have faced an unprecedented downturn, with investors gripped by fear, marking a pivotal moment in financial history. The S&P 500 experienced a dramatic decline of more than 30% in a matter of weeks, fuelled by anxieties surrounding economic downturns and unpredictable effects of the pandemic in the future. Although the worries were valid, the magnitude of the sell-off greatly exceeded reasonable forecasts, especially given that numerous major companies had sufficient liquidity to withstand turmoil. In bold, central banks and governments unleashed a wave of monetary and fiscal stimuli. As these recovery measures kicked in, the market surged dramatically, propelling the S&P 500 to unprecedented heights in just 1 month. Those who recognised the market's overreaction and invested in fundamentally solid stocks during the decline were poised to benefit from the rapid rebound.

Understanding the nuances of behavioural finance is essential for uncovering price inefficiencies that arise from emotional overreactions. Conventional financial theories, such as the efficient market hypothesis (EMH), suggest that asset prices reflect all publicly available information. Nonetheless, behavioural finance research challenges this idea, demonstrating that psychological factors play a significant role in shaping market behaviour. By weaving behavioural insights into market analysis, investors can anticipate more accurately when irrational actions cause extreme price fluctuations and adjust their strategies accordingly. Grasping the nuances of behavioural triggers such as panic selling driven by fear or the thrill of speculative euphoria empowers market players to make wiser choices. This approach minimises emotional trading and enhances the chance of spotting undervalued assets.

The market's tendency to overreact presents both dangers and opportunities. Emotional responses can heighten instability and result in significant losses, yet they also present opportunities for disciplined investors who maintain their composure during market turmoil. By differentiating between valid adjustments and unwarranted fears, market players can develop strategies to mitigate risk and capitalise on pricing discrepancies. In today's fast-paced world of information flow and automated trading, understanding the behavioural trends that lead to overreaction is essential to ensuring financial stability and securing lasting investment success.

11.2 Early Warning Signs of Market Overreaction

Financial markets are frequently characterised as the outcome of joint intellectual efforts, although historical accounts have shown that irrationality can hit them hard. Overreaction is not an insidious phenomenon; rather, it is a widespread one. On the one hand, it is a trial that remains hidden from those who do not know where to look (Zakamulin 2024). A significant shift in perception is required to identify it; for example, to distinguish between a manifestation of the natural market and an emotional market frenzy. A trader who can see these signals at the forefront can either, on the one hand, avoid unnecessary risks or, on the other hand, they can seize the opportunity that appears amid chaos.

The most clear-cut sign of market overreaction is the extreme volatility of the price whenever asset prices are shifted far from their historical averages (Hendershott et al. 2011). Even though price swings in the financial market are common, outbursts and excessive fluctuations sometimes imply more than just fundamental transformations; they are often the result of emotional trading under the pressure of heightened emotions. A typical example is a stock that has always fluctuated within a 2% range per day, only to suddenly lose 15% of its value in one session, with no prospects of any subsequent change in its long-term outlook. This type of quick transfer is not caused by logical prejudice but by fear-oriented liquidation or speculative buying. It is a classic example of overreaction, where chaotic short-term traders, instead of revealing the truth, destabilise the market with their noise.

The second notable sign is that trading volumes are unusually high. For instance, a stock, cryptocurrency, or commodity may see a steep rise or fall in buying or selling activity. At the same time, it is a firm signal that it has speculative enthusiasm more than sensible intervention. Through social media promotion and trend-following, retail traders can serve as a driving force for increasing asset prices, which are often very high due to retail investor irrationality (Yang et al. 2025). As a good example of the verbal meme stock rally, these companies had poor fundamentals but witnessed their share prices surge for the first time due to the retail investors' later joint purchase of the online stock. The waves of farsighted gambling, such as a tsunami, build up but then collapse just as dramatically. Keeping track of trading volumes can be essential if you notice a spike in an asset that previously had stable trading levels, which may indicate an overreaction to a news event.

The first clue that prices are overestimated is a significant contrast between the technical market prices of an asset and its actual value (Zhang 2010). Regardless of how thrilling the story about a single stock or the market is, the story is, to a great extent, based on the probabilities of future earnings, cash flow, and economic conditions. If a stock trades at many times its earnings, or if a company with no clear plan for generating revenue sees its value soar to match that of an established business, it raises serious questions. Price, then traders should pause a little. The price jumps that do not relate to the key parameters generally signal that sentiment, rather than logic, is ruling the market. These wrong timings can be the best moment of the year, either to short an overbought asset or to acquire a quality asset that is downtrodden by market fears for no real reason.

Then, there is usually media, both traditional financial news and the growing, dominant social media. Whether it is excessive or merely a hype of optimism, it can catalyse overreaction. The press either promotes stock as the future number one with facts or declares that the market is hopeless, and the reactions are only an exaggeration (Bradley and Oates 2021). Think of the fear of missing out and herd behaviour that are both the right knives to cut off the prices that spiralled out of control. A prudent investor is wise enough to identify the times when sentiment becomes dominant, influencing the market. The recognition of a situation where emotion is ruling the market instead of data allows such investors to act inversely, selling during periods of irrational exuberance and buying during uncertain times of depression.

Markets are emotional ecosystems, and, like any ecosystem under pressure, they can react wildly to the most minor changes. Table 11.1 presents a behavioural roadmap through this chaotic terrain, capturing the telltale signs that a market has strayed from reason and stumbled into the realm of overreaction. One of the most precise signals is unusual price volatility in the absence of the corresponding fundamental news. Picture a company missing earnings expectations by a mere cent, hardly a catastrophe, yet its stock plummets by 15% in a single day. This is not logical at work; it is the availability heuristic and loss aversion playing the puppeteer role. Investors anchor their expectations to headline figures, rather than the context; when these expectations are not met, fear triggers an outsized response. These episodes are not random; they are predictable symptoms of a crowd driven by emotion, rather than evidence. When do trading volumes spike with no new data in sight? That is, the market echoes the noise of herd behaviour, where investors trade not because they know something but because they are afraid of being left behind.

However, within this chaos lies a rare type of clarity for those who know where to look. The divergence of stock prices from intrinsic value, the breathless media coverage that portrays every dip as a disaster, and the sharp reversals without any meaningful news, each is a flare signalling irrationality (Kirilenko et al. 2017). Overreaction is not just a risk; it is also an opportunity to dress in panic. Investors who can see past fear and question the hype rather than follow it are often the ones who capitalise on these market misfires (Siegel 2024). Think back to March 2020, when pandemic-fuelled fear knocked the S&P 500 into a downward spiral. The headlines screamed for the collapse, but the fundamentals of many firms remained solid. Those who saw the noise and stepped into the storm emerged months later with remarkable gains. Table 11.1 is more than a checklist; it serves as a comprehensive guide to emotional intelligence in finance. In an era of algorithmic trading and digital frenzy, understanding these behavioural patterns offers a competitive edge, helping investors not only to survive the storm but to sail ahead of it.

The ability to recognise the signs of a sag in the market due to overreaction is an indispensable skill for any investor who wishes not only to survive but also to win in the transient condition. The markets stand, though, as a jungle where emotional control is never possible; being the one to differentiate the noise from reality is the key that will drop you on the right side of the deal most of the time.

Table 11.1 Signals of market overreaction

Signal of overreaction	Description	Market impact	Investment implication
Unusual price volatility	Sudden, extreme price changes not supported by fundamental news (e.g. a 15% drop on a minor earnings miss)	Heightened uncertainty, panic-driven selling or buying	Signals potential mispricing; opportunity for contrarian investors to enter/exit strategically
Sharp divergence from intrinsic value	Market price strays significantly from valuation metrics (e.g. P/E, book value, DCF)	Disconnect between market sentiment and true fundamentals	Indicates potential reversion to mean; investors may position for rebound or correction
High trading volumes with no new information	Surge in trades despite absence of earnings, news, or macro events	Reflects speculation rather than informed trading	Suggests emotional response; warrants caution or opportunistic entry
Media frenzy and sensational headlines	Overwhelming media coverage that amplifies fear or euphoria (e.g. 'black Monday', 'crypto to the moon')	Drives crowd behaviour, inflates bubbles or deepens sell-offs	Contrarian investors can take advantage by fading hype once fundamentals are reassessed
Overreaction to minor news or earnings misses	Severe market response to slight underperformance or neutral guidance	Triggers unjustified panic; can cause undervaluation of quality stocks	Identify quality assets on discount for long-term gain
Persistent momentum with no justified growth	Stocks or assets rallying solely on recent past performance, not on forward-looking fundamentals	Unsustainable price levels, eventual reversal or correction	Red flag for overbought positions; ideal point to take profits or short
Price recovery without fundamental change	Sharp rebound after a panic-driven sell-off despite no material news or updates	Suggests overreaction correction is underway	Opportunity to ride recovery if timing entry after panic

Source: Authors' work

11.3 Using Data to Identify Overreaction Patterns

11.3.1 Volatility Measures

Volatility is the heart rate of a financial market. It captures not only the extent to which prices fluctuate but also whether rational or emotional factors drive those shifts. When fear seizes the market, volatility is at its peak, and when the market is complacent, it becomes insignificant (Day et al. 2023). Those who want to catch the overreaction with perfect timing can look for the volatility level, like the best alarm system, which directly shows investors' mental state in real-time.

An ever-tuned barometer of market anxiety is the VIX, or Volatility Index, which is often noted as the 'fear gauge' for the market. The VIX represents the expected volatility of the S&P 500 over the next 30 days, derived from the prices of options. During calm periods, the VIX remains quiet, serving as an accurate gauge of absolute market confidence. However, when uncertainty prevails, passing through economic data shocks, geopolitical upheavals, or financial crises, the index peaks. A VIX that jumps suddenly shows a strong fear sentiment in the market, leading to brainless selling of stocks and deepening market overreaction. Earlier, the extremities of the VIX successfully predicted the best chances for long-term investors to buy. During the peak of the panic, when the VIX reaches its highest levels, it is the bold investors who swim against the current who often reap the most significant benefits.

Market overreaction is not always as apparent as a VIX spike; it sometimes collects in the past consequences of volatility. With the help of the historical volatility of an asset and its current volatility figure, investors can identify moments when the market's mood has shifted significantly. For example, a stock which often trades with an average daily price swing of 1% but, for some time, deviates to about 5% or more will experience a rather unusual situation. This is the moment when volatility enters the picture, and it becomes a diagnostic tool for investors. They can decide whether the price movement is a rational response or an emotional overreaction.

The beauty of volatility analysis is that it forces investors to disregard momentary noise and focus on the overall picture. If volatility spikes but fundamentals remain intact, it implies that the market has overreacted; hence, it presents a good opportunity to make an interesting purchase in that asset. Conversely, if volatility remains low while economic uncertainties grow, it could be a signal of a market stage setting for a probable shock in the future, presenting an intellectual challenge to extinguish emotional fires. If investors are informed about such relationships, they can make informed strategic decisions rather than being swayed by public emotions.

Volatility is far more than just a tool for measuring price changes. It is an expression of real human behaviour. Fear and greed, panic, and overjoyment impact volatility metrics (Reddy et al. 2021). Those who manage to decode these signals correctly can transform the disorder of market overreactions into smart and calculated opportunities, thereby using rational judgement in uncertain situations. In contrast, others let themselves be influenced by emotional turbulence.

11.3.2 Sentiment Analysis and Investor Surveys

The fact that emotional drivers, rather than merely numbers, move markets is a psychological breakthrough for investors. Learning to understand sentiment in financial markets is akin to having a window into the collective psyche of the market, where one can discern whether fear or greed is prevailing (Du et al. 2024). There is a traditional way of analysing the financial sector, which primarily involves balance sheets and earnings reports. However, the absolute mastery in detecting an overreaction lies in the ability of investors to gauge the collective mood of the market. This is where sentiment analysis and investor surveys were conducted.

In the current digital era, the evolution of artificial intelligence (AI) has completely soured the sentiment tracking process. The AI-driven algorithms can scan thousands of news articles, social media posts, and trading patterns in real-time. Thus, they are able to spot the shift in investor mood well ahead of it being reflected in stock prices. Analysis of the language used in financial news, social media chatter, and corporate earnings calls is one of the mechanisms through which AI can visualise the sentiments of people and businesses on a large scale (Saleh and Semaan 2024). As an illustration, if Twitter users are filled with joyful mentions of a specific stock or cryptocurrency, the AI models can show the confidence which is developing in the stock market. Instead, suppose the news is filled with people discussing a recession. In that case, the AI might sometimes observe over-pessimism, as the understatement of the company's risk is already priced in due to profits that have already been capitalised. These tools for tracking sentiment have become the mainstay of hedge funds, institutional investors, and even retail traders who aim to outperform the broader market.

Nevertheless, although AI sentiment tracking is in vogue, investor surveys remain the tried-and-true method for measuring the market's psychology. For instance, the AAII Investor Sentiment Survey, which aims to determine whether retail investors are bullish, bearish, or neutral about the market economy, is a valuable tool for exploring the average investor's perspective on the future of the stock market. A situation in which bullish sentiment skyrockets is often a sign of an overheated market, and thus, a downturn is likely to follow (Agarwal et al. 2024). Conversely, the point at which bearish sentiment is at its lowest is when fear has reached its peak; generally, this means that a buying opportunity is soon to arise. These surveys are a type of contrarian indicator that helps investors determine the best strategy to identify when the crowd either benefits too much or remains indifferent to its benefits.

Sentiment analysis, regardless of whether AI goes for it or if it is the survey method, is a capable way to find out the market overreaction. This method enables investors to distinguish between two types of market movements: one driven by rational decisions and the other influenced by emotional biases. By providing the investor with the current state of their mood, it would be easier to anticipate a situation where the investor's sentiment has become the primary reason and the market is overreacting; thus, it can be intelligently turned around.

11.3.3 Price Deviation from Intrinsic Value

Emotions dictate the markets in which self-determination is concerned. It is well known that the intrinsic worth of assets is a concept contrary to this (Sachdeva et al. 2022). There is a fundamental value for every asset based on its income, growth, and the outlook of the surrounding industry. In other words, time after time, through the influence of the crowd, prices deviate significantly from their intrinsic reality. The key to identifying mispricing lies in understanding the deviations that occur. When prices diverge considerably from their inherent value, savvy investors spot an opportunity to buy an asset they believe the market has undervalued or overvalued, which they consider to be irrational.

Mispricing exposure models are the primary tools for identifying such sources of error, and fundamental valuation models serve this purpose. Tools such as cash flow (DCF) analysis, price-to-earnings (P/E) ratios, and book value comparisons enable investors to determine the price that an asset should achieve based on quantifiable financial metrics. For instance, a stock that trades at 50 times its earnings while its industry peers average 15 P/E seems clouded in darkness. Either the stock itself is overhyped and, therefore, worth more than its actual value; otherwise, or the rest of the market is not able to figure out the company's growth potential. The exact nature of the case is a stock with increased revenue and better margins, which, however, falls suddenly due to short-term worries, but may still be a great buying option. Investors using objective fundamental data as a frame of reference can quickly identify the difference between an appropriate adjustment and an incorrect one, which can cause mispricing.

Furthermore, the valuation process is not limited to the unique enterprise level; it also relates to the entire market. Economic gauges, such as GDP growth, inflation rates, and employment statistics, provide the necessary framework for determining whether market principles are grounded in fact or fiction. Numerous cases exist where market psychology causes individuals to perceive what they think they see (Nurwulandari and Wahid 2023). Exemplifying this, when stock prices drop drastically due to high corporate profit reports or a flourishing economy, it directly conveys miscommunication. Otherwise, if high surpluses are registered simultaneously with weak market economy movements, they signal excessive enthusiasm in the index. Benchmarks are further valuable, if not invaluable, in this exercise. When an asset's performance deviates significantly from its sector, there should be an explanation from the market's origin, likely due to a luxury or fair-weather customer selling it, or perhaps for other reasons.

The market can ignore intrinsic value for extended periods, but eventually, the fundamentals prevail. Those who track these deviations gain an edge: they buy when fear has driven prices too low and sell when speculation has pushed them too high.

11.4 Tools for Mitigating Emotional Investment Decisions

In a saturated market, the most significant enemy of an investor is emotion. Most of the time, emotions such as fear and greed can cloud good judgement, leading to hasty actions that result in losses. This often involves buying high and selling low, the opposite of a successful strategy (Rehman et al. 2024). Although no one can ultimately win the battle against emotions, those who manage to stand out are those who find a way to counteract them. What distinguishes an investor from others who are subjected to short-term panic is the ability to be rational, especially in volatile markets. The secret is not just knowing but acting with discipline, frameworks, and safeguards that keep one's emotions in check.

The most effective way to hedge emotional investment is to establish disciplined investment rules, clear, pre-defined strategies that eliminate guesswork from decision-making. This approach involves establishing strict entry and exit points for stone, defining risk tolerance, and adhering to an allocation strategy regardless of market fluctuations. For example, an investor would decide to never allocate more than 5% of their portfolio to a single stock or always take gains when an asset rises by 20% beyond its value. The safeguards serve as a buffer against taking over, allowing emotions to be managed during periods of shared turbulence. A well-planned investment strategy confirms that the decisions made are based on logic, not impulse, and that investors do not pursue hype or exit at the first sign of difficulties.

Only discipline falls short; a solid understanding of behavioural finance is just as crucial for keeping a rational mind. The behavioural finance framework helps investors identify and mitigate psychological biases that lead to poor decision-making. For instance, in loss aversion, the impulse always feels the negative side of losses heavier than the positive side of gains (Bhatia et al. 2022). This bias often leads to holding onto losing positions for too long, waiting for a miracle, or losing some profits by selling winners too early because of fear. By recognising these habits, investors can practice becoming more neutral by looking at what the data show instead of what their feelings recommend. Similarly, an understanding of recency bias, the tendency to overreact to recent events, prevents investors from acting excessively in fluctuating markets. A single missed earnings does not equal a ruined company, and one strong quarter does not guarantee a secure future.

Another tool is contrarian investment, a strategy that counters the crowd when emotions are at extremes. History teaches us that the most favourable moments often come when greed or fear is at its maximum. When markets are at their most excited, the risk is frequently at its highest; however, when panic prevails, the situation is the opposite. Successful contrarian investors do not follow the crowd; instead, they identify when the mood has shifted too far in one direction and take the opposite side. This is not to say that one should buy without thinking when prices drop or sell when prices increase, but rather to spot discrepancies between the market price and intrinsic value due to collective deeds. Warren Buffett has expressed it best 'Be fearful when others are greedy, and greedy when others are fearful' which gives the best summary of this mindset.

Even in the presence of discipline and awareness, human emotions can take the front stage with extreme volatility (Rekar et al. 2023). This is where automated risk controls are implemented. Solutions such as stop-loss orders, automated rebalancing, and algorithmic trading can eliminate the tendency of human beings to make emotionally driven decisions. For instance, a stop-loss order guarantees that a position will be automatically sold if it falls below a specific threshold, thereby guarding the investor against holding onto losing positions due to denial or wishful thinking.

Automated portfolio rebalancing ensures that asset allocations are aligned with long-term goals, whereas investors sell high and buy low in the natural course of action. By integrating automation into their approach, investors can mitigate the risk of making impulsive trades that could otherwise undermine their long-term gains.

Mastery of emotional control is the most substantial asset in investing, and it is not something you acquire overnight. This involves training, self-awareness, and the use of appropriate tools to manage one's emotions. People who can separate themselves from their financial decisions will navigate market turbulence and change more effectively, rather than allowing it to dictate their destiny.

11.5 Conclusion

Financial markets serve more than just as a barometer of economic health. They are also an arena where emotions of fear, greed, euphoria, and panic often shape price movement more than other factors, for instance, pushing assets well past their actual value. It requires both technical and behavioural expertise to discern these irrational and extreme market reactions; indeed, it is a life skill that has the potential to make and break one's investment career. When one can see that prices have deviated too far from a realistic level, one can capitalise on the mispricing by purchasing underpriced assets that have been undervalued due to the fear factor or by selling when prices are inflated far beyond reason through irrational exuberance. It is not about forecasting the future that is long-term success in investing; it is about being rational while others are losing their heads.

In an environment where market trends change rapidly, emotional noise does not align with a powerful data-oriented approach. The rise of AI has led to the development of sentiment analysis, driven by social media, volatility tracking, and fundamental financial models, enabling low investors to gain insight into market behaviour. This software sifts genuine economic drivers from those caused by mass hysteria, allowing the investors to rely on the logic of the situation rather than their instincts. Whether it monitors VIX spikes, tracks social media sentiment, or examines prices in relation to earnings and industry benchmarks, videos perform heavy lifting in quantifying the market's state. If correctly managed, quantitative-based strategies yield sufficient transparency, enabling marketers to shift their focus from fear and insecurity to one of risk and return.

However, the recognition of the error is only one-half of the battle, and the other half is resisting it. The formulation of both mentality and strategy is necessary to retain financial flexibility. As long as the market is volatile, breaks will occur, providing concrete opportunities for quick decisions with fears and brows. This is the magic of the rigid set of rules for investing, the counterintuitive notion that operates in this way, and the automated risk control that legislation delivers. These are sturdy platforms that will carry you over the simply unreasonable stages of making emotional decisions. Those with self-discipline to rein in their emotions, concentrate on the long term, and thus act wisely will not merely endure a market tumult; they will actually prosper.

The essence of winning in the investment field is a simple fact: the market may misprice, but you do not have to. Those who perceive the moment when emotions drive the majority will always be ahead of the curve. Adopting a resilient outlook for navigating turbulent economic times through data-driven insights, strict discipline, and cultivating a resilient mental mindset ensures that investors can convert the chaos of market overreactions into opportunities. In the final analysis, as far as financial success is concerned, it is not who is the smartest in the room but who is the most rational.

References

Agarwal V, Taffler RJ, Wang C (2024) Investor emotions and market bubbles. Rev Quant Finan Acc 64(1):339–369

Bhatia A, Chandani A, Divekar R, Mehta M, Vijay N (2022) Digital innovation in wealth management landscape: the moderating role of robo advisors in behavioural biases and investment decision-making. Int J Innov Sci 14(3/4):693–712

Bradley C, Oates HE (2021) The multi-level marketing pandemic. Tenn Law Rev 89:321

Day MY, Huang P, Cheng Y, Ni Y (2023) Investing strategies for trading stocks, considering overreactions triggered by technical trading rules and concerns related to big data. Rom J Econ Forecast 26:148–161

Du K, Xing F, Mao R, Cambria E (2024) Financial sentiment analysis: techniques and applications. ACM Comput Surv 56(9):1–42

Hendershott T, Jones CM, Menkveld AJ (2011) Does algorithmic trading improve liquidity? J Financ 66(1):1–33

Kirilenko A, Kyle A, Samadi M, Tuzun T (2017) The flash crash: high-frequency trading in an electronic market. J Financ 72(3):967–998

Nurwulandari A, Wahid RS (2023) The effect of debt-to-equity ratio, return on asset, current ratio, and total asset turnover on stock price: the intervening effect of intrinsic value in Indonesia's retail business. Shirkah J Econ Business 9(1):1–16

Reddy K, Qamar MAJ, Mirza N, Shi F (2021) Overreaction effect: evidence from an emerging market (Shanghai stock market). Int J Manag Financ 17(3):416–437

Rehman M, Dhiman B, Nguyen ND, Dogra R, Sharma A (2024) Behavioural biases and regional diversity: an in-depth analysis of their influence on investment decisions-a SEM & MICOM approach. Qubahan Acad J 4(2):70–85

Rekar P, Pahor M, Perat M (2023) Effect of emotion regulation difficulties on financial decision-making. J Neurosci Psychol Econ 16(2):80

Sachdeva M, Fotheringham S, Li Z (2022) Do places have value? Quantifying the intrinsic value of housing neighborhoods using MGWR. J Hous Res 31(1):24–52

Saleh L, Semaan S (2024) The potential of AI in performing financial sentiment analysis for predicting entrepreneur survival. Admin Sci 14(9):220

Siegel E (2024) The AI playbook: mastering the rare art of machine learning deployment. MIT Press, Cambridge

Yang Y, Zhang Y, Wu M, Zhang K, Zhang Y, Yu H, Wang B (2025) TwinMarket: a scalable behavioural and social simulation for financial markets. arXiv preprint arXiv:2502.01506

Zakamulin V (2024) Stock price overreaction: evidence from bull and bear markets. Rev Behav Financ 16(6):998–1011

Zhang F (2010) High-frequency trading, stock volatility, and price discovery. Social Science Research Network, Working Paper Series, pp 1–44

Chapter 12
Strategies to Avoid Overreaction

12.1 Introduction

The financial market is a complex and dynamic entity comprising numerous elements, including investor psychology, external economic forces, and fundamental analysis. At the same time, overreaction behavioural bias is one of the most persistent and costly fungal infections for both private investors and institutions as it grows in this entangled web. When the relationship between speculation and stock prices becomes loose, and the illusion of truth takes hold, people often sell stocks for less than they are ultimately worth. This outcome can lead to unwarranted increases in value, bubble formation, and lateral crashes due to fear of loss. The neurophysiology of humans, despite technological advancements and the increased availability of financial data, presents fundamental reasons for market inefficiencies; thus, overreaction is an inevitable reality.

In addition, addressing the issue of overreaction remains vital with the advent of social media, algorithmic trading, and real-time news broadcasting, all of which create market sentiment hype at record speed. Investors are overwhelmed by this deluge of information, which makes it harder for them to distinguish between what is essential and what is worthless. Fear and greed, the two primary emotions driving financial decisions, are the prevailing forces that push individuals into ill-advised actions—buying high when euphoria is at its peak or selling low when panic is at its height. Funds and institutions are often perceived as more rational than individual investors, but they are also susceptible to these influences. Fund managers may become disoriented not only with the herd mentality but also under pressure from clients or short-term performance standards, which can exacerbate market conditions. Even if a person is an experienced investor, without a proper framework for handling these emotional traumas, they may make irrational decisions that will impact their long-term financial success.

The topic focuses on the primary causes of overreaction and practical actions that can be taken to make a positive impact. If you are aware of the psychological

K. L. Ooi et al., *Following the Crowd: Psychological Drivers of Herding and Market Overreaction*, https://doi.org/10.1007/978-981-95-0792-4_12

and cognitive biases that are responsible for overreaction, then you have a chance to come up with ways to keep your head cool and to be more rational when you make decisions. The presentation primarily focuses on three central routes: systematic saving and budgeting, financial knowledge and training, and adopting a long-term perspective to counteract short-term fluctuations. This means that investors develop resistance to triggering emotions and, consequently, make more balanced, logical, and profitable decisions in the investment process. In the following sections, we undertake a comprehensive analysis of each of these strategies, along with practical recommendations, to help investors manage the unpredictable market with newfound confidence and clarity.

12.2 Building Disciplined Investment Habits

The path to successful investment does not lie in having a flawless plan or making a lucky stock choice but rather in strict discipline. In financial markets, where volatility is extreme and investors' emotions frequently cloud their judgement, designing a strategy to remain firm in the face of the unknown often distinguishes the great from the rest, who are overwhelmed by their mistakes (Gurung et al. 2023). The investment discipline is not a talent cultivated by nature but rather a behaviour formed by examining and correcting weaknesses in personal practices. This is the only way to maintain a solid investment policy, which emotional reactions and market noise could otherwise compromise.

A potent method for building a discipline is to establish a set of predefined investment rules. These rules work as safeguards, making it impossible for investors to be affected by temporary fear or faulty market responses (Thaler and Sunstein 2008). For example, whether it is to decide a fixed percentage of funds for each asset, to set distinct thresholds of loss protection, or to stick to a punctual schedule of rebalancing, the presence of clear rules brings about a considerable reduction in lending one's self to confusion about fear or greed that drives an investor to act hastily. Legendary investor Warren Buffett follows one simple yet powerful rule: 'Be fearful when others are greedy, and greedy when others are fearful'. The principle of this maxim represents the need to neutralise emotional impulses through a rationally predetermined initiative.

Another key segment of the discipline is to formalise a systematic approach to trading and investing. A clearly defined strategy, whether it employs value investing, growth investing, momentum trading, or passive index tracking, ensures standardisation and helps eliminate randomness from the decision-making process. This systematic approach is a real divider between professionals and amateurs. The same is true for systematic investors, who base their informed decisions on fundamental analysis, technical analysis, macroeconomic indicators, or quantitative models rather than just reacting to headlines. Therefore, this structure not only breeds confidence but also stamps out the kind of anxiety that leads people to make emotional trades.

Herd mentality is the most critical risk factor for disciplined investment. The markets are turbulent: experts are making astonishing forecasts, the media are reporting high stock prices, and social networks are shaping trends. It can be easily carried away by a stratospherically climbing stock or the dread of falling into a broader market and then acting irrationally. Nevertheless, history has repeatedly shown that those who follow the crowd blindly are often the ones who ultimately suffer the consequences. The destruction of the value of dot-com stocks in the late 1990s, the housing market, which was wildly inflated in the mid-2000s, and cryptocurrencies, which experienced a boom and bust in recent years, serve as clear warnings about the power of the herd mentality. Investors who held on to their principles and stayed away from speculative excesses during these periods flourished much more than those who rode a wave of excitement.

The success of disciplined investors is the best affirmation of the discipline's power (Dekker 2025). Picture someone like Ray Dalio, founder of Bridgewater Associates, one of the world's most significant hedge funds. Every bit of success has primarily been attributed to the disciplined application of his investment principles, which centred on diversification, risk equalisation, and autonomous transaction-making. Another example is Benjamin Graham, the father of value investing and Warren Buffett's mentor, who amassed his wealth through rigorous fundamental analysis, avoidance of speculative trends, and a focus on intrinsic value rather than short-term price fluctuations. Their reliance on discipline created success, rather than relying on chance or the perfect timing of the market.

In the ever-changing and unpredictable environment of financial markets, discipline is the single most valuable trait for any investor. It serves as a protective hedge for making decisions outside the emotional realm, a guard against taking on unnecessary risks, and the groundwork for achieving long-term objectives. People demonstrating discipline do not just outlive the storms of the market; they thrive through them.

12.3 Educating Investors to Resist Emotional Biases

12.3.1 The Role of Behavioural Finance Education

The stock market is more than a number-counting game (Coffee 2011). Instead, it is a game of the mind. Every decision made by an investor is influenced by a complex mix of emotions, biases, and cognitive shortcuts that often lead investors to make incorrect decisions. Behavioural finance, the new science at the intersection of psychology and economics, has forever changed our understanding of investors' behaviour, bringing to light the endemic psychological biases that underlie market malfunctions (De Goey 2023). Investors who learn and apply these ideas have a powerful tool at their disposal: they are capable of recognising the mental traps they fall into and making decisions based on rationale rather than impulse. Thus, even the most sophisticated investment strategies can be compromised by the lack of this insight, as it leads to fear, greed, and overconfidence.

A significant bias in this format is loss aversion, a disposition where one feels the sting of losses more intensely than the joy equivalent gains provide. Explaining the illogic of panic selling, this bias may account for the fact that too many investors not only lock in losses but also miss the opportunity to recover them by remaining in the market. On the other hand, the overconfidence bias attracts investors to think they can outsmart the market. Thus, they end up taking extra risks without proper cognisance of the results. The next in line is confirmation bias, which deters investors from seeing any other reality but the one that they believe in, thus falling prey to unsupported assertions. By dabbling in behavioural finance, investors can uncover patterns in action and tailor-make strategies to mitigate them before they cloud their judgement.

In addition to regulating emotions, an understanding of behavioural finance also sharpens the investment skill of thinking probabilistically, which is essential for effective risk management. Markets are inherently unpredictable, and no strategy or research guarantees success (Khedlekar et al. 2024). The wisest investors are those who do not think in absolutes; instead, they consider probabilities. Rather than putting all their funds on one stock or betting on only one market forecast, they evaluate the risks in terms of what is likely to happen, thereby hedging and diversifying their portfolios to palliate uncertainty. This shift in perspective, conceiving investment as a game of probabilities rather than certainties, helps keep investors grounded during exceptional events.

The application of this principle was evident in the case of billionaire investor Howard Marks, who not only put forward the first but also the second-level thinking by considering a range of outcomes instead of just one. Like Mark's poker champion, Annie Duke, who is now a hedge fund manager, treats investment decisions as probabilities, noting that even a well-measured bet cannot guarantee a win; the goal is to make the right decisions in the long run.

The aim of teaching investors behavioural finance is not only based on theory but also to reform the way they think about risk and how they make decisions in general (Edmans 2023). Those who make an effort to recognise the cognitive traps they fall into and adjust their thinking to consider probabilities gain the ability to withstand the emotional storms of market participation, which is a rare skill. The ability to remain rational in a cluttered world, where financial news headlines, social media discussions, and economic ambiguity trigger a knee-jerk reaction, is a competitive edge that far exceeds the benefits of any specific investment decision.

12.3.2 Institutional Investor Training Programmes

In the multimillion-dollar finance sector, where transactions are often completed amid lightning-fast algorithms, it is a natural reaction to think that big institutional investors are immune to emotional traps (Schwarcz 2009). Hedge funds, asset managers, and pension funds use data-driven models, algorithms, and quantitative strategies designed to automate the decision-making process (Khan et al. 2022). Paradoxically, these tools do not help solve the problem of human overreaction but exacerbate it. The main reason is that even when advanced technology is involved in institutional finance, it is still people who make all critical decisions.

A solution to this is found in some of the leading financial institutions that implement training programmes emphasising the importance of rational and discussed decision-making. In these courses, portfolio managers and analysts are trained on how to use quantitative tools that find investment opportunities based on probabilities rather than emotions. The most essential components of these programmes are data-driven models that process market data, identify inefficiencies, and execute orders accurately (Ghodake et al. 2024). Using these models, managers cannot avoid relying on rounded guesses or intuitive feelings that often lead to poor decision-making. Institutional investors strive to make their choices as objective as possible, utilising historical trends, machine learning algorithms, and risk-adjusted metrics.

Companies such as Renaissance Technologies and Citadel, which are hedge funds, have based their operations on the idea that machines can perform tasks that humans cannot, and have developed trading models that analyse millions of variables in real-time. Similarly, organisations using factor investing strategies, such as AQR Capital Management, leverage deep statistical analysis to create portfolios that are not influenced by biases, including overreaction and herd mentality (Zhang et al. 2024). They recognise that emotional cycles, fear, greed, euphoria, and panic are the primary forces driving market trends, which is why they develop their models to capitalise on such inefficiencies rather than suffer from them.

Despite the training and technology employed, institutional investors still have the potential to overreact to market fluctuations. Historical records indicate that the fear of institutions has been a contributing factor to some of the most spectacular financial market crashes in history. For instance, during the 2008 financial crisis, investment banks and hedge funds, along with their vast resources and expertise, became entangled in a cycle of overleveraged bets, forced liquidations, and extreme risk aversion. The same was true in March 2020, when the COVID-19 crash occurred as institutions panicked and dumped their stocks quickly, while markets rebounded sky-high after a few weeks.

Therefore, if we are to examine the most skilled professionals, why do they still occasionally fall into overreaction traps? Physicists of the institutional finance system explain such phenomena. Mutual fund managers are constantly under pressure to meet quarterly performance standards, as well as high-net-worth investor expectations for a good return, and competitive benchmarks create an environment that prioritises short-term thinking over long-term strategy. Even in the most unbearable situations, such as when developing a strong investment thesis, the manager may be fearful of underperforming competitors or disappointing clients, which prompts them to make impulsive decisions, abandoning their models in favour of crowd psychology.

Furthermore, the dimensions in which these institutions operate imply that their actions may be self-reinforcing. One large seller taking off a position makes it difficult for the automated selling of many funds, which leads to chain reactions throughout the market (Park 2023). This was readily apparent in the case of the 1998 long-term capital management (LTCM) disaster, where a high-level hedge fund, managed by economists who had won a Nobel Prize, was vulnerable to market panic despite relying heavily on advanced quantitative models.

Finally, while data-driven techniques and institutional programmes can significantly diminish emotional decision-making, they are not entirely cured. The principal nature of markets is unchanged; they are pictures of human beings; they are arbitrary, unpredictable, and often go to extremes. The most competent institutional investors see this paradox and manage to strike a proper balance. They rely on technology and models for guidance, but still realise that no system is infallible. To sum up, the success of institutional investing is not just about being emotionless, but rather about managing emotions wisely.

12.4 The Role of Long-Term Thinking in Mitigating Overreaction

Navigating a reality where stock values change in an instant and financial news cycles operate at lightning speed is an exceptional yet priceless feature. However, in a world where financial markets favour delay, most people cannot overcome the repetitiveness of the loop where they act according to temporary market shifts, seek quick returns, and ultimately panic over temporary losses. Of course, the point of history is that those who choose to adopt a long-term view, not just in terms of holding time but in the entirety of how they consistently generate wealth, outperform short-term attempts. Long-term investors not only deal with unpredictable scenarios but also work to transform them into a more favourable position in the game.

The basis for long-term investment is the ability to disregard noise. Financial media perpetuates conflicts through sensationalism; each earnings miss, economic data release, or geopolitical casualty is described as a possible market-disrupting catastrophe. Social media pushes this further, disseminating fear and hype on an unprecedented scale. However, the plain fact is that most of this information is irrelevant to the broader aspects of investing (Kim et al. 2023). Stock prices are volatile on a daily basis, while general business issues take years, if not centuries. Companies that regularly generate cash flow, enjoy strong alliances, and have the ability to adapt to management will thrive, regardless of temporary headwinds. Investors who remain clear of short-term noise and perceive the full complexity of wealth creation are those who possess the insight to capture it.

Few investors can do this as well as Warren Buffett, the Oracle of Omaha, who is a symbol of this, as his legendary results are primarily based on a straightforward yet influential belief: ‘Be greedy when others are fearful, and fearful when others are greedy'. Buffett and other value investors are the beneficiaries of the market shifting towards the extreme. Thus, the apparent solution is to wait for the counter-intuitive move when a company of a high calibre is haggled below its actual price. During times of fear, such as economic recessions, financial crises, or temporary operational glitches, value investors act. They acquire great businesses at reduced prices when the majority of investors are forced to sell due to panic and market uncertainty. This approach of discipline and contrarianism has prompted them to achieve outsized returns through multiple bear markets and economic downturns, as well as during the years that have been the star of this show, Buffett's Berkshire Hathaway.

We must never minimise the strength of persistence in investment. The stocks that have had the best returns in history, such as Apple, Amazon, and Microsoft, underwent significant short-term drops. Still, they had a long-term success trajectory that ultimately mattered. Investors who held onto them, rather than acting out of fear and parting with them initially, achieved extraordinary results. This assertion holds for all asset classes: real estate, index funds, and dividend stocks are all channels that compound wealth over long periods, but only for those who resist the temptation to enter and exit based on rash market conditions.

Long-term investing is another strong pillar of diversification, an approach that not only increases profit but also decreases the risk of taking a wrong bet. Economic downturns are inevitable, but a diversified mix of investments across stocks, bonds, commodities, and other alternatives is more effective in mitigating the impact than putting all eggs in one basket (Swedroe 2024). By dispersing their portfolios across sectors, regions, and asset types, long-term investors create a protective financial framework that shields against rocky paths. They found that temporary market dips do not last, but the rule is that remaining in the market is key to a larger share of economic growth.

However, long-term thinking is more than just holding investments for a specific period; in fact, it is a mindset that is deeper than the market's fluctuations at any given moment. It must be recognised that wealth is not created by reacting to every article but by matching investments with the principles that have prevailed for ages (Kapil and Rawal 2023). It touches on the personal courage to withstand the drops, the discipline to carry on the path, and the wisdom to exploit the wrong valuation instead of being prey to it. With the world increasingly focused on immediate gratification, it is rare to see long-term investors; however, they are ultimately the true winners.

12.5 Case Study: The 2020 COVID-19 Market Crash and the Benefits of Long-Term Investing

12.5.1 Background

Forget March 2020 did not emerge as a chaotic period in financial history. The COVID-19 pandemic, which had been a distant concern for most countries around the world at the start of the year, unexpectedly evolved into a global crisis. Countries went into lockdown, businesses closed abruptly, and uncertainty spread like wildfires through every part of the economy. The stock market, which is based on stability and predictability, took its only route: a spectacular collapse that left everyone stunned.

During the crash, the S&P 500 Index dropped by nearly 30% within weeks, closing with one of the highest and fastest declines in history. Fear engulfed the market like a dark cloud, as investors struggled to grasp the economic implications of the event. Companies slashed their profit estimates, logistics systems came to a standstill, and the unemployment rate skyrocketed to its highest level ever. The economic system was in crisis, and panic selling was the norm. Mutual funds, hedge funds, and individual investors followed a similar pattern of closing positions, believing it was the only way to escape the carnage before the situation worsened. Margin calls forced even seasoned professionals to sell, creating a cascading effect that intensifies the decline. Although many investors left in a hurry, another group made affirmative investments. Long-term investors who realised, with the help of the eternal wisdom of the past, that the economy would recover remained steady.

The difference between the two categories was eye-catching. Many people, driven by panic, sold at the low in March, leaving them with the regrettable decision of missing a historic market recovery when the S&P 500 bounced back sharply in a matter of months, fuelled by massive fiscal stimulus and a wave of innovation. The ultimate message of March 2020 was timeless: the market is resilient, overreacting results in costly mistakes, and patience, combined with conviction, is the reward for those who believe in the future.

12.5.2 How Long-Term Investors Benefited

When panic takes over in the market, rationality is often the first thing to go. In March 2020, as stocks plummeted and financial headlines touted, many investors acted instinctively by selling. This fear is justifiable. The world was coming to a halt, numerous sectors were on the verge of collapse, and countless economic forecasts were being painted. However, this history had already been written. Every market crash, such as the Great Depression, the dot-com bubble, or the 2008 financial crisis, eventually recovered. Those who noticed the pattern and decided not to get carried away with the madness emerged from the crisis better than before.

The most significant blunder that retail investors likely made during the COVID-19 crash was selling at the bottom in a state of panic. As the S&P 500 dropped by more than 30% within just a few weeks, investors could no longer bear the losses and ultimately decided to liquidate their portfolios. However, they, in fact, did so irreversibly, locking in their losses forever and missing the profitable turn of events that followed. In a very short period, the market peaked and experienced the fastest recovery. The S&P 500, which appeared to be in a downward spiral in March, managed to recover all its losses by summer, thanks to aggressive stimulus measures, extremely low interest rates, and renewed investor confidence in the economy's strength. Investors who conquered fear and decided to sell were nothing but idle spectators watching stock prices shoot past their pre-crash levels.

Retail investors were disgruntled, and institutional investors spotted this opportunity. Hedge funds, pension funds, and asset managers find that panic-driven, vibrational sell-offs typically lead to extreme market misvaluations. Top-notch corporations whose fundamentals are intact essentially trade at steep discounts, giving those with the courage and capital the key to the front door. Big firms, such as BlackRock and Vanguard, amassed these assets and positioned themselves for long-term benefits by the time the market was corrected. Additionally, Warren Buffett, often portrayed as a traditional conservative investor, also exemplified the essence of patience. Berkshire Hathaway sat on its enormous pile of cash, waiting for the right opportunities to enter into quality companies at dramatically discounted rates. While Buffett did not sell in panic, he embraced a strategy of letting the market come to him. This methodology has brought him success for decades.

The recovery that followed was not just a return to normal; it was actually moving to a higher level. The technology sector provides the best demonstration. The world's turn to remote working, online shopping, and digital services has rendered tech companies the outright champions of the pandemic crisis. Stocks such as Amazon, Tesla, and Apple reached their all-time highs, thus rewarding investors who had the foresight (or just discipline) to stick to their positions. The Nasdaq, which dropped during the initial panic, rebounded in just a couple of months and then broke all previous records. Those who sold in March were not only deprived of one of the most profitable bull runs in history, but also proved once again that it is short-term, primarily fear-based concerns that present a problem for investors.

The COVID-19 crash was a historical turning point in the market realm, not because of its pace and intensity, but because it proved to be classic evidence of how long-range considerations outpace emotional volatility. Investors who exercised patience, ignoring the hype, and especially appreciated the fundamentals, turned their portfolios from red to green and saw their ROIs become overwhelmingly positive. However, those who weakly surrendered to pressure and manipulated time were given an extremely tough lesson: markets recover only if you manage to hold them long enough to see it happen.

12.5.3 Lessons on Market Cycles and Recovery Strategies

One thing that can be said about globally universal financial markets is that they exhibit a cyclical character. In the market, the ebb and flow of bullish and bearish moods, as well as the sentiments of joy and despair, have been instrumental in shaping the market throughout the years, and they continue to do so. However, every time a major crash occurs, it seems that investors are shocked anew. The feeling of panic is profound, the emotion of fear is predominant, and rationality often takes a back seat. Nonetheless, history has consistently shown that successful investors are able to maintain patience and discipline in times of crisis, while unsuccessful investors allow fear to dictate their actions.

Market downturns are not apocalyptic scenarios; they are misrepresented blessings. Every crash, regardless of how irreparable it might have appeared at the time, was eventually followed by a recovery. The Great Depression, Black Monday, the dot-com bubble, the 2008 financial crisis, and the COVID-19 crash all felt like doomsday. Still, market cycle-savvy individuals were aware that a comeback was inevitable. The investors who remained on the course, those who neither sold out of fear nor sought out deals but instead bought undervalued stocks, were the ones who prevailed. In this case, the market rewards those who can see beyond the short-term market mayhem and recognise the general trends that will exist over the years to come.

One of the worst mistakes one can make while investing is to deviate from the predetermined course due to momentary panic. It is inherent in human beings to take action in pressing situations. When markets collapse, the instinctive reaction is to sell everything, merely to stop the bleeding and escape the anguish of seeing the numbers turn red. However, an unfortunate reality is that such a quick and emotional decision often yields the opposite of what one hopes to achieve. Selling when the market is at its lowest makes sure you give up on losses forever, while staying in the game gives your portfolio a chance to recover. Indeed, in light of this historical evidence, some of the immediate gains in the stock market have occurred immediately after crises, during which the market experienced a sharp downturn. Avoiding just a handful of these recovery days can have a profound impact in the long run.

A more effective approach, consistently proven to work over time, is to stick to the basics and adhere to long-term investment strategies. Strong companies with a sound business model, high earning power, and competitors that are not easily duplicated do not just disappear when the stock market decreases. Instead of worrying about price fluctuations, disciplined investors focus value of their shareholders. This is why investment titans such as Warren Buffett and Charlie Munger advocate for purchasing quality businesses at fair prices and holding them for an extended period, rather than chasing short-term fads.

Those who comprehend the cyclic nature of the market know that bad days are not for retreat but for preparation. Intelligent speculative traders consider the strikes, as a matter of fact, to buy excellent stocks at a cut-rate price, realising that the market's emotionality will sometimes provide the best bargains. They rebalance their portfolios, gain exposure to undervalued assets, and position themselves to benefit from the recovery that will come in due time. This strategy is rooted in confidence rather than fear, confidence in the very survival of businesses, the robust economy, and the time-tested patterns that have always governed the market.

The clarity derived from past financial crises and the COVID-19 crash is always the same: patience and rationality prevail. Those who stick to the plan, those who are not swayed by emotions, and those who acknowledge that the market's cycles are inherent to the operating life of an investor are bound to flourish. Investing is not simply a matter of dealing with ups and downs, but instead accepting that, in the long run, the market is likely to trend higher. The worst thing a person can conceive of as an investor is the belief that market crashes are forever. The best and most significant capital an investor can possess is the ability to look at past and current struggles and give consent to the mechanism that drives long-term expansion.

12.6 Conclusion

Equity markets mirror human nature, driven by greed, hopefulness, fear, and insecurity. As long as traders experience emotions while investing, incorrect market moves will always occur. Some clients are concerned about the asset's initially poor performance, leading them to sell it at the very beginning. However, some clients would seek the recommendation of the most popular or favourable traders at the moment; later, they would be burdened by the spec. Flowers that are dried when the air becomes dry. However, the people who recognise the fact that the market becomes out of balance and make prior preparations for these circumstances are those who, in the end, come out victorious.

The essential path to achieving long-term financial goals is to master oneself. Financial education and discipline were also required. Investors who can implement a disciplined approach by strictly adhering to their predetermined moves, rather than letting emotions distract them from market noise, become more resilient to unpredictable market conditions. Investors who strengthen their assets through the acquisition of financial literacy, especially in relationships such as behavioural finance and risk management, learn skills to detect and counteract the biases that arise from psychological factors. The most significant benefit, and of the greatest importance, is that investors who adopt a long-term perspective, prioritising the fundamentals over short-term market movements in price, create real wealth for themselves, regardless of the short-term fluctuations in their investments. The ability to manage emotions. Although markets will always experience their ups and downs, emotional decision-making often leads to costly mistakes. Leading investors do not panic when markets fall, nor do they chase after highs that are unlikely to last. Instead, they maintain composure during turbulence, resist the temptation of short-lived gains, and focus on long-term value. Their approach is grounded in discipline, careful analysis, and the patience to wait for the right opportunities. Be aware that the primary and only keys to investment success, both in preserving and growing those assets, are time, discipline, and a rational mindset. The investment is not about responding to the market's emotions, but rather about overcoming one's own.

References

Coffee JC (2011) Systemic risk after Dodd–frank: contingent capital and the need for regulatory strategies beyond oversight. Columbia Law Rev 111(4):795–847

De Goey JJ (2023) Bullshift: how optimism bias threatens your finances, Dundurn

Dekker S (2025) Restorative just culture: from disciplinary action to meaningful accountability. CRC Press, Boca Raton

Edmans A (2023) The end of ESG. Financ Manag 52(1):3–17

Ghodake SP, Malkar VR, Santosh K, Jabasheela L, Abdufattokhov S, Gopi A (2024) Enhancing supply chain management efficiency: a data-driven approach using predictive analytics and machine learning algorithms. Int J Adv Comput Sci Appl 15:4

Gurung RA, Chick NL, Haynie A (2023) Exploring signature pedagogies: approaches to teaching disciplinary habits of mind. Taylor & Francis, Philadelphia

Kapil S, Rawal V (2023) Sustainable investment and environmental, social, and governance investing: a bibliometric and systematic literature review. Business Ethics Environ Responsib 32(4):1429–1451

Khan PA, Johl SK, Akhtar S, Asif M, Salameh AA, Kanesan T (2022) Open innovation of institutional investors and higher education system in creating open approach for SDG-4 quality education: a conceptual review. J Open Innov Technol Mark Complex 8(1):49

Khedlekar UK, Kumar L, Sharma K, Dwivedi V (2024) An optimal sustainable production policy for imperfect production system with stochastic demand, price, and machine failure with FRW policy under carbon emission. Process Integr Optimiz Sustainab 8(3):919–938

Kim A, Muhn M, Nikolaev V (2023) Bloated disclosures: can ChatGPT help investors process information?. arXiv preprint arXiv:2306.10224

Park A (2023) The conceptual flaws of decentralized automated market making. Manag Sci 69(11):6731–6751

Schwarcz SL (2009) Regulating complexity in financial markets. Wash Univ Law Rev 87(2):211–268

Swedroe LE (2024) Enrich your future: the keys to successful investing. Wiley, Hoboken

Thaler RH, Sunstein CR (2008) Nudge: improving decisions about health, wealth, and happiness. Yale University Press, New Haven

Zhang M, Lu T, Shi C (2024) Navigating the factor zoo: the science of quantitative investing. Taylor & Francis, Philadelphia

Chapter 13
Cultural Influences on Overreaction

13.1 Introduction

In the ultra-competitive environment of financial markets, where billions of dollars can be transferred in an incredibly short period, the importance of culture is often overlooked. While economic models primarily focus on figures, strategies, and market parameters, cultural factors influence how investors perceive and evaluate risk, reward, and uncertainty. Take, for example, a Wall Street trader who decides to make a gamble by trading derivatives, or a local business in Asia that decides to hedge against currency fluctuations. What really matters is the cultural value that people have, and form is the basis on which they interpret, react, and ultimately drive the financial markets. It is not just vital for you to be aware of this. Still, it is essential for anyone wishing to learn more about the irrational behaviour of the stock market and how various regions in the world manage their financial crises.

The key cultural distinction in financial behaviour lies in the difference between collectivist and individualist societies. In collectivist cultures, such as those found to a great extent in many parts of Asia and Latin America, financial decisions primarily emphasise group-oriented, sustainable, and adequate social relations and interpersonal trust. Such societies will have investors who rely more on herd behaviour as they seek social consensus and government interventions to inform their investment decisions, rather than relying on empirical data. On the other hand, individualist societies, such as the United States and Western European countries, are built on self-reliance, personal achievement, and individual risk-taking. Unlike their counterparts, investors in these markets generally display higher levels of confidence in their judgements, which often tends to drive them to more aggressive and novel behaviour and a riskier approach during times of high volatility. This rudimentary distinction leads to a significant disparity in participation rates among stocks, preventing panic selling during economic crises.

Cultural differences in risk perception have significantly altered how investors respond to market fluctuations and situations involving uncertainty. Some societies

K. L. Ooi et al., *Following the Crowd: Psychological Drivers of Herding and Market Overreaction*, https://doi.org/10.1007/978-981-95-0792-4_13

believe that risk is an essential part of success and, thus, embrace it, whereas others see risk as a threat to existence and, therefore, are willing to minimise it at any cost. In nations with a high level of uncertainty avoidance, such as Japan and Germany, investors tend to appreciate longer-term, conservative strategies that emphasise stability and support government regulation. Conversely, cultures in which risk is not feared, such as those in the United States and the United Kingdom, tend to prefer speculative investments, which can lead to more significant market fluctuations but also increase the likelihood of financial complications. These divergences are not simply hypothetical, although they are conspicuous in historical market activities, such as Europe's risk-averse banking system, which operates under heavy regulations, and is comparable to the U.S. venture capital paradigm, where everything is driven by personal interests and perceived as risky.

This chapter characterises cultural stances and their corresponding effects on overmarket overreaction, conducting a comparative study of the East's versus the West's financial systems. It examines how differences in decision-making and risk tolerance, along with regulatory positions, influence investor behaviour in contrasting ways. The focus is on critical financial events, such as the 1997–1998 Asian Financial Crisis, which not only provides insights into this psychology in action but also serves as a window into how cultural norms influence the ordering of markets. By the end of this chapter, learners will be able to draw lessons from the intersection of psychology, culture, and finance, recognising that there are compelling reasons why markets do not always act rationally. Cultural thinking is an invisible power behind the movement of the financial field.

13.2 Cultural Differences in Risk Tolerance and Decision-Making

In the finance sector, where people become millionaires and go broke with great rapidity, investors' attitudes towards risk and the way they make decisions vary significantly. Different cultures have a profound impact on how people and organisations invest their money, which in turn can be a key factor in the distinct financial activities of the West and East (Ahmed et al. 2021). These differences are apparent not only in people's portfolios but also in the economies as a whole. They stand up for the exact way the markets operate during times of crisis, how they recover after the shocks, and what the sequences of good and bad times are. According to the cultural DNA of a society, investors either view risk as a challenge and deal with it effectively or consider it a negative factor and avoid it. It is the same for investors to rely on their judgement or follow the crowd, as well as for governments to take a backseat or intervene when the market is on the verge of collapse.

The principles of individualism predominately govern trading in Western financial markets such as those in the U.S.A., Europe, and Australia. The individual trader's perspective is the highest. Investors are encouraged to take personal responsibility for their financial future by making self-directed investment decisions that represent their risk appetite and long-term goals. The same view fosters a market culture centred on independence, data-driven analysis, and diversification. It is no wonder that many treaty countries have invented derivative hedges and algorithmic trading strategies. In this part of the world, investment is viewed as both an art and a science. It emphasises the rationality of the decision, supported by models, quantitative analysis, and behavioural finance theory. Of course, the media and analysts' recommendations have their influence. Still, they do not overshadow complex data and strategic foresight, which stand at the top of the list in business decision-making.

On the other hand, eastern financial markets, such as those in China, Japan, South Korea, and much of Southeast Asia, are predominantly shaped by collectivist values of social trust, familial influence, and government involvement. Democratic perspectives foster an atmosphere of financial decisions that rely on community wisdom more than those based on individualistic calculus. Family-managed corporations are the most popular and also the most significant players, prioritising the longevity of the business over the maximisation of immediate profits. The collective view of the matter also represents an environment in which societal actions influence market movements; in this way, Eastern markets tend to be more susceptible to a herd mentality. When one sector rises, all investors rush in, thereby capturing the potential profits that are available. Retail investors behave oppositely when panic selling occurs, as they tend to sell their stock at a price lower than they originally paid for it. In these cases, the bubble increases because investment becomes speculative, and it later decreases when the correction occurs. This is the reason behind the volatility of the Central Asian stock markets, which can be caused by speculative acts that can drive the market into an extravagant state before a sudden reversal occurs.

The regulatory environment has been an additional incentive for the development of cultural contrasts, which is manifested in how markets respond to financial downturns. The planning and preparedness of the people involved primarily regulate Western markets. Marketing under full disclosure and direct emphasis on the ethics of facts flourishes while speculation swings are curtailed in the U.S.A. The Securities and Exchange Commission (SEC) and the European Securities and Markets Authority (ESMA) are two regulatory bodies that protect the current regime from excessive trends that can endanger the system. In these free markets, it is assumed that investors should responsibly access information and accordance with regulations. It is a rare case when the government should intervene in the market, as was observed during the 2008 financial crisis, where unprecedented measures were taken to avoid full-scale market failure.

For this reason, Eastern markets are opposed to this arrangement's likeness. Politically, government intervention is frequent, with monetary policies and direct regulatory actions being two crucial pillars of financial stability. In China, regulators sometimes curb excessive speculation by ordering trading halts or adjusting the rates that influence market behaviour. The Bank of Japan is known to purchase government bonds and occasionally stocks to achieve liquidity and economic stability objectives. Indeed, this hands-on approach may help prevent real crashes. Still, it creates a moral hazard because market players choose not to be mindful of their risk evaluation, as the government will ultimately serve as a cooling factor. Sometimes government intervention itself changes how people behave. Instead of acting only on the real economic situation, they also try to guess what the government will do next. This can lead to speculation, risky behaviour, and decisions based more on predicted policies than on the actual fundamentals.

The clefts of these cultural and regulatory factors are patterns of market reactions that trend alongside the overreactions of the other side. Although Western markets are known for rational decision-making, they are not immune to speculative bubbles that can cause trouble. Yet, they mostly tend to bring the situation back to normal through their built-in safeguards. In contrast, the eastern markets, which have a high social and governmental influence, are characterised by broader changes, as in many cases, the emotional component dominates the fundamental one. The short-lived boom and subsequent crash of China's stock market in 2015, as well as the high-frequency trading flash crashes in the U.S.A., are examples that illustrate the impact of culture on financial behaviour, which is difficult to grasp through advanced economic models.

Besides the complexity of individual choices, collective behaviours, and government policies, the world also has a financial system. Evaluating the cultural aspects of risk tolerance and decision-making is not just a theoretical issue; it is vital knowledge for investors, policymakers, and those navigating the complex and unpredictable financial landscape of today's finance. It is not just the figures that make markets shift; it is also the psychology of the dealers that is planted in their souls. The psychology in question, however, often has roots in the traditions from which it originates.

13.3 How Cultural Differences Impact Market Overreaction

13.3.1 Information Processing Differences

Contrary to the general assumption, the manner in which people perceive and interpret information is equally as significant as the information they receive. However, nothing comes to mind that can be more different than this; such a process is not universal. The diverse cultural backgrounds of investors shape their interpretation of financial data, which is heavily influenced by history, social organisation, and economic ideologies (Reddy et al. 2021). In America, decision-making is primarily viewed as a numerical system, where stock traders heavily rely on fundamental analysis, statistical models, and software simulations based on past market performance. On the other hand, in the majority of Asian countries, the process of making an investment decision often involves qualitative variables, such as trust and existing social networks. These variations in how to approach the issue not only create different reactions among speculators to fluctuations but also lead to varying appearances of financial crises worldwide.

In the West, the thought of investing is often viewed as a matter of logic, devoid of spirit and emotion. Financial analysts spend sleepless nights reviewing balance sheets, cash flow statements, and price-to-earnings ratios to identify undervalued stocks or eliminate potential stocks (Lim et al. 2008). This is because, while markets may deviate from rational behaviour in the short run, they will eventually return to it, and the markets are predictable based on strict data analysis. Typically, the investment decision is based on the stock's past performance, probability studies, and the use of fully automated trading that does not allow human intervention. The emerging field of machine learning and artificial intelligence in finance has provided a robust force to the existing inclination toward this format, and it is considered an adequate measure of the order in which higher-quality data yields higher-quality outcomes. This result suggests that personal contacts and informal observations indeed carry weight, but they should be quantifiable in terms of specific benefits.

In contrast, BG stocks in many Asian countries are often a two-sided affair, as it is a technical game. Variables such as business relations, government relations, and market feelings formed by trusted networks were set against financial metrics. For instance, in China, investors often seek riddle-solving tips from industry leaders and highly regarded businesspeople, who, rather than relying on financial newspaper articles, draw on their interpersonal relationships. Japanese and South Korean industries prefer mature companies with a good standing over temporary companies that have a predisposed record of being at high risk. The inversion of the narrative originates from their dependence on kinship bonds. Put differently, many transactions could be influenced by elements that external agents can hardly realise, thus inviting a situation in which personal relationships become significant as the financial reports are compiled.

Therefore, it is easy for both Western and Eastern investors to misinterpret perturbing news. For example, negative news or disappointing economic forecasts are often interpreted by European or American market traders as death sentences, which are immediately countered by a violent wave of selling. The argument is based on the sound proposition that, as quickly as possible, the stock price should be adjusted to reflect all available public information; thus, the stock price drops considerably with bad news. Market investors, accustomed to fluctuations, anticipate such price reductions, which could either serve as an alarm to step out of the deal or an opportunity to acquire the stock at a lower price. The hallmark of the system is the importance of accurate information and its rapid, cost-free dissemination. Therefore, the cleansing process is fast but often ill-natured, for instance, as the market reacts to the newest data by selling it off without any delay.

Unlike their counterparts in the West, investors in Asia often present a guarded character and are even hesitant to take a stand on adverse news. Since the general mood and collective trust influence many investment influencers, it is common to wait for a time to resolve doubts about how, especially the large and established financial companies, will act. For example, if a corporation reports some substandard earnings in China or South Korea, its investors would probably not be the first to exit the market. Still, they would instead observe the direction that the big players in the market are opting for. Will the government help the economy with this move? Will banks trust their savings with their investments, which means they have faith that the business is viable in the long run? Such actions could sometimes delay the entire mechanism of deciding what to do; nevertheless, the consequences are thorough but slower, owing to the clarified consensus. Due to the herd mentality that prevails in the community, when panic finally sets in, it seems to erupt rapidly, triggering large sell-offs and severe fluctuations in the market.

The divergence in how investors view and process information goes a long way toward clarifying discrepancies in financial overreactions across regions (Lo 2004). In nations with Western culture, the speed at which overreaction occurs is usually meteoric and often includes sharp drops in prices, immediately reversed by equally brutal rebounds. In the East, the overreaction frequently materialises slowly and gradually until the occasion decisively defines the sentiment. Then, it can literally be overwhelming all at once (Carpenter 2022). Both models are unique and have inherent advantages and challenges. Yet, one thing is sure: the culture does not merely set the stage for financial decisions, but it becomes the essence of the market's working process. Market movements can mislead investors who are unaware of these discrepancies, ultimately leading to substantial losses.

13.3.2 Psychological and Behavioural Differences

Markets are not driven solely by numbers. A human decision is made behind each buy and sell order; thus, it is an act influenced by psychology, emotion, and cultural conditioning. While rational behaviour is the root of financial theories, actual life falsifies it (Madison et al. 2021). Investors in different regions exhibit distinct preferences, which result from the specific economic conditions, historical context, and cultural norms to which they have been exposed. The best illustration of these moments can be found in the discrepancy between Western and Asian markets, where psychological forces acting on investors can produce opposing effects on the marketplace.

The majority of Western financial markets view decision-making as being strictly related to earnings data, balance sheets, and fundamental analysis. The prevailing theory is that long-term stock prices accurately reflect a company's intrinsic value. Investors primarily focus on quarterly earnings reports, cash flow projections, and key financial ratios. A market that beats average earnings expectations can observe its stock price skyrocket; on the other hand, a small near-miss can sometimes provoke a massive sell-off. Thus, the considerable emphasis on fundamentals is primarily a result of institutional investors, hedge funds, and asset managers backing it, who make their decisions based on complex financial models that attempt to quantify every variable that might impact a company's future performance. Even in cases where speculative bubbles occur, they are primarily instigated by individuals with a collective underestimation of a company's true potential, as seen in examples such as the dot-com boom and the latest rise in the AI sector.

Nonetheless, this strong analytical approach does not protect Western investors from being influenced by emotions. Emotional factors, such as fear and greed, remain prevalent in the market, but they are now often expressed through data-driven causes. Investors who hold the view that fundamentals are key seek deeper reasons when their markets decline. Is it because GDP growth is slower? Are interest rates increasing? Are firms' profits dangerous? Despite being a typical move, panic selling is often followed by fresh analyses. At a point when assets drop significantly, institutional investors who see it as an opportunity to pick up undervalued stocks enter the market. The push-pull cycle is characterised by the phenomenon of overreaction and rectification, which is the very essence of Western markets, leading them to well-known patterns of boom and bust driven by the widespread change of mood.

On the other hand, Asian markets are like a psychological wavelength in which people live in a different world. Economic activity data are plentiful, but they are not always the operating regime of the markets (Smyth 2022). Instead, investors are predominantly focused on government communication, policy lanes, and political risk. It stems from a long historical period during which the state heavily directed economic activities, particularly in countries such as China, Japan, and Korea, where government intervention laid the groundwork for their financial systems. Investors in these regions have the intuition that a government order, whether explicit or implicit, could significantly impact a stock's value more than its earnings report.

This particular psychological setting of the market gives rise to a behaviour pattern that often perplexes investors in the West (Krauss et al. 2017). For instance, local traders might be sluggish in earnings, but their shares are still balanced or even on the rise if investors expect the executive to take measures to boost the economy. In contrast, a business with sound financials may experience a decline in stock price when government regulations, changes in trade policy, or political threats unrelated to its operations arise (Sun et al. 2022). This was the case when some of China's most profitable companies lost billions of dollars in market value overnight due to uncertainty surrounding the delivery of the new policy, rather than poor earnings.

Therefore, Asian investors spend as much time reading political cues as they do reading financial statements. Government transitions, shifts in trade policies, or even subtle indications from state-run media can trigger market trends. This creates a market space that feels more like a game of risky political chess rather than just a financial sphere at times. The investors' thoughts are no longer just inquiries, such as 'How is this company performing?' but decision-making questions, including 'What are the government's intentions regarding this company?' and 'How will the state's policies affect this sector?' As a result, stock markets often exhibit tremors in response to political issues, such as changes in leadership in China, central bank interventions in Japan, or geopolitical pressures in Korea, regardless of the earnings reports from companies.

Propulsion in the psychology of investors is not only reflected in the dynamics of the market, but also causes the overreactions of the stock market to be different. In the West, the reaction of markets to economic statistics is similar to the speed of light, with prices making almost instantaneous adjustments to new financial developments (Zhang et al. 2023). However, it is in Asia, where governmental issues are a concern, that excessive speculation leads to an extended period of uncertainty. Investors observe a policy shift and wait a long time for confirmation to make their move; however, in the event of herd thinking, it grips many more barrels, and the violence is even higher than in the West. The collective attitude of the market is such that once a storyline takes shape, whether positive or negative, it disseminates rapidly. The consequences of this development are severe, with temporary market swings that can sometimes be so extreme as to be difficult to correct.

In the long run, the psychological foundations that underpin Western and Asian markets reveal a fundamental truth about investing: that markets are more than financial machines; they are, in addition, cultural extensions of society. Just as Wall Street is obsessed with earnings data, Shanghai is influenced by attitudes towards government policies; understanding these behavioural idiosyncrasies is of paramount importance for those who want to operate successfully in global financial markets. The figures may narrate part of the story, but it is psychology that draws the complete picture.

13.3.3 Government and Institutional Influence on Overreaction

Markets, by their fundamental nature, are supposed to reflect financial data such as earnings, demand, supply, and economic growth (Maor 2018). However, the actual situation is the opposite; no other force often takes precedence, and the most powerful one is government intervention. This transfiguration can be best seen in the differences between the Western and Eastern financial systems. In the West, for instance, the U.S.A. The Federal Reserve is based on the philosophy of excess caution, and its interventions are the last resort in an effort to provide support to the economy. Under such circumstances, in many Eastern economies, especially in China, the authorities often take years to plan, directing the market not only through monetary policies but also through direct regulatory actions, such as capital controls and even state-backed bailouts. These diverse policies give rise to different market behaviours: the government suppresses volatility or, in an unexpected turn, amplifies market volatility.

In Eastern markets, the government is more than just a regulator; it plays an active role in the financial system. In this regard, China represents the most straightforward case in which state intervention is considered a standard and accepted practice. The Chinese government implements various interventions, including restricting trade, halting stock sales, injecting liquidity into the market, and even directing institutional investors to stabilise the situation by stabilising share prices when companies are in decline. This creates an investment environment that becomes increasingly less like the one in which market participants react only to economic data; they are now responding to government signals as well. While state authorities indicate that they will support a particular sector, the sector is flooded with investors who drive prices higher, even if such a move is not grounded in reality.

In contrast, when the government imposes new regulations, all sectors can experience a sudden shift from high valuations to being valued at next to zero overnight. This phenomenon occurred in 2021 during the crackdown on tech giants. This interplay makes the market resilient and volatile. For instance, if the state is perceived as the caretaker, assuming that the state will bear the losses, the market can be both highly resilient and incredibly volatile at the same time, as investors constantly try to gauge the direction of the regulatory environment.

A strong government presence in Eastern markets is not only about legitimising state measures again but also building a shared conviction that the state will always cover the losses. This leads to risk-taking behaviour, which can be perceived as reckless from a Western perspective. For instance, Chinese investors tend to engage in speculative trading, which drives the price of a house or stock above the rational level, risking a market downturn, but they are convinced that the state will intervene and bail them out. The truth is that such moral hazards can lead to negative consequences (Maor 2020). When the state, for one reason or the other, decides not to intervene, either to stop the excesses or to send a particular policy signal, the result can be a catastrophic market crash. An example is the 2015 situation that ensued when a speculative bubble bursting, mainly caused by borrowing against stocks, wiping trillions off the market in a mere instant.

The situation is entirely different from Western markets, particularly in the U.S.A., which are governed by a different set of government regulations. The Federal Reserve has no intention of directly controlling stock prices or influencing market action. Their power is felt primarily through monetary policy, which involves adjusting interest rates and the liquidity of financial assets. The Fed's fundamental mission is to facilitate stability by mitigating the effects of a recession rather than intervening in the market. For example, the bottom falling out of the market in March 2020 due to COVID-19 was met mainly by the Fed's interest rate cuts to near-zero levels and their expansive asset purchases, which led to the prevention of a financial disaster. The result was a rapid market recovery, with the S&P 500 hitting record highs in just a few months.

Indeed, while the Federal Reserve seeks to ensure stability in its activities, unintended consequences may arise. Repeated experience has shown that extremely low interest rates and quantitative easing have pushed asset bubbles higher, thereby motivating people to invest in stocks, cryptocurrencies, and real estate without due caution. Market violence can be expected when the Federal Reserve finally starts to tighten its policy. The events of 2022 occurred when the Fed began raising rates to try to keep inflation in check. This time, the expected reaction was investor recalibration, which manifested in the form of sharp corrections. The Fed's problem here remains a delicate balance: they must be careful not to distort market incentives. The difference between the two systems was a predictive factor. The Federal Reserve, by the way, clears the air with transparency, laying down its policy intentions well ahead of any action (Ehrmann and Fratzscher 2005). What this means in practice is that, while an investor may be opposed to a rate hike or a policy shift, they generally have sufficient time to make adjustments. Otherwise, they do not necessarily share the same concern in Eastern markets, where government interventions vary from one to another and lack specific details, thereby misleading the investors. These types of measures can sometimes lead to sharp market fluctuations, which can extend to sky-high rallies in cases where the policies promote growth and panic-induced crashes when new regulations are introduced suddenly.

To put it bluntly, government intervention in financial markets can create opportunities while also posing hazards. At one extreme, in the West, the almost absent government role in market construction makes it appear free, but many investors are left to face the harshness of economic downturns with no support. On the other hand, the East's strong government hand acts as a cushion, but it leads to the speculative nature of the market. The speculative nature is the norm; in addition, it creates an environment where regulation is the primary arbiter, and market value can fluctuate by trillions in a day. These are the issues that investors need to be aware of to move around successfully in markets all over the world, as it turns out the same force, whether it is the invisible hand of the Federal Reserve or the visible one of the Chinese governments, can be market not tangible but the institutions behind it.

13.4 Case Study: The 2015 Swiss Franc Shock

13.4.1 Background

Only a few moments in financial history have demonstrated how the decisions of institutions affect global markets as profoundly as they did on January 15, 2015. It was on this very day that the Swiss National Bank (SNB) made a move that was beyond shocking and totally unexpected: it removed the Swiss franc's peg from the euro. Thus, in a split second, a stable currency relationship was destroyed, and the financial world was thrown into chaos. The Swiss franc, a currency often regarded as a haven, surged by over 30% against the euro in a matter of moments. Traders, institutions, and even whole economies hurried to find a way out, but by the time they could figure it out, the damage had already been done.

It was a moment that ripped through the heart of global finance like a lightning bolt. Figure 13.1 is not just a series of data points; it is a visual echo of chaos. On January 15, 2015, when the Swiss National Bank removed its long-standing peg of the franc to the euro, the market did not just blink; it convulsed. The EUR/CHF exchange rate, which had hovered at a stable 1.20 for years, plummeted within minutes to as low as 0.85. Imagine the floor vanishing beneath your feet; that is what

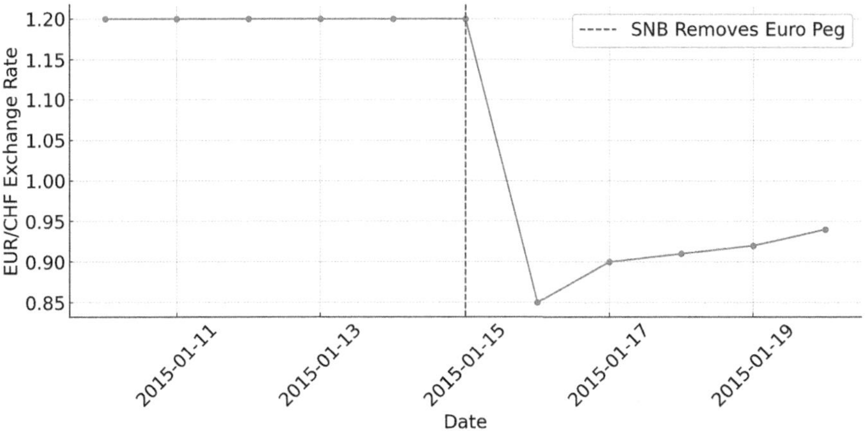

Fig. 13.1 EUR/CHF exchange rate around January 15, 2015. Source: Authors' work

traders experienced in real time. Portfolios crumbled, brokerages went bankrupt, and institutions scrambled to assess the financial wreckage. This was no ordinary correction; it was a collective, emotional detonation sparked by a central bank's decision, one that challenged the assumptions upon which countless risk models were built.

This event was a textbook case of institutional influence colliding with investors' psychology. What made it historic was not just the scale of the currency movement but also the chain reaction of fear, algorithmic liquidations, and shattered confidence. In an instant, the carefully constructed sense of policy predictability evaporated, and markets reacted not with reason but with panic. Investors did not have time to verify the fundamentals; they sold because everyone else was selling as well. Additionally, the aftershocks lingered for weeks, and the scars on Swiss exporters, global hedge funds, and retail forex traders took years to heal. The lesson? Even in an age of data-driven precision, markets are still driven by emotion when certainty is lacking. The Swiss Franc shock remains one of the most dramatic modern examples of how central bank action, when paired with investor bias and automated trading systems, can ignite a financial firestorm.

For a long time, the SNB had maintained a currency peg, which was used to keep the Swiss franc artificially weak against the euro and protect the export-driven economy. The strategy was a lifeline for Swiss businesses, which were concentrated in watchmaking, pharmaceuticals, and tourism, where price competitiveness in the European market was crucial. The pegging of the euro to the dollar assured global investors that there would be no fluctuation in the franc, thus preventing wild exchange rate swings. However, this policy involves several sacrifices. The peg was maintained only if the SNB purchased euros in large quantities to suppress the value of the franc. The situation worsened when the European Central Bank (ECB) was nearing a phase of further easing in early 2015, which made the SNB feel that it would be unsustainable to continue the peg by buying so many euros.

The SNB removed commitment from the blue. One announcement was lost in years of careful currency stabilisation. The immediate result was chaotic. The franc's value increased rapidly, leading traders to unwind their positions in a frantic attempt to minimise losses. Investors who borrowed Swiss francs under the assumption that the currency would remain weak had to deal with unprecedented debt burdens. The stock markets were in a dire situation, and the shares of Swiss multinational companies, knowing they would have to sell goods at higher prices to foreign buyers, rapidly dropped.

The market reactions were both immediate and severe. Institutional investors were the ones most surprised and rushed to liquidate their positions, as they were forced to do by the chaotic sell-offs and liquidity crises. The unexpected fluctuations in the market led to the closure of several foreign exchange brokers that were unable to cover the losses incurred by their clients. Retail investors, along with hedge funds and global corporations, were all severely impacted, with some losing millions in minutes. What was supposed to be a typical trading day soon turned into a financial market meltdown, all due to a choice made by a central bank.

The SNB's decision was a stark reminder of how significantly the central banks' policies and their credibility impacted the markets. Investors, traders, and businesses were all influenced by this move to build their strategies, forecasts, and risk models based on the idea that the peg would remain intact. Thus, when the assumption was shattered, the market reaction would not only be a recalibration of currency values based on reason, but also an emotional, fear-driven panic of full-scale form. The shock of the event revealed a fundamental reality about the financial markets: when assurance is disrupted, it is natural for overreaction to occur.

In the weeks and months to come, what unfolded was the misery of a slow and painful recovery. As businesses and investors learn to navigate the new environment of the free-floating Swiss franc, hedge funds encounter closed doors following shutdowns. Small Forex traders were removed literally. Hasty Swiss exporters found it challenging to maintain a competitive edge. In the global financial community, the SNB's surprise decision became a notable example of how institutional policy changes can, especially when implemented without prior warning, lead to significant shifts in the mechanics that extend far beyond the policymakers' intentions. Indeed, it was a lesson that government action, investor psychology, and the often unpredictable, extreme character of market reactions were all intertwined and interconnected.

13.4.2 Role of Cultural and Structural Factors in the Crisis

Stability, or at least its perception, is what the financial world relies on. This fact was clearly reflected in the period immediately preceding and during the shocking decision made by the Swiss National Bank (SNB) to cease removing the link between the Swiss franc and the euro. Switzerland, which had a legendary standing in the field of financial safety, was the country that made the Swiss franc a fundamental asset in global risk management. Investors, traders, and multinational companies, who had not previously experienced any problems, remained convinced of the country's predictability and the Swiss National Bank's commitment to this peg. Nevertheless, history has shown that such assumptions regarding market stability can pose threats, and the moment the SNB cut the string, the mirage of control experienced an instant blow-up.

The Swiss National Bank was the first to signal to the markets that the 1.20 CHF/EUR peg would remain unchanged and continue during the recession. The steadfastness of this promise lifted the burden off traders' shoulders, making them slightly complacent. As a result, market insiders started treating it like a natural law that no one would ever change the peg. This incorrect idea ultimately led to a serious contract error, which, as it was, the traders failed to recognise that the Swiss National Bank was unable or unwilling to continue this way forever. The central bank indeed played a role in creating this misconception. The central bank intervened multiple times in the currency market to settle pegs, and over time, this became a standard that traders believed would exist for an indefinite period. When the SNB finally decided to change direction, the consequent shock was not just financial but also psychological.

Misplaced trust in stability was the root cause of financial recklessness, particularly among financial institutions that viewed the Swiss franc as a haven for borrowing. The near-zero interest rates in Switzerland persuaded many hedge funds, large companies, and banks to borrow heavily in Swiss francs, placing their faith in the peg that would keep any currency fluctuations to a minimum. Then, with the trade being just one click away, they made huge profits; they borrowed Swiss francs at low rates and flipped them into high-yielding currencies, thus pocketing the difference. It was as if they were playing with free money as long as the peg was intact; however, when the peg was no longer there, the number of debts that remained payable increased exponentially. Institutional investors, who had invested a substantial amount in the franc, which was said to be permanently stable, suddenly found themselves at the edge of a sea of debts they never anticipated.

Even retail traders, small businesses, and multinational corporations are facing unforeseen circumstances. Many forex traders had the wrong impression, in fact, that the SNB was standing behind them, and so they had taken leveraged positions against the franc without incurring any risk. Equally concerning were times when they would have lost all their money in the blink of an eye, as on January 15, 2015, when they opened their email and found empty forex accounts. Small and large businesses, on the other hand, saw the book of debts grow, primarily entities from Eastern Europe that had signed loans denominated in Swiss francs, which was advantageous during a stable exchange rate. However, when the Swiss franc rallied, the debt burden skyrocketed. Unexpectedly, some firms that managed to survive by offering good products and services to clients faced sudden bankruptcy because they made a simple, though disastrous, assumption. Their thoughts this time, about seemingly impossible Swiss issues being unshakeable, finally instilled the wrong idea in their minds.

The shock triggered a chain of forced liquidations that began in the Swiss franc market and quickly spread to global financial markets. Forex brokers were the first to suffer major losses. Many had allowed clients to take highly leveraged positions in the Swiss franc, often with minimal margin requirements. When the Swiss National Bank removed the euro peg and the currency's value surged, these positions moved sharply against the traders. Margin calls were triggered instantly, and as losses exceeded account balances, clients exited in large numbers. Brokers were left absorbing the shortfall, forcing some into insolvency and creating ripple effects across the broader forex industry. Some brokers were victims of massive losses that they could not bear. Funds that had bought franc shorts in massive amounts were blitzed because their stop-losses did not catch on quickly enough due to extreme volatility. Even though the big banks were having a tough time, some of them suffered losses in the range of billions just trying to get rid of the bad positions. The financial industry learned its lessons in the most painful way that stability is not always guaranteed.

The 2015 Swiss franc crisis was not only about the currency markets, but also a poignant and profound lesson in the dangers of collective overconfidence and the herding effect. Investors, from the smallest retail traders to the largest banks and financial institutions, came together to create a card house based on a single tenet: the Swiss National Bank would never break the peg. This assumption collapsed, as did the entire global market regime. The consequence of the collapse of the assumption was that the chaos that followed was not solely an economic reaction. Still, it was a reckoning that showed all the fragile psychological structures behind even the most sophisticated financial systems.

13.4.3 Market Overreaction and Consequences

The Swiss National Bank's (SNB) decision to break the franc's link to the euro on January 15, 2015, was swift and decisive. It detonated a bomb in the global financial markets, triggering one of the most astonishing overreactions in the currency area since modern times. The extreme velocity and scale of the market's reaction transformed a potential smooth restoration into a broad financial disaster, with companies collapsing, agencies scrambling to adapt, and investors incurring substantial losses. It was a brutal example of the extraordinary intimacy of global markets and how a single policy act could generate such enormous financial chaos.

The first and most severe consequence of the franc shock was the collapse of numerous financial institutions, particularly those involved in foreign exchange trading. Alpari UK, one of the leading forex companies, was declared bankrupt just hours after the SNB's announcement, having lost numerous clients due to the sudden drop in the franc. Traders who short-sold the currency with considerable leverage were forced out of the game due to volatility, leaving brokers with enormous unpaid debts. The problem was worse, even for large players. FXCM, one of the world's top retail forex trading platforms, lost $225 million in a single day as client accounts became overwhelmingly negative. FXCM was under such tremendous pressure that it needed external funding to continue operations. Other trading firms faced a similar fate, highlighting the fragile state of the retail forex market and the destructive impact that excessive leverage has on the currency industry.

However, beyond the issue of currency trading, the franc's sudden surge also caused significant damage to businesses in Europe, including those that were more directly exposed to the Swiss franc. Swatch Group and Richemont did not spare Swiss luxury brands, as their market prices fell by 15–20% in short order. The explanation was pretty straightforward: strong franc meant that international buyers had to pay way more for their watches, jewellery, and luxury articles that were meant for them, thus affecting the companies' sales and net profit. The timing could not have been worse, as luxury goods had already suffered a slight downturn in Asia, and the shock added to margins for companies that had been long on exchange rate advantages.

It was not just a Swiss company that experienced hardship. European airlines, such as Air France-KLM, experienced financial turmoil as the cost of fuel payments and currency hedging, which were often tied to international exchange rates, increased beyond expectations. Firms that borrowed in Swiss francs, particularly those located in Eastern Europe, were surprised to find that they had to pay considerably higher amounts than they had originally borrowed. Side by side, homeowners in Poland and Hungary, who had previously opted for Swiss franc mortgages to take advantage of low interest rates, felt the brunt of the monetary shock, which led to household debt crises in these European regions.

The chain reactions subsequently spread to the global currency markets, as traders were in a state of frenzy, which created record-high volatility. The immediate decline of the euro against the franc prompted investors to seek refuge in other safe-haven currencies, resulting in unprecedented surges in the value of the Japanese yen and the U.S. dollar. Central banks in the European region were in chaos. At the same time, the franc's speculative revaluation was poised to undermine the already fragile economies, which were suffering from inadequate inflation and lacklustre growth. The European Central Bank (ECB), which was set to launch massive Quantitative Easing programmes, got its path interrupted as the event stressed the weakness of the Eurozone's financial system.

The 2015 Swiss franc shock was not merely a financial event but a poignant psychological lesson in the market, highlighting the severe consequences of exaggerated reactions. The early onset of panic selling, margin calls, and companies going bankrupt was not solely the outcome of economic fundamentals, but rather the widely held fear that the game would be fumbled for everyone's survival. Investors, enterprises, and entire financial institutions did not expect the SNB to act in such a manner. When the truth was revealed, they did not react with accurate amendments but panicked irrationally. The crisis again demonstrated how easily trust in the financial system can shift, as it has been shown once more that when the market's equilibrium is suddenly called into doubt, they do not merely react but overreact.

13.5 Lessons from Global Financial Markets

The 2015 Swiss franc crisis was not merely a financial crisis; instead, it was a demonstration of the diverse ways in which cultures, institutions, and regulatory frameworks respond to economic turmoil. When markets spiral into chaos, the devices set forth for their stabilisation reflect the value of the culture prevalent in each premise, similar to the way investors react and, consequently, the way economies recover. The differential contrast between Western and Eastern management of financial crises is striking: on the one hand, there is an emphasis on honesty and self-correcting free markets, while on the other hand, there is a belief in direct interventions and regulatory control. It is not just a matter of race; the perception of these distinctions is a crucial tool in the toolkits of multinational investors navigating a world in which financial stability is never taken for granted.

It is not just a matter of investors' culture; the Swiss franc crisis shows how deeply structural biases influence financial decision-making. Many investors from the West sincerely believed that Switzerland's commitment to economic stability was such that the peg was not to be touched; thus, they took heavily leveraged positions without weighing the risks of a policy reversal. On the other hand, the Eastern traders, who are generally more accustomed to government intervention, might have found it less surprising if the government had made a sudden policy change. Still, they should have foreseen the possibility of recovery measures. Understanding how different financial systems function and how governments respond to crises enables investors to hedge risks more effectively, invest in suitable projects, and avoid catastrophic miscalculations.

One significant finding of the global economic crisis is learning how to understand the different risk perceptions of other cultures. Risk is not objectively measurable; while one financial market sees a certain level of uncertainty as manageable, another may find it fundamentally destructive. Western financial market specialists are accustomed to respecting volatility and correcting it through the market; as such, they are prepared to react with calculated moves. The eastern ones, who-to-state intervention, will either expect the government to take action or, as a last resort, panic selling in the absence of action. Managers of funds and investors, in general, will notice key differences in the potential for seizing an opportunity due to the inherent nature of risk measurement.

The Swiss franc crisis was not the first case to show cultural chasms in financial markets, nor will it be the last. It does not matter whether it is a central bank policy twist, a global economic meltdown, or a swift market correction; investors will always react to them, influenced by their deeply ingrained cultural beliefs. The major takeaway? The markets do not just function on numbers and economic statistics; psychological factors, trust, and numerous other intangible cultural beliefs also drive them. Investors who understand this are those who not only withstand financial shocks but also do so in a situation where stability is continuously one decision away from being an illusion.

13.6 Conclusion

Financial markets are commonly perceived as rational entities consisting of numbers, economic data, and corporate performance. However, the history of financial markets is often proof that they are far from logical. The role of culture usually seems out of sight, yet it is indeed a significant factor in financial events, risk perception, and government responses to crises. The 2015 Swiss franc shock, similar to other market disruptions, was not merely a currency issue, but rather a matter of the investors' psyche, the atmosphere within financial organisations, and the cultural contexts that define different attitudes toward economic stability.

The most important fact to learn from worldwide financial crises is that not all investors are subject to the same level of risk. Western investors, who are brought up in a culture that idolises openness and self-regulation, are prone to assuming that the markets are like their own self-healing agencies; thus, they do not fear the immediate losses that can lead to adjustment. On the other hand, investors from the East typically expect more state directives in the markets and a government-supported vote of confidence, rather than the causative factors of economic turmoil. Such dissimilarities result not only in the ways in which problems are treated but also in how the markets recover. In the West, financial markets become disproportionately oversold and bow to massive sell-offs before carefully reintroducing themselves. Conversely, the East may first be hindered by uncertainty and only thereafter may herd instinct lead to extreme fluctuations, which in turn are often handled by explicit regulations.

The government is also a significant contributor to regional disparities. In the Western environment, central banks, such as the U.S. Federal Reserve, swear using the indirect approach, where the market, in essence, allocates resources. On the other hand, in the East, particularly in China and other economies that favour government intervention, state machinery appears to be much more involved, including the will to control the market, direct the support of institutional investors, and uphold stock values when necessary. The absence of these policy discrepancies implies that the same market shock can elicit two entirely distinct reactions, whether in Western or Eastern markets.

Global investors must have a thorough understanding of the typical culture of the target country, encompassing not only financial markets but also all aspects of business. The best investors are those who understand that the decisions made by companies do not simply influence the financial habits of people but instead revolve around psychology and society's natural configuration. A trader who comprehends that Swiss confidence can be deceptive, that the Chinese market is equally responsive to government hints and financial reports, or that the Western market is a frequent victim of algorithmic overweening will be at the disposal of the unrivalled talents in navigating through uncertainty. The ultimate weapon in the world of finance is flexibility, and cultural perceptiveness is the most valuable asset that an investor can possess.

There will always be uncertainty in financial markets, and crises will arise from different corners of the world. Nevertheless, one truth has remained unalterable: investors do not equate solely with numbers; they act on the foundation of their beliefs, customs, and, of course, hidden cultural factors. Those who have a knack for understanding these impacts will not only weather market fluctuations but also discover opportunities when others see only chaos.

References

Ahmed, Z., Noreen, U., Ramakrishnan, S. A., & Abdullah, D. F. B. (2021). What explains the investment decision-making behaviour? The role of financial literacy and financial risk tolerance. Afro-Asian Journal of Finance and Accounting, 11(1), 1–19.

Carpenter TG (2022) Unreliable watchdog: the news media and US foreign policy. Cato Institute, Washington

Ehrmann M, Fratzscher M (2005) Transparency, disclosure and the Federal Reserve. Monet Econ 3(1):179–225

Krauss C, Do XA, Huck N (2017) Deep neural networks, gradient-boosted trees, random forests: statistical arbitrage on the S&P 500. Eur J Oper Res 259(2):689–702

Lim KP, Brooks RD, Kim JH (2008) Financial market efficiency and the adaptive market hypothesis: evidence from Asian stock markets. J Int Money Financ 27(6):856–870

Lo AW (2004) The adaptive markets hypothesis: market efficiency from an evolutionary perspective. J Portf Manag 30(5):15–29

Madison AA, Shrout MR, Renna ME, Kiecolt-Glaser JK (2021) Psychological and behavioural predictors of vaccine efficacy: considerations for COVID-19. Perspect Psychol Sci 16(2):191–203

Maor M (2018) Overreaction and bubbles in politics and policy. In: The Oxford handbook of behavioural political science. Oxford University Press, Oxford

Maor M (2020) Policy overreaction styles during manufactured crises. Policy Polit 48:523–539

Reddy K, Qamar MAJ, Mirza N, Shi F (2021) Overreaction effect: evidence from an emerging market (Shanghai stock market). Int J Manag Financ 17(3):416–437

Smyth R (2022) Business theologies. In: The invisible Republic: the economics of socialism and republicanism in the 21st century. Springer, Cham, pp 151–182

Sun L, Fang S, Iqbal S, Bilal AR (2022) Financial stability role on climate risks, and climate change mitigation: implications for green economic recovery. Environ Sci Pollut Res 29(22):33063–33074

Zhang W, Luckert M, Qiu F (2023) Asymmetric price transmission and impulse responses from US crude oil to jet fuel and diesel markets. Energy 283:128425

Chapter 14
The Psychology of Greenwashing and ESG Disclosures

14.1 Introduction

In 1970, when Earth Day was first established, it is reported that companies spent eight times more on advertising their environmental efforts than on preserving the environment. This kind of spending is later categorised as one of the greenwashing activities, coined by Jay Westervelt, a New York environmental activist, in 1986. Nevertheless, things have turned out for the better.

Greenwashing can be viewed from various perspectives or through the lenses of different stakeholders (Forliano et al. 2025). Still, generally, it describes the misrepresentation of products, services, activities, and funding to inflate an organisation's positive image, reputation, and profits through environmental-friendly and preservation initiatives to attract a group of interests. The misleading information is exaggerated or falsified to indicate excellent environmental performance, whether in terms of practices or benefits to planetary health. This action could enhance the legitimacy of the organisations in the eyes of the stakeholders.

The stakeholders, as the target audience, are the groups of interest in greenwashing, including institutional investors, retail investors, index companies, rating agencies, policymakers, authorities, environmental activists, non-governmental organisations (NGOs), and the general public, who are the ultimate consumers. To financial market players, greenwashing is often evident through misinformation in the non-financial disclosures prepared by companies. Meanwhile, government-related entities and NGOs may be deceived by the level of activities and funding reported by companies to preserve the environment (Bin Osman 2022). Additionally, public members may be misled by products and advertisements labelled as sustainable, green, eco-friendly, or environmentally friendly. Nevertheless, no third-party certifications or assurances are obtained to verify such claims.

Within a financial context, greenwashing poses detrimental effects to market players, as this deception not only compromises market integrity, causing loss to

K. L. Ooi et al., *Following the Crowd: Psychological Drivers of Herding and Market Overreaction*, https://doi.org/10.1007/978-981-95-0792-4_14

investors, but also creates long-term risks to the company. Furthermore, investors would lose not only their funds but also confidence in the regulators' ability to contain such misleading claims, which would impact their investment decisions (Rangapur et al. 2023). From the investors' perspective, there should be robust legal frameworks to guide the disclosures and allegations related to environmental protection and preservation made by the companies. At the same time, the companies would suffer a blow to their reputation, which would take some time to recover. This incident could deter environmentally conscious potential investors from placing their money and trust in future projects. At the same time, it would promote the culture of non-compliance amongst the firms in continuing to provide overclaims and misleading information about their green initiatives.

The cause of this situation could be attributed to the fact that professional investors typically rely on non-financial disclosures that report environmental-related projects and activities. Environmental-related information is documented as part of ESG disclosures and is incorporated into either sustainability reporting or integrated reporting (Halkos and Aslanidis 2025). The former solely focuses on ESG activities, while the latter combines both financial reporting and ESG disclosures.

The ESG concept was first introduced in the report by the United Nations Global Compact in 2004. This concept outlines how companies can fulfil their environmental and social responsibilities towards their communities while also enhancing their corporate governance. Disclosures for ESG activities can be categorised into mandatory, mandated by regulators, and voluntary information, which companies choose to provide (Krueger et al. 2024). Another way to view ESG disclosures is to classify them into financial and non-financial information. Financial ESG disclosure quantifies the ESG practices and performance of companies, for example, the rate of carbon emissions, the percentage of board diversity, or the number of employee misconducts (Ooi, 2024). On the other hand, non-financial ESG disclosures can be described as narrative disclosures that depict ESG achievements in words and visuals, meeting the various needs of the stakeholders the company serves. The companies leverage ESG disclosures to enhance their image, strengthen brand loyalty, maintain a positive societal perception, and, most importantly, improve their financial standing through increased investment and sales.

Having stated this, the level of ESG disclosures depends on the institutional and firm-level factors. External influences, including regulations, industry norms, accounting frameworks, and the prevailing economic climate, shape institutional factors (Badulescu et al. 2021). Firm-level factors, on the other hand, refer to internal factors such as the cost of capital, market visibility, growth orientation, and the strength of corporate governance. Investors interested in environmentally friendly projects tend to perceive ESG disclosures positively and rely on these reports to make informed decisions. The practice of greenwashing by companies would render ESG disclosures uncredible and unreliable, hindering solid and accurate predictions of the company's real market value.

14.2 The Psychology of Greenwashing

Before delving deeper into the effects of greenwashing on investors, let us understand the forms of greenwashing and the reasons behind this unethical action by companies. The misrepresentation of information regarding environmental and sustainability practices also encompasses statements, declarations, actions, and communications to stakeholders in all forms of media, including online reach, particularly through the company's website and social media accounts (Nuseir and Qasim 2021). Indications of greenwashing can be seen through the exaggeration of statements, obscurity of declarations, irrelevance of practices towards sustainable goals, concealment of illegal and unethical acts, and, lastly, the misleading or falsification of disclosures.

Let us examine a few probable scenarios of these greenwashing forms that occur around us. Exaggeration of statements could be seen when an apparel company boasts of 'eco-friendly clothing lines and collections' when in actuality, it comprises less than a quarter of it. Vague or obscure statements occur when a hotel claims to be sustainable without specifying the actions, efforts, or products that support such a declaration. The irrelevance of greenwashing decisions occurs when a mineral water producer packages the product in recyclable materials, but the buying community lacks access to recyclable infrastructure and facilities (Afianto and Waskito 2025). In contrast, the unethical practice could be the employment of child labour by a multinational consumer goods manufacturer, yet not reported through any of the communication channels to shareholders. Moreover, lastly, falsified claims could be committed by a cosmetics and skincare company that claims no animal testing was conducted, yet outsources the tasks to third-party labs in developing countries where such actions are permitted.

Hence, what are the reasons behind such decisions by the company? Let us consider the scenario where Ally, the fund manager of a reputable institutional investor, is currently seeking to allocate her client's funds to a green equity stock. Her client is keen on an airline company that claims to support 'carbon-neutral' projects by planting acres of trees in the operating country (Nyamdorj et al. 2021). Thus, Ally reviews the company by examining multiple ESG disclosures, sustainability reports, analysts' reports, and checking the company's websites. However, upon checking with a representative of a related NGO, she finds out that the airline company only planted a quarter of the intended amount. What should Ally do? In the interest of her client's intention to invest towards planetary health, she should inform her client of the greenwashing act through exaggeration of claims.

14.3 Investor Perceptions of ESG Disclosures

Knowing what happens to Ally, the fund manager who has to deal with greenwashing, it is imperative that investors be discerning in examining the reports provided by companies for their green initiatives. In this case, it is the ESG disclosures report.

Apart from financial information, ESG disclosures carry significant weight in influencing investors' economic decisions (Ellili 2022). Essentially, all investors will weigh the risks and returns, as well as the benefits and harms, along with the long-term profits to be gained, in order to make informed decisions (Ooi 2025). Hence, it is the company's responsibility to prepare accurate, transparent, and clear reports that contain no incoherent or vague information, thereby enabling investors to make informed decisions.

This pertains not only to investors but also to other stakeholders who require relevant information for non-financial decisions. For instance, policymakers collating certain industry practices for environmental protection, or an NGO scrutinising the company's treatment of marginalised communities. The decision-making process begins with the acquisition of information, followed by the evaluation of data and information, and concludes with assessing the reliability, validity, and credibility of this information.

Referring to the reliability and credibility assessment by investors, the practice of obtaining external or third-party assurance for the ESG and sustainability information prepared by the company can mitigate the risks of greenwashing and lead to more accurate and reliable investment-related details. While companies are required to obtain third-party assurance and verification for their financial information, there is no requirement to do so for non-financial details, such as environmental, social, and governance (ESG) disclosures (Darnall et al. 2022). However, engaging a third party to verify the information could enhance the credibility and readability of the disclosures. It is also noteworthy that ESG investors tend to focus on the management and governance quality of a company rather than examining industry-level standards before making an investment (Van Duuren et al. 2016).

We can also describe the quality of ESG disclosures based on the metrics designed by Mercer (2004) and Misiuda and Lachmann (2022). Another essential quality of ESG disclosures is the readability or presentation of the information. Vague and inconsistent statements may indicate elements of greenwashing committed by the company, which hides certain unethical acts.

Assuming the ESG reports are readable, transparent, credible, and verified by a third party, investors may still face other issues and challenges. Possible causes for such errors could be non-compliance by companies in preparing the report, resulting from their negligence in interpreting the stipulated requirements set by regulators (Jahidi et al. 2024). The non-compliance could also be caused by unintentional mistakes or, worse, intentional omissions due to cost-benefit considerations. Preparing ESG disclosures requires meticulous efforts, mobilising concerted inputs from various departments that span environmental, social, and governance aspects of the company, hence explaining the costs involved.

Apart from the non-compliance issue caused by the companies, consider the scenario where an environmental NGO is exploring the possibility of raising funds to protect tigers, an endangered species in a tropical country. The NGO was keen on one multinational company that has been promoting itself on websites and social media through its monetary contributions and employee social activities (Gathoni 2020). Similar information was disclosed in the sustainability reporting under the environmental chapter. However, further checking and verification from the fund recipients, as well as the co-organisers, revealed inconsistent and inaccurate reports of the contributions and activities. What actually happened here?

This situation can be described as a misperception of stakeholders, in this case, the NGO, regarding the company's massive green image portrayed in the media. At the same time, the NGO had to handle the vast amount of information shared by the company, which compromised the credibility of the reports (Clarke 2021). Assurance and verification from a third party for the reports might mitigate this from happening. Furthermore, what could happen if the interested parties in the company are institutional and retail investors, rather than an NGO? Could the company be penalised for greenwashing and deceiving them through inaccurate ESG disclosures? Are there adequate legal protections and punishments prescribed by the regulators?

14.4 Regulatory Challenges in Tackling Greenwashing

Considering that investors seek quality and credible information for solid investment decision-making, they rely on authorities to ensure that trusted information is disseminated to the public. However, the current legal environment indicates a lack of clear regulations and penalties imposed for greenwashing activities committed by companies. The lack of penalties and fines for greenwashing would lead to investors being continuously misled (Alaudhli 2024). The closest framework that could deter the misrepresentation of ESG-related activities in company reports would be the requirements of the accounting framework, which necessitate verifications and reviews.

Let us first examine the current framework from an international perspective, considering both the financial reporting standard and the regulator's viewpoint. In terms of financial reporting, the most relevant framework is the International Financial Reporting Standard (IFRS), overseen by the International Accounting Standards Board (IASB). In June 2023, the International Sustainability Standards Board introduced the IFRS Sustainability Disclosure Standards, which include IFRS S1 and IFRS S2 (Fridson and Alvarez 2022). Moreover, the standards outline the general content and presentation requirements for these sustainability-related disclosures, ensuring that they are presented clearly and in a manner that benefits investors and other stakeholders. IFRS S1 outlines the complete requirements for companies to disclose information about sustainability-related risks and opportunities that could impact their cash flows, access to finance, or cost of capital over the short, medium, and long term. In comparison, IFRS S2 provides detailed guidelines for climate-related disclosures. Like IFRS S1, IFRS S2 requires companies to disclose information about climate-related risks and opportunities that could reasonably be expected to impact their cash flows, access to finance, or cost of capital over the short, medium, or long term.

At the regional and country levels, the most prominent example is the European Union (EU), which has several legal instruments in place to curb greenwashing activities. The first is the EU Directive 2014/95/EU, which mandates the disclosure of non-financial and diversity information for certain large companies. They also have the guideline COM/2001/0336, issued in 2001, which provides the legal definition of corporate social responsibility. This guideline was later revised in 2011 through Communication from the Commission to the European Parliament, the Council, the European Economic and Social Committee and the Committee of the Regions—A renewed EU strategy 2011–14 for Corporate Social Responsibility. In 2005, the EU also imposed Directive 2005/29/EC to outline the legal repercussions for traders involved in making unfair environmental claims. Later, in 2016, the EU took the extra step through its SWD 163, where it defined the terms of friendliness and green labelling for companies to adhere to. As a whole, there is no integrated legal framework specifically formulated to combat greenwashing across the industry.

Across the strait, the United Kingdom (UK) issued the directive regarding sustainability-related disclosures under its Companies Act. The Companies Act 2006 (Regulations 2013) outlines guidance for the disclosure of greenhouse gas (GHG) emissions, gender breakdowns, and human rights issues. Specifically, (1) environmental matters including the impact of the company's business on the environment), (2) the company's employees, and (3) social, community and human rights issues, plus the information about any policies of the company in relation to those matters and the effectiveness of those policies. In addition, their Financial Reporting Council (FRC) has published 'Guidance on the Strategic Report', while the Department for Environment, Food & Rural Affairs (DEFRA) has provided 'Environmental Reporting Guidelines' (Lin 2022). Again, it is evident that the legal guidelines are dispersed across multiple legal acts rather than being integrated into a single framework to govern any industry.

In short, most regulations pertaining to greenwashing fall under the purview of misleading advertisements aimed at consumers or reside under acts covering specific investment instruments, rather than addressing the broader issue of misrepresentations of disclosures and information disseminated to the public. What is now evident is the need for IOSCO (International Organisation of Securities Commissions) to serve as the collective body of regulators worldwide, enacting the much-needed regulations, particularly in this era where the financial community is focusing on ESG-related investments. IOSCO should consider convening with its members to detail the greenwashing from a legal perspective by issuing regulatory guidelines, enforcement frameworks, and standardised definitions to assist regulators in identifying, preventing, and penalising misleading sustainability claims in the capital markets. The issued guidelines and legal frameworks should cover all financial players in the market within the stipulated duration of the greenwashing act, which could impact the intended audience. Not to be forgotten, the regulations should list all forms of potential greenwashing that the respective entities may design.

14.5 The Case of (Mis)Perceptions: H&M and the Conscious Collection 2021

Let us first examine the case of (mis)perceptions of buyers and investors in relation to the ESG branding of a reputable H&M clothing retailer. H&M is a multinational fashion retailer that sells apparel, accessories, and homewares, headquartered in Stockholm, Sweden. This brand is present in nearly 75 countries worldwide, serving almost 100,000 potential customers. In 2010, the company released a collection of 'Conscious' apparel, claiming to be eco-friendly due to its use of at least 50% bio-based materials, such as recycled polyester and organic cotton, and its production with reduced water usage.

Over the years, H&M has promoted this growing collection, touting it as sustainable and environmentally friendly products that are a worthwhile purchase for environmentally conscious customers. However, in July 2022, a marketing student sued the company for greenwashing, alleging that it overcharged customers for its Conscious Collection under the pretext of being eco-friendly. H&M was sued for an estimated amount of USE $5 million. The plaintiff claimed that production is not operating on the less water principle as claimed by the company (Loang 2025). Such a claim by H&M is misleading, as it entices the buyer with exaggerated and false declarations. Nevertheless, the case was closed in 2023 with no public settlement or court ruling.

Now, what happened to the H&M stock price during the first two months following the lawsuit?

H&M stock declined by 5% within the two months after the lawsuit, reflecting investors' reactions to the greenwashing allegations. Distrust of the public towards H&M has intensified due to the company's overclaiming of sustainability initiatives for its clothing line. The possibility of H&M having to pay penalties will impact its financial statements and erode the company's profitability, a primary concern for investors.

Regardless of the outcome, in the long term, H&M faced severe reputational damage that could only be recovered through excellent public relations handling. Nevertheless, a positive result from this case was the concerted efforts by EU regulators, who have since pushed for more stringent marketing standards, calling for clear statements and verifications from third parties on any green products, services, and benefits provided by companies.

14.6 The Case of Biased Judgement: Volkswagen Clean Diesel Scandal

Another notable case of greenwashing is Volkswagen's deception of its diesel car lines, a German car manufacturer. Volkswagen is Europe's largest car manufacturer, offering a range of brands that span from compact to luxurious cars. Starting in

2009, Volkswagen began marketing its diesel cars as low-emission, eco-friendly vehicles due to the 'Clean Diesel Technology' developed by their R&D team. The set of information on this achievement is widely available in their ESG reports, easily accessible to the public and potential investors. Thus, the investors eagerly positioned Volkswagen as a green automotive company.

However, in 2015, the US Environmental Protection Agency (EPA) discovered that Volkswagen had installed software to cheat on the carbon emission test, resulting in the underreporting of CO_2 emissions compared to the claimed values. Worse, at the time of revelation, more than 590,000 of the cars had emitted CO_2 40 times more than what is permitted on the road. As a result, Volkswagen was instructed to pay $ 2.7 billion in 2017, marking it as the most significant penalty in the automotive industry for greenwashing consumers, manipulating investors, and violating regulatory acts. Volkswagen's stock price declined by almost 20% of its market value within two days after the announcement by the EPA. Additionally, a global recall of 11 million vehicles has cost Volkswagen a total of € 6.7 billion.

Industry observers describe Volkswagen's greenwashing act as a deceptive manipulation through its ESG reports. Consistent leadership statements on Volkswagen's environmental sustainability have successfully convinced shareholders and potential investors to invest in the company. Essentially, Volkswagen's intentional falsification of information regarding carbon emissions was a grave and unethical decision. At the same time, it also demonstrates the confirmation bias and overreliance on corporate disclosures by the investors. Another way to look at this incident is that the consistent and persistent ESG messaging across all channels, ranging from disclosures in reports to advertisements in physical and online media, could overshadow critical analysis and requirements for third-party verification. This approach led to a biased assessment of Volkswagen's actual environmental performance.

14.7 Conclusion

As we conclude this chapter and move on to subsequent discussions on the role of sustainable finance in shaping a stable financial market, it is clear that both buyers, in this case, investors, and sellers, the companies that prepare the report, should be aware of the repercussions of greenwashing in ESG disclosures. Any forms of greenwashing must be minimised in attracting incoming funding or when polishing reputation, where it can be mitigated with solid and robust legal frameworks imposed by regulators. Clear and stringent clauses on the dos and don'ts should be spelt out for companies to adhere to. Furthermore, a stronger international standardisation to regulate greenwashing should be implemented and enforced effectively. ESG disclosures issued by the company should uphold the values of reliability, accountability, and transparency expected from any company that claims to support environmental preservation, societal justice, and strong governance controls.

Apart from ESG disclosures, another disclosure that investors should be mindful of is carbon disclosure and risk mitigation in response to climate change, as well as tracking the industry's carbon footprint. While this type of disclosure is very niche and the requirements vary depending on the regulators' enforcement, its future implications might pose bigger impacts compared to the general ESG disclosures.

References

Afianto RA, Waskito J (2025) Impact of greenwashing and perceived value on purchase intention in the bottled drinking water industry: mediating role of trust. J Enterpr Dev 7(1):79–91

Alaudhli RJ (2024) Greenwashing risk and its mitigation for sustainable finance. AJRSP 6(61):05–33

Badulescu D, Akhtar MN, Ahmad M, Soharwardi MA (2021) Accounting policies, institutional factors, and firm performance: qualitative insights in a developing country. J Risk Financ Manag 14(10):473

Bin Osman AZ (2022) Accountability through reporting: the case of foundations in Malaysia. Asia-Pacific Manag Acc J 17(2):32

Clarke G (2021) The credibility of international non-governmental organizations (INGOs) and the Oxfam scandal of 2018. J Civ Soc 17(3–4):219–237

Darnall N, Ji H, Iwata K, Arimura TH (2022) Do ESG reporting guidelines and verifications enhance firms' information disclosure? Corp Soc Responsib Environ Manag 29(5):1214–1230

Ellili NOD (2022) Impact of ESG disclosure and financial reporting quality on investment efficiency. Corp Gov Int J Business Soc 22(5):1094–1111

Forliano C, Battisti E, De Bernardi P, Kliestik T (2025) Mapping the greenwashing research landscape: a theoretical and field analysis. Rev Manag Sci. https://doi.org/10.1007/s11846-025-00856-3

Fridson MS, Alvarez F (2022) Financial statement analysis: a practitioner's guide. Wiley, Hoboken

Gathoni M (2020) Use of social media for fundraising by non-governmental wildlife conservation organizations in Karen (Doctoral dissertation, Daystar University, School of Communication)

Halkos G, Aslanidis PS (2025) Integrating environmental economics into ESG reporting in Europe: the environmental topic-specific cross-sector European sustainability reporting standards (ESRS)

Jahidi Z, Danuri MSM, Abd Karim SB (2024) Regulatory non-compliance and its limitations towards risk minimisation in the oil and gas industry. J Project Manag Pract 4(1):42–61

Krueger P, Sautner Z, Tang DY, Zhong R (2024) The effects of mandatory ESG disclosure around the world. J Account Res 62(5):1795–1847

Lin W (2022) Corporate non-financial reporting in the UK: diversions from the EU sustainability reporting framework. Sustainability 14(15):9134

Loang OK (2025) From tweets to trades: the dynamic dance of investor sentiment, attention, and news sentiment in ESG stocks. China Financ Econ Rev 14(1):70–91

Mercer M (2004) How do investors assess the credibility of management disclosures? Account Horiz 18(3):185–196

Misiuda M, Lachmann M (2022) Investors' perceptions of sustainability reporting—a review of the experimental literature. Sustainability 14(24):16746

Nuseir M, Qasim A (2021) Investor relations in the era of social media: systematic literature review of social media as a strategic corporate disclosure tool. J Financ Report Acc 19(5):819–838

Nyamdorj B, Anaka W, Stoica A, Sushant S, Ortega J, Helm B, Moreira P (2021) Carbon neutrality, reduction and offset-aviation solutions in the 21st century. SAE Int J Adv Curr Pract Mob 3:1293–1306

Ooi KL (2024) Demystifying behavioral finance. Springer, Cham

Ooi KL (2025) Market, news sentiments, and twitter happiness on adaptive herding behaviour of investors in Shariah-compliant stocks. J Islam Acc Business Res. https://doi.org/10.1108/JIABR-06-2024-0219

Rangapur A, Wang H, Shu K (2023) Investigating online financial misinformation and its consequences: a computational perspective. arXiv preprint arXiv:2309.12363

Van Duuren E, Plantinga A, Scholtens B (2016) ESG integration and the investment management process: Fundamental investing reinvented. J. Bus. Ethics 138(3):525–533

Chapter 15
The Psychology of Greenwashing and Investor Perception

15.1 Introduction

The rising prominence of sustainable finance has ushered in a new era where ESG criteria have become central to investment decision-making and corporate accountability (Xiao et al. 2023). Within this context, greenwashing—the practice by which firms exaggerate or fabricate their sustainability credentials—has emerged as a formidable challenge that undermines the foundational goals of ESG investing. Greenwashing is not merely a marketing tactic or an ethical transgression; it is a phenomenon with profound psychological and regulatory implications that distorts market signals and investor judgement. As the volume and complexity of ESG disclosures have grown, so too have the opportunities for firms to manipulate these narratives to their advantage. This manipulation undermines the authenticity of sustainable finance and risks diluting the very purpose it aims to achieve: redirecting capital toward environmentally and socially responsible activities.

Investor perception lies at the heart of this dilemma. How investors interpret, internalise, and act upon ESG information directly influences whether greenwashing is successful or not. For instance, investors often rely on company-issued sustainability reports, third-party ESG ratings, and media representations when evaluating a firm's commitment to sustainability. However, these sources are frequently characterised by ambiguity, selective disclosure, and inconsistencies in measurement frameworks. In the absence of standardised reporting protocols, investors are left to navigate a fragmented information environment, where the boundary between genuine ESG performance and performative signalling is increasingly blurred (Chopra et al. 2024). Consequently, investor perception becomes a malleable and powerful force capable of either reinforcing misleading corporate behaviour or resisting it through critical scrutiny and informed scepticism.

The inherent problem of information asymmetry exacerbates this dynamic. Corporations, as the primary producers of ESG disclosures, possess more information about their actual environmental and social practices than external

K. L. Ooi et al., *Following the Crowd: Psychological Drivers of Herding and Market Overreaction*, https://doi.org/10.1007/978-981-95-0792-4_15

stakeholders. When these firms strategically withhold negative information or embellish positive achievements, they create an informational imbalance that impairs rational assessment (Zhou et al. 2024). This asymmetry not only limits investors' ability to differentiate between authentic and superficial ESG efforts but also distorts capital flows and risk evaluations across financial markets. Investors may unknowingly allocate capital to firms engaged in greenwashing while penalising those with more cautious or conservative disclosure strategies, thereby creating perverse incentives that reward deception over transparency.

The complexity of greenwashing as both a psychological and regulatory issue necessitates a multidimensional analytical framework. The chapter explores this phenomenon through three interrelated dimensions. First, it examines investor reactions to ESG communication, focusing on how disclosure tone, frequency, and salience shape market behaviour among retail, institutional, and algorithmic investors. Second, it delves into the cognitive biases and behavioural distortions that contribute to investor misjudgement, drawing on psychological theories such as bounded rationality and prospect theory to explain why even sophisticated market participants may fall prey to sustainability narratives. Third, it assesses the regulatory landscape, analysing how current legal frameworks, institutional mechanisms, and global ESG standards either succeed or fail in mitigating greenwashing (Poiriazi et al. 2025). These three dimensions collectively provide a comprehensive foundation for understanding the interplay between corporate strategy, investor psychology, and regulatory oversight in the evolving field of sustainable finance. Through this lens, the chapter aims to illuminate the underlying mechanisms that enable greenwashing and propose pathways for strengthening investor discernment and regulatory efficacy.

15.2 How Market Participants React to Corporate ESG Disclosures

The heterogeneous nature of financial markets implies that investors do not uniformly interpret or react to corporate ESG disclosures. Distinct categories of market participants, including retail investors, institutional investors, and algorithmic traders, exhibit divergent behavioural patterns and informational processing mechanisms when confronted with ESG narratives (Loang 2025a). Each group's response is shaped by a unique set of cognitive, informational, and strategic constraints that mediate their interpretation of sustainability-related information. Empirical research increasingly underscores the differentiated impact of ESG communication on capital allocation across these investor classes, revealing both rational and behaviourally biased reactions.

Retail investors, typically characterised by limited access to granular firm-level data and lower financial sophistication, often rely on public-facing disclosures, media narratives, and ESG branding as proxies for corporate virtue. Studies indicate that retail investors demonstrate a pronounced sensitivity to the tone and framing of ESG announcements, with positive disclosures leading to increased retail order flow and upward price adjustments (Moss et al. 2024). This behaviour is magnified by media amplification; firms that issue ESG disclosures in highly publicised contexts or with emotionally charged language tend to attract disproportionate attention and capital from individual investors. Behavioural finance theories, particularly the affect heuristic and framing effects, provide a plausible explanation for these tendencies. Retail investors may anchor their investment decisions on superficial attributes of the disclosure, such as optimistic language or visually appealing sustainability reports, rather than on objective assessments of ESG performance. This can result in a potential overreaction to positive cues and underreaction to risks embedded in boilerplate or ambiguous ESG statements.

Institutional investors, including mutual funds, pension funds, and insurance companies, are traditionally seen as more analytical and better resourced in their evaluation of ESG disclosures. Nevertheless, empirical findings suggest that even institutional actors are not immune to behavioural distortions. While many institutions have integrated ESG criteria into their investment mandates, their reactions are often influenced by peer benchmarking, reputational concerns, and strategic herding (Rau and Yu 2024). For example, large asset managers may increase their holdings in firms with high ESG scores or those that frequently communicate sustainability, not solely on intrinsic value grounds, but to signal their alignment with industry trends or stakeholder expectations. Research has documented positive abnormal returns following ESG disclosure events that coincide with high institutional ownership, suggesting a form of informed momentum trading. However, such patterns may also reflect herding behaviour, where institutions follow each other's ESG-driven investment moves, potentially exacerbating market mispricing. The bounded rationality of institutional decision-making, coupled with imperfect ESG metrics, creates conditions where overreaction to popular ESG themes such as carbon neutrality or diversity pledges can drive capital toward firms with symbolic rather than substantive sustainability commitments.

Algorithmic investors, by contrast, react to ESG disclosures through data-driven, rule-based strategies that parse textual, numerical, and sentiment-based signals in real time. The increasing use of natural language processing (NLP) and sentiment analysis tools enables these investors to detect disclosure tone, frequency of ESG keyword usage, and media co-occurrence patterns with high precision. While algorithmic trading ostensibly eliminates human biases, it introduces a new layer of systemic dynamics whereby ESG disclosures, particularly those optimised for favourable sentiment scores, can trigger rapid capital reallocations and high-frequency trading anomalies. Algorithms may amplify short-term price swings if they are calibrated to react positively to any ESG communication without contextual understanding of its materiality or veracity (Tamura 2024). Such reactions can lead to temporary overvaluation of firms engaging in greenwashing or strategic signalling, only to be corrected in subsequent trading cycles as deeper inconsistencies emerge. This mechanistic approach to ESG interpretation raises concerns about the unintended consequences of ESG disclosure gamification, where firms tailor language and frequency of communication to exploit algorithmic decision rules rather than to convey meaningful sustainability progress.

Across all investor categories, the tone and frequency of ESG disclosure play pivotal roles in shaping perceptions and capital flows. Firms that maintain consistent, transparent, and frequent sustainability communication are often rewarded with increased investor trust and reduced cost of capital. Conversely, sporadic or excessively promotional ESG disclosures can invite scepticism, especially in the presence of contradictory financial or operational performance indicators (Rino 2021). Behavioural finance offers a valuable lens through which to interpret these phenomena. The representativeness heuristic, for instance, can cause investors to equate stylistic presentation with substantive ESG performance. At the same time, availability bias may lead them to overweight recent or salient ESG events in their valuation models. These biases contribute to well-documented underreaction and overreaction patterns: markets may initially underreact to understated or complex ESG disclosures, only to later overreact once media coverage or peer consensus amplifies the information.

15.3 Behavioural Factors Leading to Investor Misjudgement of Sustainable Initiatives

Investor misperceptions of corporate sustainability claims are often not the result of deliberate ignorance or lack of data but rather stem from deeply rooted cognitive biases and heuristic shortcuts that shape how individuals process complex and uncertain information. In the context of ESG disclosures and green branding, these mental shortcuts frequently distort rational evaluation, leading to systematic errors in judgement and decision-making. Among the most influential cognitive distortions are confirmation bias, the halo effect, and framing bias, all of which play a prominent role in reinforcing greenwashing practices and obscuring the accurate sustainability profile of firms.

Confirmation bias is particularly salient in the ESG investment landscape, where investors tend to seek out and give greater weight to information that aligns with their pre-existing beliefs about a company's sustainability posture. For example, once a firm earns a reputation as an environmentally responsible leader, whether through early adoption of renewable energy policies or high ESG ratings, investors may disproportionately favour new information that confirms this perception while discounting contradictory data, such as involvement in environmental violations or supply chain abuses. This selective information processing impedes objective assessment and creates a fertile ground for greenwashing, as firms can rely on reputational inertia to shield themselves from critical scrutiny (Aliano et al. 2024). Behavioural finance theory suggests that such bias is amplified in high-uncertainty environments where ESG metrics are non-standardised and difficult to verify, further compromising market discipline.

The halo effect operates similarly by allowing a single favourable attribute, such as a high-profile sustainability initiative or charismatic ESG-focused leadership, to cast a positive glow over unrelated corporate domains. Investors influenced by the halo effect may conflate corporate social responsibility with overall firm quality, leading them to overestimate financial performance, governance strength, or long-term risk management capabilities (Puspitasari et al., 2024; Shapira 2022). This distortion has profound implications for capital allocation, as it can lead to the overvaluation of firms based not on their financial fundamentals but on perceived moral legitimacy. Prospect theory provides additional insight into this behaviour by highlighting how investors are prone to overweighing gains and underestimating losses in emotionally charged contexts. The aspirational appeal of investing in a 'green' or 'ethical' company may cause individuals to focus disproportionately on potential social or environmental benefits, while overlooking the inadequately disclosed or understood financial risks that remain.

Framing bias further compounds these misperceptions by influencing how investors interpret ESG-related information based on its presentation rather than its content. The framing of ESG disclosures, whether as opportunities for positive impact, obligations for compliance, or narratives of innovation, can significantly alter investor reactions (Sun 2024). For instance, firms that present their sustainability efforts through aspirational storytelling or emotionally resonant visuals are more likely to elicit favourable investor sentiment, even when the underlying data lacks substance. This susceptibility to narrative framing undermines the analytical rigour that should underpin investment decisions, enabling firms to obfuscate underperformance with stylistic embellishment. The emotional resonance of ESG branding, which aligns with identity, values, and social signalling, can therefore overwhelm rational risk assessment, especially in markets where investors seek not just returns but also meaning and moral alignment from their portfolios.

Bounded rationality, as articulated by Herbert Simon, offers a structural explanation for these behavioural anomalies. Given the cognitive limitations of individuals and the overwhelming volume of ESG data, investors often rely on simplified heuristics and brand cues to navigate sustainability information. This reliance is not irrational per se, but it exposes decision-making to systematic manipulation when firms strategically frame or curate their ESG communications to exploit these heuristics. Similarly, prospect theory, with its emphasis on loss aversion and reference dependency, explains why investors may irrationally cling to firms they perceive as ESG leaders despite emerging evidence to the contrary. The fear of losing a perceived moral high ground or admitting misjudgement may reinforce cognitive inertia and delay corrective action in portfolios.

15.4 Regulatory Challenges in Combating Greenwashing

The regulatory landscape confronting greenwashing is characterised by fragmentation, ambiguity, and institutional undercapacity, all of which contribute to the persistent difficulty in identifying and penalising misleading sustainability claims. At the core of this challenge lies the legal and definitional opacity surrounding what constitutes greenwashing (Shanor and Light 2022). Unlike traditional financial fraud, which is often governed by well-established statutory and case law precedents, greenwashing occupies a regulatory grey zone where enforcement depends on evolving ESG taxonomies, soft law instruments, and interpretive discretion. This legal indeterminacy hinders regulators' ability to establish clear thresholds between legitimate sustainability disclosures and deceptive marketing practices, thereby limiting their capacity to impose consistent penalties and deter misconduct.

One of the primary impediments to effective regulation is the lack of standardised ESG taxonomies. While taxonomies aim to create a unified framework for defining sustainable economic activities, their current state remains underdeveloped and jurisdictionally fragmented (Li 2024). The European Union's Sustainable Finance Taxonomy represents the most ambitious attempt to establish science-based criteria for labelling activities as 'environmentally sustainable'. However, the implementation of this taxonomy has been beset by political contestation, scope limitations, and technical complexity, resulting in partial coverage that omits specific sectors and social dimensions. Furthermore, its reliance on firm self-reporting poses verification challenges.

In contrast, the United States has not developed a comprehensive taxonomy; instead, it has focused on mandating climate-related risk disclosures through the Securities and Exchange Commission (SEC). The SEC's proposed climate disclosure rule emphasises standardised reporting on greenhouse gas emissions and climate governance. However, it stops short of defining what qualifies as a sustainable activity, thereby creating interpretive leeway that firms may exploit to project a green image without adhering to substantive criteria.

Voluntary disclosure regimes exacerbate these challenges by allowing firms considerable discretion in determining the content, scope, and tone of their ESG communications. Frameworks such as the Global Reporting Initiative (GRI), the Task Force on Climate-related Financial Disclosures (TCFD), and the Sustainability Accounting Standards Board (SASB) have encouraged greater transparency; however, they lack effective enforcement mechanisms, thereby creating a compliance environment driven more by reputational incentives than legal obligations. While some firms engage with these frameworks in good faith, others utilise the flexibility to disclose favourable metrics while selectively omitting material sustainability risks. This practice, often referred to as 'selective transparency', is challenging to regulate under voluntary regimes and creates asymmetries in the information available to investors. Moreover, the absence of assurance standards or third-party audits for ESG reports allows inconsistent or inflated claims to circulate unchecked, diluting the credibility of the entire ESG disclosure ecosystem.

Third-party ESG ratings, intended to provide investors with independent assessments of corporate sustainability performance, have themselves become a source of confusion and regulatory concern. Ratings agencies employ divergent methodologies, opaque algorithms, and inconsistent criteria, which often result in low correlation across ESG scores for the same firm. This inconsistency undermines the reliability of ratings as decision-making tools and facilitates arbitrage by companies that tailor disclosures to align with specific rating models. Furthermore, the lack of regulatory oversight over ESG rating providers means that conflicts of interest, such as payment-for-rating models, remain largely unaddressed. These structural limitations hinder investors' ability to verify ESG claims, emboldening firms to strategically manage perceptions without improving actual performance.

Comparative regulatory analysis reveals significant variation in the stringency, coherence, and enforceability of ESG disclosure rules across jurisdictions. The EU's Sustainable Finance Disclosure Regulation (SFDR) requires asset managers and financial advisors to categorise their investment products based on their level of sustainability integration and to provide detailed disclosure of ESG risks. The SFDR operates within a broader taxonomy-based regulatory architecture, making it one of the most comprehensive frameworks globally. However, its effectiveness has been constrained by inconsistent implementation across member states and the transitional nature of supporting guidelines. In contrast, the U.S. SEC's climate disclosure rule, though narrower in scope, signals a move toward mandatory ESG reporting within the financial materiality paradigm.

Nevertheless, it remains vulnerable to legal challenges and political reversals, given the contentious nature of climate regulation in the United States. Other jurisdictions, such as Japan and Canada, have adopted hybrid approaches that blend voluntary guidelines with incremental mandatory elements. Still, these efforts lack the enforcement teeth required to deter greenwashing meaningfully.

Regulatory gaps both within and between jurisdictions amplify investor vulnerability. The absence of globally harmonised ESG standards creates opportunities for regulatory arbitrage, where firms can exploit jurisdictional inconsistencies to present divergent sustainability profiles across markets. This dynamic undermines investor trust, complicates cross-border capital allocation, and weakens the effectiveness of ESG as a risk mitigation tool. In addition, under-resourced regulatory agencies often lack the technical expertise and institutional capacity to conduct deep audits of ESG disclosures or to pursue legal action against offenders, especially in emerging markets where enforcement infrastructures are less developed.

The legal and institutional barriers to curbing greenwashing are deeply embedded in the current architecture of ESG regulation. The limitations of existing taxonomies, the voluntary nature of most disclosure frameworks, and the deficiencies in third-party rating systems create a permissive environment for strategic misrepresentation. Global inconsistencies and institutional inertia further weaken deterrence. Addressing these challenges will require not only stronger regulatory coordination and standard-setting at the international level but also the development of enforcement capabilities, audit mechanisms, and legal definitions that can withstand judicial scrutiny. Only through such comprehensive reform can the integrity of sustainable finance be safeguarded and investor protection be meaningfully advanced.

15.5 Conclusion

The interplay between investor psychology and greenwashing represents a critical juncture in the evolution of sustainable finance. As demonstrated throughout this chapter, the mechanisms that allow greenwashing to flourish are deeply rooted in cognitive biases, structural asymmetries, and regulatory fragmentation (Malmlund 2024). Misaligned incentives within both corporate and financial sectors encourage strategic sustainability signalling over genuine transformation. Simultaneously, behavioural distortions such as confirmation bias, the halo effect, and framing susceptibility impair investors' ability to distinguish between substantive ESG performance and superficial branding. These psychological patterns are not merely individual aberrations; they represent systemic vulnerabilities that compromise the efficiency of capital allocation and erode the credibility of ESG markets.

The lack of coherent and enforceable regulatory frameworks further compounds the pervasiveness of greenwashing. As evidenced by the divergence between the EU's taxonomy-driven Sustainable Finance Disclosure Regulation (SFDR) and the U.S. Securities and Exchange Commission's (SEC) climate disclosure rule, jurisdictions remain fragmented in their definitions, enforcement mechanisms, and scope of coverage. Voluntary disclosure regimes and inconsistent third-party ESG ratings add layers of opacity rather than clarity. In such an environment, investor trust becomes fragile, susceptible to collapse under the weight of repeated credibility shocks and market corrections triggered by ESG controversies. The current configuration of ESG governance, therefore, lacks the necessary institutional alignment to support a transparent and accountable sustainable finance ecosystem.

Restoring integrity in ESG investing demands a reconfiguration of both behavioural and regulatory infrastructures. On the behavioural front, future research should prioritise the development of diagnostic tools capable of detecting greenwashing narratives before they gain traction in capital markets (Alaudhli 2024). These tools may include sentiment analytics calibrated to identify disingenuous language, heuristics-mitigating investor education platforms, and decision-support systems embedded with behavioural guardrails. Academic inquiry into the psychological triggers of ESG perception should also be deepened to uncover the emotional and cognitive levers most susceptible to manipulation.

On the regulatory front, establishing universally accepted ESG disclosure standards is imperative. Harmonising taxonomies, enhancing audit requirements for sustainability reports, and increasing oversight of ESG rating agencies will be vital steps toward minimising the interpretive and informational discretion that greenwashing exploits. Furthermore, regulators must be equipped with both the technical capacity and legal authority to pursue enforcement actions that transcend jurisdictional boundaries and hold firms accountable for deceptive ESG narratives.

The chapter argues that the sustainability agenda can only be realised if the psychological and institutional pathways through which greenwashing operates are addressed simultaneously. Sustainable finance is not just a matter of improving data quality or refining metrics; it is a challenge of aligning human cognition, market structures, and regulatory norms to a shared vision of long-term value creation. The credibility and effectiveness of ESG markets will depend not only on what is disclosed but on how investors interpret those disclosures and how institutions respond to their misuse. The convergence of behavioural finance and regulatory design must therefore be central to any forward-looking strategy for combating greenwashing.

References

Alaudhli RJ (2024) Greenwashing risk and its mitigation for sustainable finance. AJRSP 6(61):05–33

Aliano M, Cestari G, Madonna S (2024) Greenwashing. In: Sustainable finance for SMEs: the role of capital for sustainable and inclusive growth. Springer, Cham, pp 103–124

Chopra SS, Senadheera SS, Dissanayake PD, Withana PA, Chib R, Rhee JH, Ok YS (2024) Navigating the challenges of environmental, social, and governance (ESG) reporting: the path to broader sustainable development. Sustainability 16(2):606

Li D (2024) Sustainable ecosystems and the economics of state ownership: a three-stage structural framework and innovative insights. J Knowl Econ 15(3):11090–11127

Loang OK (2025a) Can machine learning surpass human investors? Evidence from adaptive herding behaviour in US, China and India. J Appl Econ 28(1):2435796

Loang OK, Candra S (2025) Religion and green: the dual power of ESG and Shariah-compliant stocks in brand values of Malaysia, Indonesia, and Saudi Arabia. J Islam Monet Econ Financ 11(2):419–448

Malmlund R (2024) Uncovering greenwashing–approaches for understanding and addressing the complexity of deceptive environmental practices

Moss A, Naughton JP, Wang C (2024) The irrelevance of environmental, social, and governance disclosure to retail investors. Manag Sci 70(4):2626–2644

Poiriazi E, Zournatzidou G, Konteos G, Sariannidis N (2025) Analyzing the interconnection between environmental, social, and governance (ESG) criteria and corporate corruption: revealing the significant impact of greenwashing. Admin Sci 15(3):100

Puspitasari N, Harymawan I, Ab Aziz N (2024) Islamic governance and leverage: the interacting role of corporate social responsibility disclosure. J Islam Account Bus Res 15(6):1028–1049

Rau PR, Yu T (2024) A survey on ESG: investors, institutions and firms. China Financ Rev Int 14(1):3–33

Rino A (2021) "I know something you don't know": analysis of perceptions of environmental, social and governance (ESG) reporting in the Canadian oil and gas industry through signaling, dramaturgy, and reception theories (Doctoral dissertation, Mount Saint Vincent University)

Shanor A, Light SE (2022) Greenwashing and the first amendment. Columbia Law Rev 122(7):2033–2118

Shapira R (2022) The challenge of holding big business accountable. Cardozo Law Rev 44:203

Sun Y (2024) The real effect of innovation in environmental, social, and governance (ESG) disclosures on ESG performance: an integrated reporting perspective. J Clean Prod 460:142592

Tamura Y (2024) How can we promote impact/ESG investing?-clarifying the skeptical reasons and benefits of addressing impact & ESG investing in the age of artificial intelligence (Doctoral dissertation, Massachusetts Institute of Technology)

Xiao R, Deng J, Zhou Y, Chen M (2023) Analyzing contemporary trends in sustainable finance and ESG investment. Law Econ 2(11):44–52

Zhou Y, Chen L, Zhang Y, Li W (2024) "Environmental disclosure greenwashing" and corporate value: the premium effect and premium devalue of environmental information. Corp Soc Responsib Environ Manag 31(3):2424–2438

Chapter 16
The Role of Sustainable Finance in Market Stability

16.1 Introduction

The past two decades have been marked by a succession of systemic disruptions that have exposed the vulnerabilities inherent in modern financial markets (Loang 2025a). The 2008 global economic crisis, triggered by a collapse in the subprime mortgage sector and fuelled by excessive leverage, opacity, and moral hazard, revealed the consequences of unregulated financial innovation and short-term profit orientation. More recently, the COVID-19 pandemic unleashed a shockwave of economic uncertainty, liquidity stress, and capital flight, highlighting the fragility of supply chains, labour markets, and healthcare systems upon which financial systems are deeply interdependent. These crises, although distinct in origin, share a common implication: traditional risk assessment frameworks and market practices have repeatedly failed to anticipate and mitigate systemic risks that are broad-based and systemic. In response to this recurring instability, sustainable finance has emerged as a paradigmatic shift, integrating ESG considerations into investment and policy decisions to promote economic durability and long-term value creation (Xiao et al. 2023).

Sustainable finance can be defined as the alignment of financial decision-making with the principles of sustainability, wherein capital is allocated not merely according to risk-adjusted returns, but also with regard to societal and environmental externalities. At the centre of this approach lies ESG investing, a practice that embeds non-financial criteria into portfolio construction, risk management, and corporate governance engagement. ESG investing challenges the neoclassical assumption of investor rationality and market efficiency by introducing multidimensional objectives that transcend immediate profitability (Visconti 2021). Rather than functioning as a marginal ethical preference, ESG investing is increasingly positioned as a systemic necessity a mechanism for internalising long-horizon risks, such as climate change, social unrest, and governance failures, that have historically been excluded from traditional valuation models. As such, ESG integration is not only a

K. L. Ooi et al., *Following the Crowd: Psychological Drivers of Herding and Market Overreaction*, https://doi.org/10.1007/978-981-95-0792-4_16

response to normative demands for responsible capitalism but a strategic imperative for market stability.

The research problem addressed in this chapter revolves around the effectiveness of sustainable finance in mitigating systemic risk and enhancing the resilience of financial markets. Specifically, it examines whether and how ESG considerations serve as stabilising forces that reduce volatility, prevent contagion, and facilitate more efficient capital allocation during periods of stress. This question gains significance in light of empirical evidence suggesting that ESG-aligned assets tend to outperform or exhibit lower downside risk during crises, thereby offering protective features that are not fully captured by conventional financial analysis. However, this empirical association is not yet theoretically consolidated nor universally observed, raising critical questions about causality, measurement heterogeneity, and the role of institutional actors in shaping ESG outcomes.

The scope of the chapter is threefold. First, it lays the theoretical groundwork by examining the conceptual and normative foundations that link sustainable finance to financial stability, drawing on frameworks such as Modern Portfolio Theory, Stakeholder Theory, and Systemic Risk Theory. Second, it engages in an empirical review of ESG performance during major financial shocks, with a particular focus on risk-adjusted returns, volatility metrics, and capital flows. This analysis considers both firm-level and asset-class level data to unpack heterogeneity in ESG resilience (Gianfrate et al. 2024). Third, the chapter examines the role of institutional investors and financial regulators in integrating ESG principles into market structures through fiduciary stewardship, disclosure mandates, and the taxonomic classification of sustainable activities. In doing so, it assesses the effectiveness of policy instruments, including the EU Sustainable Finance Disclosure Regulation (SFDR), the Task Force on Climate-related Financial Disclosures (TCFD), and central bank interventions aimed at integrating green monetary policy.

16.2 Theoretical Foundations Linking Sustainable Finance to Market Volatility Reduction

The integration of sustainable finance into mainstream financial decision-making is underpinned by several foundational theories that highlight its potential to mitigate volatility and foster systemic stability. Chief among these is Modern Portfolio Theory (MPT), which posits that investors optimise portfolios by maximising expected returns for a given level of risk through diversification. While traditional interpretations of MPT emphasise financial metrics, recent extensions of the theory incorporate ESG factors as an additional dimension of risk assessment. ESG variables such as exposure to climate regulation, reputational risk from poor labour practices, or governance deficiencies introduce latent, non-linear risks that are often unaccounted for in standard models (Loang and Candra 2025). Incorporating these variables into portfolio construction allows investors to anticipate and mitigate material downside exposures that would otherwise remain hidden. Empirical evidence increasingly supports the notion that portfolios with strong ESG integration exhibit lower idiosyncratic risk, reduced drawdowns during periods of market stress, and enhanced Sharpe ratios, particularly in sectors susceptible to regulatory or environmental disruption. Thus, ESG inclusion does not deviate from the MPT framework but rather enhances its predictive and protective capacity by broadening the definition of relevant risks.

Stakeholder Theory provides a complementary lens by recasting the firm not solely as an agent of shareholder value maximisation, but as a nexus of relationships with diverse stakeholders, including employees, customers, regulators, communities, and the environment. From this perspective, firms that prioritise ESG principles cultivate long-term trust, operational resilience, and license to operate, thereby reducing both firm-specific and systemic uncertainty (Hughes et al. 2025). Sustainable firms often enjoy more stable cash flows, lower capital costs, and reduced litigation or regulatory penalties, all of which contribute to their financial robustness. Furthermore, by proactively managing externalities and engaging with social and environmental risks, these firms enhance their adaptability in the face of shocks, which in turn stabilises investor expectations. Stakeholder-centric governance thus serves not merely as an ethical imperative but as a risk mitigation strategy that aligns corporate behaviour with broader economic resilience (Loang & Ahmad 2020). In aggregate, the widespread adoption of stakeholder-oriented practices across firms can temper market exuberance, foster alignment between private incentives and public welfare, and dampen the boom-bust cycles associated with short-term profit chasing.

The Market Efficiency Hypothesis (MEH), which posits that asset prices fully reflect all available information, encounters a more nuanced interface with sustainable finance. While ESG information is increasingly disseminated, it is neither universally standardised nor instantly incorporated into market valuations, resulting in persistent inefficiencies. These inefficiencies arise from heterogeneous disclosure standards, inconsistent third-party ratings, and varying investor interpretations of ESG materiality. However, these frictions also offer an opportunity: by systematically integrating ESG data into investment decisions, informed investors can arbitrage inefficiencies and facilitate more accurate price discovery. In this sense, sustainable finance contributes to the dynamic efficiency of markets by accelerating the internalisation of long-horizon risks and aligning prices more closely with fundamental value. Moreover, the long-term orientation inherent in ESG strategies counteracts the short-termism that often drives speculative bubbles and market volatility. By extending investment horizons and privileging stable, value-preserving firms, ESG investors foster a more patient capital base that acts as a stabilising anchor during market corrections.

Critically, ESG integration modifies the traditional risk-return trade-off by challenging the assumption that maximising returns must come at the cost of higher risk. Instead, sustainable finance reframes risk as multidimensional, encompassing financial, environmental, social, and governance exposures (Ooi 2025). ESG integration prompts a re-evaluation of what constitutes a 'high-return' asset, recognising that short-term gains achieved through unsustainable practices may entail long-term liabilities not yet reflected in the market. For instance, a fossil fuel-intensive firm may offer attractive dividends, but if its business model is incompatible with future regulatory or technological developments, its earnings stream may be unsustainable. ESG analysis enables investors to anticipate these transition risks and recalibrate portfolios accordingly. Consequently, capital is more likely to be allocated toward firms that exhibit long-term strategic alignment with sustainable development goals, thereby reinforcing structural resilience within the financial ecosystem.

The theoretical foundations of sustainable finance articulate a coherent rationale for its stabilising influence on markets. Through the diversification logic of MPT, the relational robustness emphasised by Stakeholder Theory, and the informational refinement envisioned by MEH, ESG integration emerges not as an ancillary consideration but as a critical tool for risk management and financial stability. However, realising these theoretical benefits in practice depends on the continued evolution of ESG data quality, regulatory harmonisation, and investor sophistication (Chiu 2025). Only then can sustainable finance fulfil its promise as a bulwark against systemic instability and a conduit for durable economic value.

16.3 Literature Review on ESG Performance during Financial Crises

The empirical performance of ESG investments during financial downturns has attracted increasing scholarly attention, particularly in the aftermath of the 2008 global economic crisis and the COVID-19 pandemic. The growing body of literature since 2020 has provided a nuanced understanding of how sustainability-focused portfolios behave under conditions of market stress, with researchers seeking to evaluate whether ESG integration offers genuine downside protection or merely correlates with other risk-mitigating attributes. These investigations have drawn on a variety of datasets, asset classes, and geographies, producing a spectrum of findings that inform the ongoing debate about the financial materiality of ESG considerations.

A substantial portion of the literature converges on the conclusion that ESG investments have exhibited relative resilience during major economic shocks. For example, Broadstock et al. (2021) analysed Chinese equity markets during the COVID-19 pandemic. They found that high-ESG stocks outperformed their low-ESG counterparts in terms of both returns and risk-adjusted performance. Similarly, Albuquerque et al. (2020) provided evidence from the U.S. market showing that firms with superior ESG scores experienced smaller stock price declines and lower volatility in the early months of the pandemic (Loang 2025b). They attribute this resilience to stronger customer loyalty, stakeholder engagement, and risk management capabilities inherent in ESG-leading firms. These findings are echoed by Baer et al. (2021), who examined global mutual fund flows and demonstrated that ESG funds faced significantly lower redemptions during COVID-19-induced market turbulence, suggesting that investors perceived these funds as more trustworthy and stable in times of crisis.

Beyond the COVID-19 period, studies that retrospectively examine the 2008 financial crisis offer additional insight. While ESG data were less robust and standardised at that time, retrospective scoring methodologies enable comparative analyses. Nofsinger and Varma (2014), although predating the post-2020 literature, laid a foundational argument by showing that socially responsible mutual funds outperformed conventional funds during the crisis period, even though they underperformed during non-crisis times. More recent studies have attempted to validate and extend these findings with improved datasets and methodologies (Pachouly et al. 2022). For instance, Capelle-Blancard and Petit (2019) revisited ESG fund performance during both the 2008 and 2011 crises using a global sample. They confirmed that funds with ESG mandates experienced less severe drawdowns and quicker recoveries. These outcomes suggest that ESG strategies may function as a form of insurance, offering capital preservation benefits that become particularly salient when market confidence deteriorates.

However, the literature is not without dissent. Some studies challenge the notion that ESG investments offer intrinsic risk protection, arguing instead that observed resilience may be an artefact of sectoral biases or other confounding variables. ESG funds tend to be overweight in technology and underweight in energy and financial sectors that were, respectively, favoured and punished during the COVID-19 downturn. Once these sector exposures are controlled for, the performance differential between ESG and non-ESG portfolios diminishes. Similarly, Pedersen et al. (2021) propose a three-factor model that decomposes ESG performance into traditional risk, ESG-specific alpha, and taste components. They find that while ESG characteristics correlate with risk aversion and investor preferences, the standalone alpha attributable to ESG strategies is modest and often context-dependent. These findings underscore the importance of disentangling ESG-related effects from other structural portfolio characteristics when interpreting performance results.

Another dimension of divergence in the literature concerns regional and temporal variability. ESG resilience is not uniformly observed across all markets and timeframes. For instance, European ESG funds have generally outperformed their North American counterparts in downturns, possibly due to stronger regulatory support and more mature investor demand in the EU. Meanwhile, emerging markets present a more heterogeneous picture, where governance challenges and data inconsistencies complicate the evaluation of ESG. Furthermore, the durability of ESG performance through multiple crisis phases, including shock onset, recovery, and post-crisis normalisation, remains an open question. While ESG portfolios often outperform during sharp declines, their relative advantage may taper off or reverse as risk appetite returns and traditional cyclical sectors regain favour.

Despite these complexities, the post-2020 empirical literature affirms the hypothesis that ESG integration contributes to portfolio resilience during systemic disruptions. ESG-aligned assets generally demonstrate lower downside risk, reduced idiosyncratic volatility, and more stable capital flows during periods of financial stress (Jormakka 2025). This performance is likely attributable to a confluence of factors, including superior risk management practices, enhanced stakeholder relationships, and growing investor conviction in sustainability as a strategic imperative. Nevertheless, the robustness of these findings depends critically on the quality of ESG data, the specificity of scoring methodologies, and the context in which investments are made.

While consensus has emerged around the stabilising role of ESG strategies during crises such as COVID-19 and the 2008 financial meltdown, significant divergences persist regarding the sources, magnitude, and generalisability of this effect. The empirical evidence is increasingly compelling, yet it invites further refinement through more granular, longitudinal, and multi-market analyses. A deeper understanding of how ESG dynamics interact with financial contagion, liquidity constraints, and behavioural biases during market downturns will be essential for both scholars and practitioners seeking to harness sustainable finance as a tool for mitigating systemic risk.

16.4 The Role of Institutional Investors in Promoting Sustainable Market Practices

Institutional investors have emerged as pivotal actors in shaping the trajectory of sustainable financial markets. With their vast assets under management (AUM), long investment horizons, and strategic market influence, these entities—comprising pension funds, sovereign wealth funds, insurance companies, and asset managers—possess the structural capacity to internalise ESG risks and catalyse corporate behavioural change (Loang and Candra 2025). Central to their influence is the fiduciary duty they owe to beneficiaries, which traditionally emphasised the maximisation of risk-adjusted returns. However, recent developments in fiduciary interpretation have broadened this mandate to include sustainability considerations, reflecting a growing consensus that ESG risks are financially material and therefore inseparable from prudent investment practice.

The evolving understanding of fiduciary duty is particularly evident in jurisdictions where regulatory bodies and courts have recognised ESG factors as consistent with, or even necessary for, fulfilling long-term fiduciary responsibilities. For example, the U.K.'s Department for Work and Pensions and the U.S. Department of Labour have issued guidance allowing pension funds to integrate ESG criteria without violating fiduciary obligations, provided such integration is grounded in economic rationale (Muir 2022). This shift has legitimised ESG investing as a fiduciary imperative, enabling institutions like CalPERS to embed sustainability into their investment policies formally. CalPERS' Investment Beliefs framework, for instance, explicitly acknowledges that long-term value creation depends on the effective management of ESG risks, thus institutionalising sustainability within its fiduciary logic.

Portfolio rebalancing practices offer another mechanism through which institutional investors shape sustainable markets. By reallocating capital toward ESG-compliant firms and funds, institutional investors influence asset pricing and corporate access to capital. Empirical studies, such as those by Dyck et al. (2019), demonstrate that institutional ownership is positively associated with improved ESG performance at the firm level, suggesting that firms respond strategically to the preferences of their institutional shareholders. Moreover, research by Bolton and Kacperczyk (2021) during the COVID-19 crisis revealed that firms with higher institutional ESG ownership experienced less severe stock price declines, implying that institutional ESG preferences can confer downside protection and pricing premiums. These dynamics create a self-reinforcing loop: as firms recognise the capital advantages associated with ESG alignment, they are incentivised to improve their disclosure and performance, thereby expanding the universe of investable sustainable assets.

Institutional investors also exert influence through their roles as stewards and engaged participants. As large blockholders, they possess the voting power and organisational bandwidth to actively engage with portfolio companies on ESG issues (Loang 2025a). This stewardship function is increasingly formalised through proxy voting policies, shareholder proposals, and direct dialogues. BlackRock, the world's largest asset manager, exemplifies this trend through its annual stewardship reports, which disclose engagement outcomes and voting behaviour on ESG matters. In 2021, BlackRock announced its intent to hold boards accountable for a lack of progress on climate-related disclosures and diversity targets, reinforcing the reputational and governance consequences of ESG underperformance. These stewardship actions extend beyond symbolic gestures; empirical evidence from Dimson et al. (2020) demonstrates that successful ESG engagements by institutional investors result in positive abnormal returns and improvements in governance, validating engagement as a credible tool for ESG enhancement.

Institutional pressure on corporate ESG disclosures also plays a crucial role in improving market transparency and accountability. By demanding consistent, decision-useful sustainability data, institutional investors encourage firms to adopt internationally recognised reporting frameworks, such as the Task Force on Climate-related Financial Disclosures (TCFD), the Global Reporting Initiative (GRI), and the Sustainability Accounting Standards Board (SASB). Asset owners and managers have increasingly collaborated through networks such as the Climate Action 100+ and the Principles for Responsible Investment (PRI) to standardise expectations and escalate pressure on lagging firms. These coordinated initiatives aim to reduce informational asymmetries and align ESG reporting with investor needs, thereby improving the quality of sustainability signals that guide portfolio decisions.

Nevertheless, institutional influence is not without limitations or contradictions. Some critics argue that asset managers face inherent conflicts of interest between ESG advocacy and short-term financial performance mandates. Furthermore, stewardship intensity varies significantly across institutions, with many engagements remaining private and difficult to verify. There is also a concern of ESG 'box-ticking', wherein institutions adopt sustainability rhetoric without substantive follow-through, particularly in passive investing contexts where shareholder engagement is less aggressive. These challenges underscore the need for stronger regulatory frameworks that mandate ESG stewardship transparency and harmonise reporting standards, ensuring that institutional influence translates into genuine corporate sustainability improvements.

Institutional investors are central architects of sustainable financial markets. Through their fiduciary evolution, capital allocation strategies, stewardship practices, and demand for transparency, they embed ESG considerations into market operations and corporate governance. Entities such as BlackRock and CalPERS exemplify how institutional leverage can shift norms and redirect financial flows toward sustainability objectives. However, to fully realise this potential, institutional efforts must be complemented by regulatory coherence, accountability mechanisms, and continued academic scrutiny into the causal pathways linking investor behaviour to systemic sustainability outcomes.

16.5 Regulatory and Policy Mechanisms for Strengthening Financial Stability through ESG Integration

The integration of ESG principles into financial markets has increasingly relied on an evolving ecosystem of regulatory and policy instruments designed to align capital allocation with sustainability objectives (Baer et al. 2021). These tools, ranging from green finance taxonomies and disclosure mandates to carbon pricing schemes and central bank interventions, constitute a multi-level governance architecture that seeks to internalise ESG externalities, reduce informational asymmetries, and embed systemic risk mitigation into market structures. However, their effectiveness in promoting long-term financial stability remains heterogeneous, contingent on regulatory coherence, institutional capacity, and political commitment.

Green finance taxonomies have emerged as foundational tools in standardising definitions of sustainable economic activities. By providing a precise classification of which sectors and projects qualify as environmentally sustainable, taxonomies seek to reduce greenwashing and improve the comparability of financial products. The European Union's Sustainable Finance Taxonomy, the most developed of its kind, delineates technical screening criteria across six environmental objectives, including climate mitigation and biodiversity conservation. Early assessments suggest that the taxonomy has improved transparency and catalysed product innovation in green bonds and ESG-linked loans. However, its practical implementation faces several limitations. The political compromise required to classify specific contentious sectors, such as natural gas and nuclear energy, has diluted the scientific rigour of the taxonomy. Furthermore, the compliance burden on firms and the reliance on self-reporting introduce risks of selective disclosure and measurement inconsistency. While the taxonomy is a necessary step toward market discipline, its impact on systemic stability will depend on how rigorously it is embedded in supervisory and investment mandates.

Disclosure mandates such as the Task Force on Climate-related Financial Disclosures (TCFD) and the Sustainable Finance Disclosure Regulation (SFDR) are critical in addressing the information asymmetry that hinders ESG integration. TCFD, initiated by the Financial Stability Board, encourages firms to report climate-related risks and opportunities across governance, strategy, risk management, and metrics. Its widespread adoption by financial institutions and corporates, now exceeding 3000 organisations globally, has fostered convergence in climate risk reporting. Empirical studies indicate that TCFD adoption improves the quality of firm-level climate risk data and enhances investors' ability to price transition and physical risks. However, the voluntary nature of the framework limits its enforcement and comparability. The SFDR, by contrast, imposes mandatory ESG disclosures on asset managers operating in the EU, requiring classification of investment products under Articles 6, 8, or 9 depending on the level of ESG integration. While the SFDR represents a regulatory leap in ESG transparency, it has also generated confusion due to evolving guidance, interpretive ambiguity, and a lack of alignment with the EU taxonomy (Macpherson 2024). Moreover, without third-party verification or assurance standards, the reliability of disclosed data remains uncertain. Both frameworks contribute to systemic risk awareness, but their stabilising influence is undermined by inconsistent implementation and limited enforcement mechanisms.

Carbon pricing, whether through carbon taxes or emissions trading systems (ETS), represents one of the most direct policy instruments for internalising environmental externalities. By assigning a market price to carbon emissions, these mechanisms incentivise low-carbon investments and penalise high-emission activities. The European Union Emissions Trading System (EU ETS) has played a crucial role in reducing industrial emissions, and recent reforms have tightened the cap and introduced a market stability reserve to mitigate price volatility. Empirical analyses demonstrate that higher and more stable carbon prices correlate with increased investment in renewable energy and low-carbon technologies. Nonetheless, the global carbon pricing landscape remains fragmented. Many jurisdictions either lack carbon pricing altogether or implement it at levels far below the social cost of carbon, leading to carbon leakage and regulatory arbitrage. Inconsistent carbon pricing undermines its function as a systemic stabiliser, as firms and investors are unable to accurately forecast regulatory risk or integrate carbon costs into financial models across jurisdictions. Thus, while carbon pricing is theoretically potent in promoting market correction and long-term stability, its effectiveness is conditional on global coordination and price adequacy.

Central banks and financial supervisors have increasingly taken on a proactive role in integrating ESG considerations into their financial oversight. The Network for Greening the Financial System (NGFS), comprising over 140 central banks and regulators, advocates for climate scenario analysis, stress testing, and the integration of ESG risks into prudential regulation. The Bank of England and the European Central Bank (ECB), for example, have begun integrating climate risk into monetary policy frameworks and supervisory review processes. The ECB's climate stress test in 2022 revealed that most banks were underprepared for transition risks and lacked the granular data necessary to manage their exposure. While these findings have spurred supervisory action, central bank interventions remain constrained by legal mandates and concerns over market neutrality. Critics argue that central banks risk overstepping their remit by favouring green assets, potentially distorting market signals. Nevertheless, given the financial system's vulnerability to climate-related shocks, central banks' involvement is increasingly viewed as essential to safeguarding macroprudential stability.

The current regulatory and policy toolkit for ESG integration offers a partial but evolving infrastructure for enhancing financial market resilience. Taxonomies bring definitional clarity but suffer from scope and political compromise (Coady 2021). Disclosure mandates improve transparency but require harmonisation and assurance mechanisms to enhance trust. Carbon pricing holds systemic potential but is hindered by global fragmentation and political inertia. Central bank interventions offer supervisory rigour but face institutional and normative constraints. For these tools to collectively promote systemic stability, greater policy coherence, international alignment, and robust enforcement will be indispensable. Without these reforms, the ambition of sustainable finance to act as a stabilising force in global markets will remain aspirational rather than operational.

16.6 Conclusion

This chapter has advanced a comprehensive analysis of sustainable finance as a mechanism for enhancing financial market stability through the integration of ESG principles. Drawing from theoretical frameworks such as Modern Portfolio Theory, Stakeholder Theory, and the Market Efficiency Hypothesis, the discussion has demonstrated how ESG integration modifies traditional risk-return dynamics, extends investor horizons, and fosters a more resilient financial architecture. By internalising long-horizon risks that are often externalised in conventional models, ranging from climate volatility to governance failures, sustainable finance reorients market behaviour toward strategic stability and long-term value preservation.

The empirical evidence presented affirms that ESG-aligned portfolios tend to outperform or exhibit lower downside volatility during periods of financial crisis, such as the 2008 global economic meltdown and the COVID-19 shock. These findings support the claim that ESG integration serves not only as an ethical or reputational strategy but also as a credible instrument for mitigating systemic risk (Ma 2024). Notably, the analysis of institutional investor behaviour highlights how fiduciary evolution, capital reallocation, and stewardship practices are key transmission channels through which ESG norms are embedded into market governance. The growing influence of asset owners like BlackRock and CalPERS signals a paradigmatic shift in how sustainability imperatives are being internalised at scale.

Nevertheless, the robustness of sustainable finance as a stabilising force is contingent on the effectiveness of regulatory and policy instruments. Green finance taxonomies, disclosure mandates such as TCFD and SFDR, carbon pricing mechanisms, and central bank interventions all play essential roles in shaping incentives and reducing informational asymmetries. Yet, as critically examined, these tools remain unevenly implemented, politically contested, and institutionally constrained. Without greater coherence, enforcement capacity, and global alignment, their capacity to ensure credible ESG integration and systemic resilience will remain limited.

Looking forward, several directions warrant further attention. First, future research must deepen our understanding of ESG materiality across diverse asset classes and geographies, especially in emerging markets where data limitations persist. Longitudinal studies that track the evolution of ESG risk exposure and financial performance across business cycles will be instrumental in reinforcing the theoretical foundation of sustainable finance. Second, policy frameworks must prioritise standardisation and verification in ESG reporting to enhance comparability and reduce the risk of greenwashing. This includes the development of globally accepted assurance protocols and third-party audit mechanisms (Ilori et al. 2024). Third, central banks and financial regulators must expand their mandates to incorporate sustainability-linked macroprudential supervision, thereby embedding climate risk into the core of financial stability assessments.

Sustainable finance holds transformative potential not only to reallocate capital toward socially and environmentally beneficial outcomes but also to fortify the structural integrity of financial systems. By aligning investment practices with risk mitigation and long-term value creation, ESG integration offers a viable path toward reconciling financial profitability with systemic resilience (Emma 2024). Realising this promise, however, will require a sustained commitment from policymakers, institutional investors, and academic researchers alike to refine tools, test assumptions, and institutionalise sustainability at every level of financial governance. Only then can sustainable finance evolve from a normative aspiration to an operational foundation for stable and equitable markets.

References

Albuquerque R, Koskinen Y, Yang S, Zhang C (2020) Resiliency of environmental and social stocks: An analysis of the exogenous COVID-19 market crash. Rev Corp Financ Stud 9(3):593–621

Baer M, Campiglio E, Deyris J (2021) It takes two to dance: institutional dynamics and climate-related financial policies. Ecol Econ 190:107210

Bolton P, Kacperczyk M (2021) Do investors care about carbon risk? J Financ Econ 142(2):517–549

Broadstock DC, Chan K, Cheng LT, Wang X (2021) The role of ESG performance during times of financial crisis: Evidence from COVID-19 in China. Finance research letters, 38, 101716

Capelle-Blancard G, Petit A (2019) Every little helps? ESG news and stock market reaction. J Bus Ethics 157(2):543–565

Chiu IHY (2025) Regulating ESG rating and data product providers: critically examining EU regulation through the lens of functional regulatory consistency. Eur J Risk Regul 16(1):242–262

Coady CAJ (2021) The meaning of terrorism. Oxford University Press, Oxford

Dimson E, Marsh P, Staunton M (2020) Divergent ESG ratings

Dyck A, Lins KV, Roth L, Wagner HF (2019) Do institutional investors drive corporate social responsibility? International evidence. J Financ Econ 131(3):693–714

Emma L (2024) Integrating sustainable financial strategies for long-term corporate growth and stakeholder value

Gianfrate G, Rubin M, Ruzzi D, van Dijk M (2024) On the resilience of ESG firms during the COVID-19 crisis: evidence across countries and asset classes. J Int Bus Stud 55(8):1069–1084

Hughes M, Hu Q, Simeonova B, Ge B, Issah WB, Jack S, Dai S (2025) ESG in family firms: a review of research, regulations and practice guidance

Ilori O, Nwosu NT, Naiho HNN (2024) Third-party vendor risks in IT security: a comprehensive audit review and mitigation strategies. World J Adv Res Rev 22(3):213–224

Jormakka E (2025) Integrating ESG criteria into investment portfolios to reduce investor financial risk in emerging markets: CASE: stock exchange-listed companies in India (2012-2022)

Loang OK, Ahmad Z (2020) Social factors and herd behaviour in developed markets, advanced emerging markets and secondary emerging markets. J Contemp East Asia 19(1)

Loang OK (2025a) Can machine learning surpass human investors? Evidence from adaptive herding behaviour in US, China and India. J Appl Econ 28(1):2435796

Loang OK (2025b) Financial stability at risk: evidence from market overreaction and herding behaviour in developed and emerging markets. China Financ Rev Int 15(1):67–92

Loang OK, Candra S (2025) Religion and green: the dual power of ESG and Shariah-compliant stocks in brand values of Malaysia, Indonesia, and Saudi Arabia. J Islam Monet Econ Financ 11(2):419–448

Ma Q (2024) Exploring the multi-dimensional effects of ESG on corporate valuation: insights into investor expectations, risk mitigation, and long-term value creation. Adv Econ Manag Polit Sci 103:8–15

Macpherson M (2024) Meeting the EU's sustainability disclosure rules-a mission (im) possible? In: Research handbook on sustainability reporting. Edward Elgar Publishing, Cheltenham, pp 224–249

Muir DM (2022) Sustainable investing and fiduciary obligations in pension funds: the need for sustainable regulation. Am Bus Law J 59(4):621–677

Nofsinger J, Varma A (2014) Socially responsible funds and market crises. Rev Corp Financ Stud 48:180–193

Ooi KL (2025) Market, news sentiments, and twitter happiness on adaptive herding behaviour of investors in Shariah-compliant stocks. J Islam Acc Business Res. https://doi.org/10.1108/JIABR-06-2024-0219

Pachouly J, Ahirrao S, Kotecha K, Selvachandran G, Abraham A (2022) A systematic literature review on software defect prediction using artificial intelligence: datasets, data validation methods, approaches, and tools. Eng Appl Artif Intell 111:104773

Pedersen LH, Fitzgibbons S, Pomorski L (2021) Responsible investing: The ESG-efficient frontier. J Financ Econ 142(2):572–597

Visconti RM (2021) ESG capital and the corporate finance paradigm shift: from father profit to mother nature? Università Cattolica del Sacro Cuore, Milano

Xiao R, Deng J, Zhou Y, Chen M (2023) Analyzing contemporary trends in sustainable finance and ESG investment. Law Econ 2(11):44–52

Chapter 17
The Future of Behavioural Finance in a Sustainable World

17.1 Introduction

The evolving dynamics of global finance increasingly demand a re-evaluation of conventional assumptions concerning investor behaviour, risk perception, and market rationality. In recent years, the growing consideration of ESG factors has fundamentally reshaped the decision-making landscape in financial markets, compelling investors, institutions, and policymakers to incorporate sustainability criteria into their portfolio construction, asset valuation, and capital allocation. This transformation, while driven in part by regulatory shifts and stakeholder pressure, is equally a consequence of profound psychological and behavioural realignments among market participants (Xi 2024). As climate risks intensify, social justice narratives gain prominence, and ethical considerations take centre stage in corporate governance discourse, investors are progressively reorienting their preferences and heuristics in ways that challenge the core postulates of traditional behavioural finance.

At the intersection of these shifts lies a pressing theoretical question: How does behavioural finance, which has historically focused on bounded rationality, heuristics, and cognitive biases in a value-neutral market context, adapt to the normative and multidimensional demands of sustainable investing? Classical frameworks, such as prospect theory, overconfidence bias, mental accounting, and herding behaviour, offer powerful tools for understanding anomalies in investor behaviour. However, these models were mainly developed in environments where financial returns were the primary, if not sole, motivator of economic behaviour. In contrast, sustainable investing introduces an expanded utility function that includes ethical alignment, reputational concerns, intergenerational responsibility, and long-term environmental outcomes. Consequently, investor behaviour in ESG contexts must be examined through a more nuanced behavioural lens that accounts for affective decision-making, moral reasoning, and the evolving psychology of risk under climate uncertainty.

K. L. Ooi et al., *Following the Crowd: Psychological Drivers of Herding and Market Overreaction*, https://doi.org/10.1007/978-981-95-0792-4_17

The adaptation of investor behaviour to sustainability imperatives is increasingly evident across various domains. Retail and institutional investors alike are increasingly sensitive to non-financial disclosures, prioritising ESG metrics in fund selection and engaging in values-driven capital deployment. Behavioural cues, such as green labelling, ESG scoring systems, and sustainability-themed narratives, now influence market sentiment, investment flows, and asset pricing, often independently of conventional fundamentals. Simultaneously, climate-related uncertainties ranging from physical risk to policy transition risk have introduced new dimensions of ambiguity and salience that shape investor attention and judgement (Zhang 2022). These developments suggest that traditional behavioural constructs must be recalibrated to reflect a shifting informational environment in which sustainability narratives, ethical heuristics, and long-termism play a central role in shaping perceived value and utility.

This chapter aims to critically examine the theoretical and empirical implications of this behavioural transformation (Loang 2025a). It investigates how established behavioural finance theories are being reinterpreted in light of ESG integration and what new conceptual frameworks are emerging to account for sustainability-oriented biases and preferences. It explores the role of artificial intelligence and financial technology in mediating or amplifying behavioural responses to ESG information. Furthermore, the chapter considers the importance of financial literacy, investor education, and policy nudges in cultivating behaviourally robust sustainable investment practices. By synthesising insights from behavioural economics, sustainability studies, and finance, the chapter proposes a forward-looking paradigm for behavioural finance, one that is attuned to the ethical, environmental, and systemic complexities of a sustainability-driven financial ecosystem.

17.2 The Impact of Artificial Intelligence on Sustainable Investment Behaviour

AI is fundamentally reshaping the architecture of sustainable investment decisions, introducing unprecedented capabilities in data processing, pattern recognition, and decision automation. In the context of ESG investing, where informational complexity, qualitative assessments, and non-financial metrics abound, AI-driven systems offer a technological scaffolding to support investor decision-making in the face of behavioural constraints. The deployment of AI tools, particularly robo-advisors, sentiment analysis engines, and predictive algorithms, is increasingly positioned as a remedy to cognitive biases such as overconfidence, framing effects, recency bias, and affective forecasting errors that historically impair sustainability-oriented investment judgements. Yet, while AI systems offer significant potential to enhance decision accuracy and rationality, they also introduce novel risks that may perpetuate or amplify systemic distortions, particularly when embedded with opaque logics, algorithmic biases, or misaligned incentives.

Robo-advisors have emerged as one of the most visible manifestations of AI in retail sustainable investing. These automated portfolio management platforms utilise machine learning algorithms to assess individual investor profiles, risk preferences, and sustainability inclinations, and to generate ESG-optimised asset allocations accordingly (Dalne 2023). Platforms such as Betterment, Wealthfront, and the ESG-focused EarthFolio allow investors to access diversified portfolios aligned with values-based criteria, often at lower fees than traditional human advisors. Robo-advisors reduce the influence of emotion-laden decisions by standardising rebalancing procedures and eliminating reactive trading in response to market noise. From a behavioural finance perspective, this automation reduces susceptibility to panic selling, anchoring on past performance, and mental accounting errors. Moreover, by integrating ESG-specific constraints into optimisation models, robo-advisors embed sustainable preferences into rationalised portfolio structures, potentially enhancing consistency between stated investor goals and actual allocations.

Sentiment analysis tools further extend the scope of AI in sustainable investing by enabling investors and asset managers to quantify market perception and narrative momentum surrounding ESG issues. Utilising natural language processing (NLP), these tools analyse vast quantities of unstructured data, including news articles, earnings call transcripts, social media posts, and ESG disclosures, to extract real-time sentiment signals. For instance, firms such as Truvalue Labs and RepRisk provide ESG sentiment scores that inform asset selection and risk monitoring (Loang 2025b). These systems mitigate availability and salience biases by systematically aggregating dispersed information and highlighting material ESG developments that might otherwise be overlooked. However, sentiment-driven trading also raises concerns about herd behaviour and reflexivity, wherein market actors react to each other's AI-generated interpretations, potentially reinforcing feedback loops that amplify volatility or misprice ESG risks. Suppose sentiment signals are disproportionately driven by media hype or superficial keyword associations. In that case, they may distort rather than clarify the sustainability profile of assets, leading to overreaction and ESG branding bubbles.

Predictive models represent a third frontier where AI is transforming sustainable finance by anticipating long-term ESG risks and performance trajectories. These models incorporate structured and unstructured ESG data, macroeconomic indicators, and firm-level fundamentals to forecast sustainability-related outcomes such as carbon transition risk, regulatory exposure, or social licence erosion. In the insurance and fixed income sectors, AI models are already being utilised to estimate climate-related credit risk and physical asset vulnerability with precise geographic granularity. While such predictive capabilities enhance forward-looking risk management, they are not immune to overfitting, data biases, or interpretability problems. AI systems trained on historical data may underperform when exposed to non-linear ESG transitions or policy shocks not present in the training set. Additionally, the opacity of deep learning models, commonly referred to as the 'black box' problem, complicates their use in fiduciary contexts where transparency and auditability are essential.

Critically, the promise of AI to reduce behavioural bias must be tempered by recognition that AI systems are not epistemically neutral; they reflect the preferences, assumptions, and data environments of their designers. Algorithmic decision-making may replicate cognitive shortcuts and discriminatory patterns if ESG data sources are incomplete, inconsistent, or biased (Singh 2025). For example, AI models trained predominantly on Western ESG frameworks may misclassify or undervalue firms operating in emerging markets with different regulatory regimes or cultural sustainability norms. Furthermore, AI can foster overreliance or automation bias, whereby investors excessively defer to machine outputs without questioning their assumptions or limitations. This dynamic may erode active engagement, critical judgement, and the moral reasoning that is central to authentic, sustainable investing.

Recent developments underscore both the promise and peril of AI in this domain. In 2023, BlackRock expanded its Aladdin Climate platform, incorporating machine learning tools to project climate-adjusted risk-return profiles across asset classes. Similarly, Nasdaq launched ESG Data Hub, an AI-powered platform that curates ESG datasets from alternative providers to enhance investor analytics. Conversely, controversies surrounding AI bias in sustainability scoring, such as discrepancies among ESG ratings providers revealed by the MIT Sloan study, illustrate how AI can reinforce opacity and investor confusion if not subject to robust oversight and standardisation.

AI constitutes a transformative force in sustainable investing by equipping investors with enhanced analytical precision, behavioural discipline, and data synthesis capabilities. It holds considerable promise in mitigating known cognitive biases and enabling more consistent, values-aligned investment decisions. However, the introduction of AI also necessitates new forms of behavioural vigilance and governance, as it carries the risk of embedding systemic blind spots, automating flawed heuristics, and diffusing responsibility across algorithmic infrastructures. The future of behavioural finance in a sustainable world thus requires a dual emphasis on technological innovation and ethical design, ensuring that AI not only enhances rationality but also upholds the normative commitments at the core of ESG investing.

17.3 Behavioural Finance Theories in Sustainability-Oriented Economies

Foundational theories of behavioural finance, namely prospect theory, overconfidence bias, and mental accounting, provide critical interpretive frameworks for understanding investor behaviour in sustainability-oriented financial markets (Loang and Candra 2025). As ESG investing becomes more deeply embedded within both retail and institutional practices, these theories illuminate the psychological underpinnings that shape how investors perceive value, assess risk, and react to sustainability narratives. The integration of ESG criteria into financial decision-making does not eliminate cognitive distortions; instead, it often amplifies or reframes them through moral, reputational, and affective lenses (Imade 2024). The resulting behavioural dynamics contribute to distinct patterns in ESG investment flows, valuation anomalies in green assets, and differentiated risk perceptions tied to sustainability concerns.

Prospect theory, introduced by Kahneman and Tversky, posits that individuals evaluate outcomes relative to a reference point and exhibit loss aversion, disproportionately fearing losses compared to equivalent gains. In ESG investing, this framework helps explain the asymmetric perception of sustainability-related risks. Investors may view potential ESG failures, such as a carbon emission scandal or labour rights violation, as more damaging than commensurate ESG gains, such as a new green initiative or diversity milestone. This asymmetry drives heightened sensitivity to negative ESG news and can prompt rapid divestment in response to perceived sustainability lapses, even when the financial fundamentals remain intact. Additionally, prospect theory sheds light on the framing of ESG opportunities: investors are more likely to adopt ESG strategies when they are framed as a means to avoid losses (e.g. stranded assets, climate transition risk) rather than as a means to achieve gains (e.g. superior long-term returns). This loss-avoidant framing reinforces the trend toward defensive ESG investing, particularly during periods of regulatory change or environmental instability.

Overconfidence bias, the tendency for individuals to overestimate their knowledge or ability to predict outcomes, is another salient behavioural force in ESG markets. ESG investing often requires interpreting complex, multidimensional data and making long-horizon forecasts about non-financial risks. Investors, especially institutional asset managers and ESG fund providers, may exhibit overconfidence in their ability to evaluate sustainability metrics, project climate-adjusted returns, or differentiate genuinely green firms from those engaged in strategic greenwashing. This overconfidence can lead to suboptimal diversification, excessive concentration in trending ESG themes (such as renewable energy or electric vehicles), and underestimation of systemic risks associated with ESG misclassification. Empirical studies have shown that fund managers with strong ESG convictions are prone to conviction-induced trading, reinforcing performance-chasing behaviour and exposing portfolios to valuation reversals when sustainability expectations are not met. In this way, overconfidence contributes to both the momentum and fragility of ESG investment bubbles.

Mental accounting, the cognitive process by which individuals categorise and treat money differently depending on its source or intended use, also plays a pivotal role in shaping ESG investment behaviour. Investors often segment their portfolios into 'core' financial assets and 'satellite' ESG or impact allocations, applying different performance expectations and evaluative criteria to each. This compartmentalisation enables investors to pursue sustainability goals without applying uniform return thresholds, thereby creating psychological space for values-driven investing that may not conform to classical utility maximisation. While this behaviour can support the growth of ESG markets, it also introduces inconsistencies in risk tolerance and monitoring rigour across portfolio segments. For example, investors may accept underperformance in ESG funds as the 'cost' of ethical alignment, while demanding alpha generation from traditional holdings, which potentially distorts overall portfolio efficiency (Xxx 2023). Mental accounting also influences charitable giving and social impact investing, where returns are sometimes deprioritised in favour of perceived moral utility, further complicating the integration of ESG into standard financial optimisation frameworks.

These behavioural mechanisms collectively contribute to herding phenomena in ESG markets, particularly in the form of excessive capital flows into green stocks or ESG-themed funds during periods of heightened environmental awareness or policy signalling (Loang 2025c). As investors observe others shifting toward sustainable assets, whether due to media narratives, regulatory developments, or institutional endorsements, they may interpret this movement as an informational signal, thereby reinforcing the trend through mimetic behaviour. Such herding amplifies price momentum and creates feedback loops that can lead to mispricing, volatility, and subsequent corrections. The Tesla case, wherein valuations soared amid ESG enthusiasm before experiencing sharp declines, illustrates how behavioural feedback and herd dynamics can influence sustainability-linked assets in ways not fully accounted for by fundamentals.

Risk perception in sustainability-oriented markets is also deeply coloured by these behavioural biases. Investors often overweigh vivid, emotionally salient ESG risks, such as climate disasters or reputational crises, while underestimating slower-moving, structural risks, like supply chain inequality or governance deficiencies. This bias reflects the affect heuristic, whereby emotional reactions guide risk assessment more than probabilistic reasoning. Consequently, ESG risk perception is not always aligned with objective exposure, leading to capital misallocation and inconsistent risk pricing across sectors and regions.

17.4 ESG Investment Through Financial Literacy and Investor Education

Financial literacy and investor education occupy a pivotal role in the behavioural architecture of sustainable investing. As ESG investing becomes an increasingly influential paradigm in global financial markets, the ability of individuals and institutions to process sustainability-related information, interpret ESG metrics, and integrate non-financial criteria into portfolio decision-making hinges on cognitive competencies that are deeply affected by education. Behavioural finance research consistently demonstrates that financially literate individuals exhibit lower susceptibility to heuristics such as the disposition effect, overconfidence, and mental accounting errors (Suresh 2024). Within the ESG context, education serves not merely as a mechanism for technical comprehension but also as a behavioural intervention capable of reshaping preferences, improving self-regulation, and anchoring investor behaviour in a long-term, ethically aligned framework.

Investor education programmes that specifically address the complexities of ESG criteria, ranging from climate risk and human rights exposure to governance practices and the detection of greenwashing, help narrow the intention-action gap that plagues sustainable investing. Many retail investors express interest in aligning their portfolios with personal values or environmental goals, yet struggle to execute these preferences due to information overload, inconsistent ESG ratings, or a lack of interpretive skills. Targeted education initiatives can demystify ESG terminologies, clarify the materiality of sustainability factors, and offer actionable frameworks for ESG portfolio construction. Studies show that when investors are equipped with precise, decision-useful ESG knowledge, they are more likely to adopt sustainable investment strategies and remain committed to them, even during periods of underperformance or heightened market volatility. Furthermore, ESG-specific education reduces reliance on superficial green branding or heuristics, enabling investors to engage with sustainability at a substantive analytical level.

The psychology of ethical investing further underscores the importance of education in mitigating behavioural biases. Ethical investing is often driven by affective and identity-based motivations, such as moral satisfaction, reputational signalling, or congruence with deeply held beliefs (Ooi 2025). While these motives can foster engagement, they can also distort rational risk assessment and return expectations, leading to herding, narrative-driven overreaction, or neglect of financial fundamentals. Financial literacy serves as a cognitive moderating variable, enabling investors to balance their ethical inclinations with analytical rigour. For instance, a well-informed investor may pursue ESG investments not only to express environmental values but also to anticipate regulatory trends, reputational risk, or evolving consumer preferences. In this way, education transforms moral preference into strategic foresight, tempering behavioural volatility with informed intentionality.

Generational differences further highlight the crucial role of education in fostering sustainable investing. Younger cohorts, particularly millennials and Generation Z, have demonstrated a stronger inclination toward ESG-aligned investment products, driven by heightened environmental awareness, increased digital engagement, and shifting social norms. However, this demographic also exhibits relatively lower levels of financial literacy, especially in areas such as portfolio diversification, risk-adjusted returns, and time horizon calibration. Without adequate education, their enthusiasm for sustainable investing may be channelled into speculative, poorly diversified ESG assets or be influenced by social media-driven sentiment rather than evidence-based decision-making. Conversely, older generations, while possessing greater financial experience, may exhibit inertia or scepticism toward ESG integration due to entrenched habits or unfamiliarity with sustainability metrics (Soares 2022). Tailored investor education sensitive to generational contexts and cognitive frames can bridge these gaps by offering both normative appeal and practical competency, ensuring that ESG investing is both inclusive and effective across age groups.

Framing effects also play a crucial role in determining how investors receive and respond to ESG information. Behavioural research shows that the presentation of information, whether framed as a gain, a loss, a risk, or a moral imperative, profoundly influences decision outcomes. ESG data framed in terms of avoided losses (e.g. stranded assets, litigation risks, or reputational damage) tends to elicit stronger engagement than when presented as opportunity narratives (e.g. green growth or impact returns). Financial literacy enhances investors' ability to interpret such frames critically, recognise framing manipulation, and seek the underlying substance. Education programmes that teach investors how to deconstruct ESG narratives, identify framing techniques, and evaluate risk disclosures through multiple lenses contribute to a more resilient and discerning investment culture. This framing literacy also supports more democratic participation in sustainable finance, allowing diverse investor segments to navigate the proliferating ecosystem of ESG products with confidence and agency.

17.5 ESG Strategy Development and Policy Design

Behavioural insights have become increasingly integral to the design of ESG strategies and financial policy frameworks, offering a pragmatic toolkit to address the cognitive and motivational barriers that inhibit sustainable investment behaviours. By leveraging findings from behavioural economics and psychology, regulators and asset managers can design interventions commonly referred to as 'nudges' that steer investors toward more responsible decisions without restricting choice or altering financial incentives in coercive ways. Nudging mechanisms capitalise on predictable behavioural patterns such as inertia, default bias, social norm adherence, and framing sensitivity, allowing ESG principles to be embedded into the architecture of decision-making environments. The use of default settings, for instance, has proven highly effective in influencing investment allocation (Mohsin et al. 2023). Empirical studies reveal that when retirement savings plans automatically enrol participants into ESG-themed portfolios with the option to opt out, rather than opt in, participation rates in sustainable investment vehicles rise significantly. This default effect exploits status quo bias, where investors are inclined to stick with pre-selected options, thereby promoting ESG engagement without requiring deliberate, cognitively demanding action on the part of the investor.

Incorporating social norms into ESG strategy is another behaviourally grounded intervention that has shown promising results. Disclosure of peer behaviour, such as providing information that a majority of investors in a demographic group favour ESG funds, can activate conformity biases and drive adoption through social proof. Financial institutions have also begun experimenting with message framing that emphasises collective impact and ethical responsibility (Brugman 2024). For example, platforms that frame ESG investing as a form of civic duty or intergenerational responsibility are more likely to elicit engagement from individuals who identify with environmental or social causes. Such framing is particularly effective when combined with visual aids, storytelling, and simplified ESG metrics, reducing decision fatigue and facilitating heuristic-based engagement that is directionally aligned with long-term sustainability goals.

Regulators have also begun to institutionalise behaviourally informed policies in the ESG domain. The United Kingdom's Financial Conduct Authority (FCA), for instance, has developed guidance on 'consumer duty' that encourages asset managers to act in the best interest of clients by simplifying ESG disclosures and offering sustainability-labelled funds as a prominent default option. In the Netherlands, the Pension Agreement includes provisions that utilise default ESG options in retirement portfolios, structured around the recognition that most savers exhibit low financial literacy and high inertia (Khiavi 2025). Furthermore, the European Commission's Sustainable Finance Action Plan explicitly incorporates behavioural insights in its strategy, recognising that choice architecture and information framing are essential for empowering retail investors to make sustainable choices. These regulatory interventions are often accompanied by requirements for plain-language ESG labelling, simplified risk disclosures, and dashboard-style fund comparison tools, as well as behavioural features designed to reduce informational asymmetries and cognitive overload.

At the policy level, behavioural insights have also influenced the design of climate risk communication tools. Central banks and supervisory authorities such as the Bank of England and the European Central Bank have begun integrating behavioural considerations into stress testing and climate scenario analyses. By emphasising tail risks, cascading system failures, and long-term financial consequences in their disclosures, these institutions aim to reframe climate-related financial risk as an immediate and salient concern, thereby counteracting the temporal discounting and optimism bias that often delay investors' responses to climate threats. These framing strategies are complemented by probabilistic visualisations and scenario narratives that help investors concretise abstract, long-horizon ESG risks, thereby enhancing comprehension and salience.

17.6 Conclusion

As global finance continues its paradigmatic shift toward sustainability, the discipline of behavioural finance faces a compelling imperative to expand its theoretical scope and practical applications. Traditional models of investor psychology, rooted in bounded rationality, heuristic-driven choices, and emotional framing, must evolve to reflect the multifaceted nature of ESG investing. In this context, ethical motives, intertemporal trade-offs, and complex risk perceptions fundamentally reshape how decisions are made. This chapter has argued that behavioural finance is not only capable of adapting to this new financial terrain but also essential in decoding its emerging complexities (Sutton 2025). The convergence of artificial intelligence, progressive regulatory policy, and targeted financial education creates a transformative ecosystem that can nudge, inform, and optimise investor behaviour in alignment with long-term sustainability goals.

Artificial intelligence occupies a central role in this behavioural transformation, both as a corrective to human biases and as a potential source of new cognitive distortions. AI tools, ranging from robo-advisors to sentiment analysis engines, can reduce the influence of panic, inertia, and overconfidence in ESG investment decisions by offering data-driven, personalised portfolio strategies. Yet, these same technologies risk amplifying opacity, herding, and automation bias if not properly governed (Sifat 2023). The future of sustainable behavioural finance will thus require not only innovation in AI applications but also rigorous oversight and transparency to ensure that algorithmic decision-making aligns with normative and ethical standards. Significantly, the behavioural effects of AI are mediated by the investor's cognitive literacy, further reinforcing the centrality of education in this evolving domain.

Indeed, financial literacy and ESG-focused investor education constitute the foundational behavioural infrastructure of sustainable finance. As the chapter has demonstrated, informed investors are better positioned to interpret ESG disclosures, evaluate risk beyond short-term metrics, and resist superficial greenwashing narratives. Education mitigates biases such as framing effects, mental accounting, and loss aversion by equipping individuals with the analytical and ethical tools needed to engage critically with sustainability claims. Moreover, intergenerational and demographic variations in ESG motivation highlight the need to tailor educational interventions to the unique psychological and cultural contexts of each group. The rise of digitally native, value-driven investor cohorts demands not only new content but new modes of delivery, including interactive platforms, gamified simulations, and AI-guided financial coaching.

Policy design, informed by behavioural science, serves as a crucial third pillar in shaping the future of sustainable investing. Regulatory tools that embed nudges such as ESG default options, simplified disclosures, and norm-based messaging can shift investor behaviour without compromising autonomy (Mormann 2023). Behavioural interventions allow regulators to address cognitive friction, informational overload, and status quo bias in subtle yet powerful ways. As demonstrated by initiatives from the EU, the UK Financial Conduct Authority, and the Network for Greening the Financial System, behaviourally informed policy can enhance ESG integration at scale, particularly when combined with technological innovation and public education campaigns. However, these policies must be continuously evaluated for efficacy, transparency, and fairness, ensuring that behavioural influence does not devolve into manipulation or technocratic paternalism.

Looking forward, the psychology of investing in a sustainable world will increasingly reflect a dual commitment to cognitive efficiency and normative orientation. Investor behaviour will be shaped not only by utility-maximising logic but also by identity expression, moral reasoning, and collective risk consciousness (Davis 2024). As climate instability, social fragmentation, and governance crises become more salient investment considerations, financial decision-making will move further away from the rational-agent model and toward a complex, multidimensional behavioural framework. This evolution presents both a challenge and an opportunity for behavioural finance: a challenge to expand its empirical and theoretical boundaries, and a chance to play a formative role in constructing the cognitive foundations of sustainable markets.

References

Brugman BC (2024) How the effects of emphasizing ethics are examined: a systematic review of moral framing experiments. Ann Int Commun Assoc 48(4):436–455

Dalne G (2023) ESG-integrated machine learning portfolio opimization strategies: performance analysis and applications

Davis JB (2024) Identity, capabilities, and changing economics: reflexive, adaptive, socially embedded individuals. Cambridge University Press, Cambridge

Imade O (2024) Impact of cognitive biases on ESG investment decisions. Available at SSRN 4907383

Khiavi E (2025) Democratising pension funds by quadratic voting: giving a louder voice to occupational pension scheme members contents. Available at SSRN 5259888

Loang OK (2025a) Can machine learning surpass human investors? Evidence from adaptive herding behaviour in US, China and India. J Appl Econ 28(1):2435796

Loang OK (2025b) Financial stability at risk: evidence from market overreaction and herding behaviour in developed and emerging markets. China Financ Rev Int 15(1):67–92

Loang OK (2025c) From tweets to trades: the dynamic dance of investor sentiment, attention, and news sentiment in ESG stocks. China Finance Econ Rev 14(1):70–91

Loang OK, Candra S (2025) Religion and green: the dual power of ESG and Shariah-compliant stocks in brand values of Malaysia, Indonesia, and Saudi Arabia. J Islam Monet Econ Financ 11(2):419–448

Mohsin M, Dilanchiev A, Umair M (2023) The impact of green climate fund portfolio structure on green finance: empirical evidence from EU countries. Ekonomika 102(2):130–144

Mormann F (2023) Climate choice architecture. BCL Rev 64:1

Ooi KL (2025) Market, news sentiments, and twitter happiness on adaptive herding behaviour of investors in Shariah-compliant stocks. J Islam Acc Business Res. https://doi.org/10.1108/JIABR-06-2024-0219

Sifat I (2023) Artificial intelligence (AI) and retail investment. Available at SSRN 4539625

Singh SS (2025) Novel data mining methodologies for environmental, social and governance analytics: a comprehensive framework for sustainable investment

Soares GD (2022) ESG is in the eye of the beholder: the ambiguities within concept, culture and evaluation (Doctoral dissertation, Doctoral dissertation). Universidade Nova de Lisboa

Suresh G (2024) Impact of financial literacy and behavioural biases on investment decision-making. FIIB Business Rev 13(1):72–86

Sutton CV (2025) Navigating financial turbulence with confidence: preparing for future market challenges, crashes & crises. NuovoNova Ltd, Poole

Xi W (2024) Regulatory changes and compliance challenges. In: Strategic financial management: a managerial approach. Emerald Publishing Limited, Leeds, pp 119–134

Xxx S (2023) ESG investment and its impacts on equity holders, creditors and other institutional investors (Doctoral dissertation, Politecnico di Torino)

Zhang SY (2022) Are investors sensitive to climate-related transition and physical risks? Evidence from global stock markets. Res Int Bus Financ 62:101710

GPSR Compliance

The European Union's (EU) General Product Safety Regulation (GPSR) is a set of rules that requires consumer products to be safe and our obligations to ensure this.

If you have any concerns about our products, you can contact us on ProductSafety@springernature.com

In case Publisher is established outside the EU, the EU authorized representative is:

Springer Nature Customer Service Center GmbH
Europaplatz 3
69115 Heidelberg, Germany

Batch number: 10725802

Printed by Printforce, the Netherlands